THE DICKENS COMPANIONS

General editor Susan Shatto, Associate editor Michael Cotsell

---

The Companion to *Our Mutual Friend*

THE DICKENS COMPANIONS

The Companion to
Our Mutual Friend

MICHAEL COTSELL

London
ALLEN & UNWIN
Boston   Sydney

Allen & Unwin (Publishers) Ltd,
40 Museum Street, London WC1A 1LU, UK

Allen & Unwin (Publishers) Ltd,
Park Lane, Hemel Hempstead, Herts HP2 4TE, UK

Allen & Unwin, Inc.,
8 Winchester Place, Winchester, Mass 01890, USA

Allen & Unwin (Australia) Ltd,
8 Napier Street, North Sydney, NSW 2060, Australia

First published in 1986

British Library Cataloguing in Publication Data

Cotsell, Michael
    The Companion to Our mutual friend.—(Dickens companions; 1)
1. Dickens, Charles, *1812–1870*. Our mutual friend
I. Title
823'.8   PR4568
ISBN 0-04-800035-8

Library of Congress Cataloging in Publication Data

Cotsell, Michael.
    The companion to Our mutual friend.
    (Dickens companions)
Bibliography: p.
Includes index.
1. Dickens, Charles, 1812–1870. Our mutual friend. I. Dickens, Charles,
1812–1870. Our mutual friend. II. Title. III. Title: Our mutual friend.
IV. Series.
PR4568.C67 1986   823'.8   85-11178
ISBN 0-04-800035-3 (alk. paper)

Set in 10 on 11 point Erhardt by Fotographics (Bedford) Ltd
and printed in Great Britain by Anchor Brendon, Tiptree, Essex

To my Mother and Father

CONTENTS

LIST OF ILLUSTRATIONS

GENERAL PREFACE
BY THE EDITORS

The Dickens Companions series provides the most comprehensive annotation of the works of Dickens ever undertaken. Separate volumes are devoted to each of Dickens's fifteen novels, to *Sketches by Boz* and to *The Uncommercial Traveller*; the five Christmas books are treated together in one volume. The series will be completed by a General Index, making nineteen volumes in all.

The nature of the annotation is factual rather than critical. The series undertakes what the general editors of the Clarendon Dickens have called 'the immense task of explanatory annotation' of Dickens's works. Each Companion will elucidate obscurities and allusions which were doubtless intelligible to the nineteenth-century reader but which have changed or lost their meaning in a later age. The 'world' of Dickens passed away more than a century ago, and our perceptions and interpretations of his works can be sharpened by our having recalled for us a precise context or piece of information.

The annotation identifies allusions to current events and intellectual and religious issues, and supplies information on topography, social customs, costume, furniture, transportation, the illustrations to the novel, and so on. Identifications are provided for allusions to plays, poems, songs, the Bible, the Book of Common Prayer and other literary sources. Elements of Dickens's plots, characterization and style which are influenced by the works of other writers are also identified. When an aspect of the text can be shown to have been influenced by Dickens's own experience, this is indicated. The work of Dickens's illustrators is also discussed. Finally, although the Companions do not attempt the work of a modern scholarly edition, material from Dickens's manuscripts and proofs is included when it is of major significance.

The main part of the information in each Companion is arranged in the form of notes presented for convenient use with any edition of Dickens's works. The information is thus placed where it is most relevant, enabling the notes to be used to elucidate a local difficulty, or to pursue the use of a certain kind of material or the development of a particular idea. To facilitate their use, the notes are cross-referenced, and each Companion contains a comprehensive index. The introduction to each Companion traces the major influences and concerns revealed by the annotation and, where appropriate, demonstrates their place in the genesis and composition of the text.

Dickens's vital and imaginative response to his culture is a familiar fact, but The Dickens Companions demonstrate and explore this response more fully and in far greater detail than has ever been attempted. Hitherto, Dickens's works have been annotated only on a modest scale. Many modern editions of the novels contain some notes, but there is not space in one volume for both the text of a novel and a comprehensive annotation of the text. Because most volumes of The

Dickens Companions are devoted to a single work, the series can provide the full-scale, thoroughgoing annotation which the works of Dickens require. The completed series will compose a uniquely comprehensive archive of information about Dickens's world, affording the modern reader an unparalleled record of Dickens's concerns and the sources of his artistry. For many kinds of scholar, not merely Dickensians, The Dickens Companions will provide a fundamental tool for future critical and historical scholarship on various aspects of nineteenth-century British culture.

To undertake the 'immense task' of annotation, the Editors have assembled a team of Dickens scholars who work closely together and with the Editors in order to enhance the depth and scope of each Companion. The series is not a variorum commentary on Dickens: it does not consist of a survey or a selection of comments by other annotators and scholars. Previous scholarship is, in general, cited only when it is considered to identify an important piece of information about the historical, literary and biographical influences on Dickens's works.

The annotation in The Dickens Companions is based on original research which derives for the most part from the writings of Dickens's own time, the reading available to him and the books he is known to have read. The annotation is not perfunctorily minimal: a large number of notes are substantial essays and all are written in a readable style. Nor does the annotation consist of narrow definitions of what the reader (in the opinion of another reader) 'needs to know' in order to 'understand' the text. Rather, the annotation attempts to open up the actual and imaginative worlds which provided the sources and the backgrounds of Dickens's works in the belief that what interested, engaged and amused Dickens can hardly fail to interest, engage and amuse his readers. Our largest hope for The Dickens Companions is that the volumes will be read with a pleasure akin to that with which Dickens's own writings are read, and that they will be genuine Companions to both his works and his readers.

The idea of providing each of Dickens's major works with a companion volume of annotation originated with the late Professor T. J. B. Spencer. It is to his memory that the series is gratefully and affectionately dedicated.

SUSAN SHATTO
MICHAEL COTSELL

ACKNOWLEDGEMENTS

I am grateful to the Pierpont Morgan Library, New York, for permission to quote from the manuscript of *Our Mutual Friend* and to transcribe the number plans and to the Henry W. and Albert A. Berg Collection, New York Public Library, Astor, Lennox and Tilden Foundations, for permission to quote from the proof sheets. I am much indebted to the librarian and staff of those institutions and of the British Library, the Dickens House, and the University of Ulster Library (Coleraine).

This study owes a great deal to four people: the late Professor T. J. B. Spencer, whose idea it was; Susan Shatto, the best of general editors and friends, who has given me invaluable help and more support than I can possibly acknowledge here; Professor K. J. Fielding, who kindly read through the typescript and made many important suggestions; and my friend and colleague, John McVeagh. Without their scholarship and encouragement *Our Mutual Friend* would as yet have no Companion.

Many Dickens scholars and friends have helped me with information and advice, in particular Professor P. A. W. Collins. I am also indebted to Robin Gilmour, Wendy Jacobson, David Paroissien, Robert Patten, Andrew Sanders, Paul Schlicke and Michael Slater. Every annotator of Dickens owes a great deal to the scholarship of other Dickensians. The notes of T. W. Hill and the topographical work of Robert Allbut have been particularly useful, and I am, of course, much indebted to the work of Professor Collins on education. Recent studies by James A. Davies, Nancy Metz and Deirdre David have also been very useful. I am indebted for information to Peter Roebuck and John Springhall of the Department of History, University of Ulster. I am very grateful to Keith Ashfield for his support of the Companions in their early days and his continuing friendship. Jane Harris-Matthews has been a most kind and efficient editor. Maeve Boyle has aided my understanding of the novel and given me much encouragement. My colleagues Simon Gatrell and Professor A. W. Thomson have helped me in a number of respects. Rosemary Gilmore provided an excellent typescript. Finally, I am very grateful to Kevin Harris for an amusing and instructive index.

English Studies,   MICHAEL COTSELL
University of Ulster

ABBREVIATIONS FOR DICKENS'S WORKS AND RELATED MATERIAL

1. Works: Principal

AN	*American Notes*
BH	*Bleak House*
BL	*The Battle of Life*
BR	*Barnaby Rudge*
C	*The Chimes*
CC	*A Christmas Carol*
CH	*The Cricket on the Hearth*
CHE	*A Child's History of England*
DC	*David Copperfield*
DS	*Dombey and Son*
GE	*Great Expectations*
HM	*The Haunted Man*
HT	*Hard Times*
LD	*Little Dorrit*
MC	*Martin Chuzzlewit*
MED	*The Mystery of Edwin Drood*
MHC	*Master Humphrey's Clock*
NN	*Nicholas Nickleby*
OCS	*The Old Curiosity Shop*
OMF	*Our Mutual Friend*
OT	*Oliver Twist*
PI	*Pictures from Italy*
PP	*The Pickwick Papers*
SB	*Sketches by Boz*
TTC	*A Tale of Two Cities*
UT	*The Uncommercial Traveller*

2. Works: Miscellaneous Writings

CP	*Collected Papers*
MP	*Miscellaneous Papers*
RP	*Reprinted Pieces*

AYR	*All the Year Round*
HW	*Household Words*

CD	Charles Dickens Edition, 21 vols (1867–[74])

3.   Related Material: Basic Sources

Forster   John Forster, *The Life of Charles Dickens*, 3 vols (1872–4)
Letters   *The Letters of Charles Dickens*, ed. Madeline House and others, Pilgrim
                   Edition (1965–   )
Letters: Coutts *Letters from Charles Dickens to Angela Burdett-Coutts, 1841–1865*, ed.
                   Edgar Johnson (1953)
Nonesuch   *The Letters of Charles Dickens*, ed. Walter Dexter, Nonesuch Edition,
                   3 vols (1938)
Speeches   *The Speeches of Charles Dickens*, ed. K. J. Fielding (1960)

BIBLIOGRAPHICAL SYMBOLS
AND ABBREVIATIONS

MS   Manuscript
< >   Deletion in MS or proof
∧ or ∧   Addition or substitution in MS
∧ OR ∧   Addition or substitution in proof
illegible word   Signifies an unreadable word in MS

INTRODUCTION

Our Mutual Friend, Dickens's last completed novel, was begun in the winter of 1863–4. As early as August 1863, Dickens was eager to finish his contribution to that year's Christmas number of *All the Year Round* so that he could begin the novel: 'When I can clear the Christmas stone out of the road, I think I can dash into it on the grander journey,' he wrote to Forster (30 August, *Nonesuch* 3.361). His excitement is obvious in another letter he wrote to Forster in October:

> I am exceedingly anxious to begin my book. I am bent upon getting to work at it. I want to prepare it for the spring; but I am determined not to begin to publish with less than five numbers done. I see my opening perfectly, with the one main line on which the story is to turn; and if I don't strike while the iron (meaning myself) is hot, I shall drift off again, and have to go through all this uneasiness once more.
>
> (October 1863, Forster 3.339–40)

The new novel was to be Dickens's first return to the novel of twenty monthly parts since *Little Dorrit* (1855–7), and it was to be his last attempt at a novel of that length: *The Mystery of Edwin Drood* was intended for publication in twelve monthly parts. Dickens was himself aware of the magnitude of the task that he had set himself, but he was also confident of his powers. With the first two numbers completed, and at work on the third, he wrote to Wilkie Collins:

> It is a combination of drollery with romance which requires a great deal of pains and a perfect throwing away of points that might be amplified; but I hope it is *very good*. I confess, in short, that I think it is. Strange to say, I felt at first quite dazed in getting back to the large canvas and the big brushes; and even now, I have a sensation as of acting at the San Carlo after Tavistock House, which I could hardly have supposed would have come upon so old a stager.
>
> (24 January 1864, *Nonesuch* 3.378–9)

The manuscript and proofs bear out Dickens's remark about 'a perfect throwing away of points'. He overwrote the first number (chapters 1–4) by four pages, and was forced to make substantial cuts, mainly from the scene when John Harmon, as John Rokesmith, visits the Wilfers in chapter 4, but also from the riverside scenes in chapter 3. The second number (chapters 5–7) was also overwritten: the Lammles' wedding, 'A Marriage Contract', was to have been chapter 7, but had to be postponed to the next number, where it became chapter 10. Searching around for a subject for the new chapter 7, Dickens took a hint from his illustrator, Marcus Stone, and introduced Mr Venus – an inspired improvisation. This pattern of overwriting continued throughout book 1. The third number (chapters 8–10) passed without problems, but the fourth number (chapters 11–13) was again overwritten, and Dickens was forced to divide his account of the pursuit of Gaffer (the planned chapter 13) and introduce the remaining material into the fifth number (chapters 14–17) in another chapter (chapter 14). This, in turn, forced him to make cuts elsewhere in the fifth number: once again he chose to delete passages from scenes in which Harmon is involved.

Some of the overwriting must be attributed to the lapse of seven years since Dickens had last written in monthly parts. His intention to have book 1 completed before publication began in May 1864 must be attributed to his awareness of the task that lay before him. He reiterated his intention in a letter to Forster in March:

> If I were to lose a page of the five numbers I have purposed to myself to be ready by the publication day, I should feel that I had fallen short. I have grown hard to satisfy, and write very slowly. And I have so much – not fiction – that *will* be thought of, when I don't want to think of it, that I am forced to take more care than I once took.
>
> (29 March 1864, Forster 3.340–1)

The difficulties of composition and the distractions from it are evident from this letter. By July, writing again to Forster, Dickens did confess some slacking of invention:

> Although I have not been wanting in industry, I have been wanting in invention, and have fallen back with the book. Looming large before me is the Christmas work, and I can hardly hope to do it without losing a number of *Our Friend*. I have very nearly lost one already, and two would take one half of my whole advance. This week I have been very unwell; am still out of sorts; and, as I know from two days' slow experience, have a very mountain to climb before I shall see the open country of my work.
>
> (29 July 1864, Forster 3.341)

Dickens had just completed a season of 'severe dinner-eating', 'public speechifying, private eating and drinking, and perpetual simmering in hot rooms' that led him, like some of his characters, to look forward to a 'release from this dining life with an inexpressible longing after quiet and my own pursuits' (17 June 1864, 15 May 1864, *Nonesuch* 3.392, 389).

He found a further distraction in the summer heat, asking Mrs Wills in a letter of August to assure her husband that he would '*try* to work at my book (for I can't do it in this heat, though I make believe every day)' (*Nonesuch* 3.395), but from that month onwards a characteristic note of commitment is heard in his letters. Declining an invitation, he wrote to the dedicatee of *Our Mutual Friend*, Sir James Emerson Tennent:

> The mere knowledge that I had such a thing before me would put me out. It is not the length of time consumed, or the distance traversed, but it is the departure from a settled habit and a continuous sacrifice of pleasures that comes in question. This is an old story with me. I have never divided a book of my writing with anything else, but have always wrought at it to the exclusion of everything else; and it is now too late to change.
>
> (26 August 1864, *Nonesuch* 3.396)

Dickens made the same order of declaration to Mrs Procter:

> I have registered a vow (in which there is not the least merit, for I couldn't help it) that when I am, as I am now, very hard at work upon a book, I never will dine out more than one day in a week . . . I always have given my work the first place in my life.
>
> (15 February 1865, *Nonesuch* 3.415)

He told both Macready and Wills that he was 'working like a dragon' (*Nonesuch* 3.419, 434). The death of his friend John Leech, the *Punch* cartoonist, delayed his work on a number in November 1864, but Dickens was well into the 'open country' of his novel before there were any further signs of distress. Then, in early summer of 1865, he complained to Forster that 'Work and worry, without exercise, would soon make an end of me. If I were not going away now, I should break down. No one knows as I know to-day how near to it I have been' (May 1865, Forster 3.342). On 9 June 1865, returning from France with Ellen Ternan and possibly her mother, he was involved in the Staplehurst railway accident to which he made allusion in the 'Postscript'. It is perhaps not surprising that shortly afterwards he wrote to Forster, 'alas! for the two numbers you write of! There is only one in existence. I have but just begun the other,' and added 'Fancy! fancy my having under-written number sixteen by two and a half pages – a thing I have not done since *Pickwick*!' (July 1865, Forster 3.343). The underwritten number was completed by the addition of six short passages, and the letters then record an unbroken commitment to the end: 'I have been working my head off, but finished my book on the Second of this month,' he wrote to Thomas Beard on 21 September 1865 (*Nonesuch* 3.436). Overall, there is little in the record of composition to suggest the flagging of inspiration that the young Henry James thought he detected not only in *Our Mutual Friend* but also in *Bleak House* and in *Little Dorrit* (review in the *Nation*, 21 December 1865, 786–7; reprinted in Collins, 1971, 469–73). Some critics, like the Leavises, who omitted *Our Mutual Friend* from their discussion of the 'mature novels', have felt that there was a falling-off of some kind: they have, perhaps, failed to respond to that 'combination of drollery and romance' with which Dickens painted his 'large canvas'.

Our Mutual Friend opens with the words 'In these times of ours . . .'. It is indeed a novel of the 1860s. But present political dissatisfactions and personal difficulties (too familiar to be rehearsed here) were often for Dickens's creative imagination the road back to the past. In 1862 he wrote to Forster:

> I must entreat you to pause for an instant, and go back to what you know of my childish days, and to ask yourself whether it is natural that something of the character formed in me then, and lost under happier circumstances, should have reappeared in the last five years. The never to be forgotten misery of that old time, bred a certain shrinking sensitiveness in a certain ill-clad ill-fed child, that I have found come back in the never to be forgotten misery of this later time. (1.53)

The inspiration for major elements in the novel can be traced to experiences in Dickens's childhood and early manhood. These experiences began to come together in some tentative ideas which Dickens recorded between January and May of 1855 in the *Book of Memoranda* he started at that time (dating following Kaplan's edition, 1981). Two events, one personal, one public, made the spring of 1855 a period of significance in Dickens's life: one was the reappearance of Maria Beadnell, now Mrs Winter; the other was his considerable political dissatisfaction with events at the time of the Crimean War. The ideas recorded in early 1855 lay dormant until, in 1862, as the *Book of Memoranda* indicates, Dickens recognized that he had the potential of a 'LEADING INCIDENT FOR A STORY'.

The two main plots of *Our Mutual Friend*, the one concerning John Harmon, Bella and the Boffins, and the one concerning Gaffer Hexam, Lizzie and Eugene, both derive from plays by James Sheridan Knowles (noted by Davis, 1964, 266–8). They are, respectively, *The Hunchback* (1832) and *The Daughter* (1837). *The Hunchback* tells the story of a young woman, Julia, who is taught the value of true love by her guardian's pretence that he has become mercenary. She is thus reunited with her lover, who has presented himself to her in the guise of a rich man's secretary (see p. 203). *The Hunchback* was first performed at Covent Garden in 1832, with Fanny Kemble in the leading role. Her performance was much appreciated by an admirer of her art, Arthur Henry Hallam:

> The scene in the second Act, where Fanny Kemble plays the fine lady, was excellent, but the tragic parts yet finer: for instance where Clifford comes in as Secretary, and afterwards where she expostulates with Master Walter. Her 'Clifford, why don't you speak to me?' and 'Clifford, is it you?' and her 'Do it,' with all the accompanying speech, I shall never forget. (Hallam, Lord Tennyson, *Memoir*, 1.83)

In March of that year Dickens himself had applied to Covent Garden for an opportunity to demonstrate his acting talents, so he very likely saw the play in production. At any rate, he had a marked copy of the 1832 edition of the play in his library at Gad's Hill. Dickens was at that time unhappily involved with Maria Beadnell, and it is possible that his heightened emotions gave the play a special significance for him.

The plot of *The Daughter* centres on the story of the daughter of a wrecker in Cornwall, who is deceived into believing that her father murders someone who has been wrecked. The villainous wrecker, who is responsible for both the murder and the deception, resembles in certain respects Rogue Riderhood. It is not known when Dickens first encountered the play. Probably as great an influence on the riverside plot of *Our Mutual Friend* as *The Daughter* was a passage from the *Memoirs of Grimaldi*, which Dickens edited in 1837. Grimaldi's brother, who had run away to sea fourteen years previously, unexpectedly returned to Grimaldi's greenroom, with a companion dressed, as Grimaldi later realized, in identical clothes. Having made an arrangement to meet up with Grimaldi, the brother left with his companion, but never returned. Grimaldi was forced to conclude that he had been murdered, perhaps with the connivance of the sinister companion. This would seem to be the source of the incidents Harmon describes in book 2, chapter 13.

Perhaps neither *The Daughter* nor the passage from Grimaldi would have had significance for Dickens had he not imaginatively connected them with Limehouse. Dickens's godfather, John Huffam, was a prosperous 'rigger, and mast, oar, and block-maker' (Forster 1.21) who lived at 5 Church Row (now Newell Street). At the end of Church Row was St Anne's, Limehouse, the 'tall spectral' tower Harmon gazes at in book 2, chapter 13. Limehouse had a particular significance in Dickens's boyhood, because it was for him an alternative to the London of the Marshalsea and the blacking warehouse: in *Dombey and Son*, when Solomon Gills falls into the hands of his creditors, it is to Limehouse and Captain Cuttle that Walter Gay runs for assistance. An attractively naïve fantasy of running away to sea and returning to win a bride can be discerned in Dickens's writings when Limehouse is the scene.

The development of what Dickens was to call 'the one main line on which the story is to turn' begins in the 1855 entries in the *Book of Memoranda*. There, on one page, he noted: 'Found Drowned. The descriptive bill upon the wall, by the water-side.' A little below comes another entry: 'A "long shore" man – woman – child – or family < ? Query ? Found xx > qy. connect the Found Drowned Bill with this?' (8) In the third chapter of *Little Dorrit*, written at that time, Arthur Clennam, whose life is dominated by an implacable parent, the Marshalsea and the memory of an old love, passes, on his weary way home, 'a narrow alley leading to the river, where a wretched little bill, FOUND DROWNED, was weeping on the wet wall'. These two entries in the *Book of Memoranda* raise the possibility of connecting a saddened, exiled character, like Clennam or Harmon, with the riverside world of the Hexams. Another entry a few pages earlier suggests the relation of Charley Hexam and his father, as well as the relation of Pip to both Magwitch and Joe in *Great Expectations*: 'The uneducated father (or uncle?) in fustian, and the educated boy in spectacles. Whom Leech and I saw at Chatham' (6).

The list of 'General Titles' which appears on the same page as this entry suggests that Dickens had by 1855 established the Harmon story, though he had not yet connected it with the riverside. The titles include 'The Grindstone', 'Rokesmith's Forge', 'The Cinder Heap', 'Two Generations', 'Broken Crockery', 'Dust', 'The Young Person', 'My Neighbour', 'The Children of the Fathers', 'No Thoroughfare', 'Co' and 'Our Mutual Friend'. Clearly Podsnappery was already a major part of Dickens's idea, and two pages earlier he had noted: '– And by denying a thing, supposes that he altogether puts it out of existence' – an entry which he later marked off with the words 'Done in Podsnap'.

Dust-heaps and river came together in Harmon's story in 1862. The note in the *Book of Memoranda* reads:

LEADING INCIDENT FOR A STORY. A man – young and eccentric? – feigns to be dead, and *is* dead to all intents and purposes external to himself, and < xx > for years retains that singular view of life and character. *Done Rokesmith.* (19)

This is immediately preceded by a note relating to Podsnap and followed by one that represents the gist of the Lammles' story. The next page has at its top the title 'Our Mutual Friend', and that page and the next are fertile with ideas for the novel, including those of some 'perfectly New people' and of two characters who read Gibbon.

By adding the riverside to the dusty world of the 1855 ideas for 'Our Mutual Friend', Dickens had arrived at profound symbolism and deep regenerative possibilities. The experiences recorded in some of the essays in *The Uncommercial Traveller* (1862) may well have brought the riverside world back to his mind. The themes of death by drowning and of the fate of sailors at sea and on land run through that collection. As well, Dickens had been led by contemporary conditions in the East End to re-explore Limehouse and the adjacent districts. He was dismayed by the suffering he saw there and shocked by the character of the population of the waterside districts. *Our Mutual Friend* was to be a way of finding hope not only for his young heroes but also for the Limehouse of his affections.

The East End also brought forcibly to Dickens's mind the need for the centralization of Poor Law administration in London, thereby adding a dimension to his case against Podsnappery. Dickens's attention to Poor Law administration in *The Uncommercial Traveller* is reinforced by articles by other authors in *All the Year Round*. Although Betty Higden's home is transposed to Brentford, in the *All the Year Round* articles the parishes which are mentioned as suffering particularly from the current arrangements are always those of the East End riverside. Dickens's attack on the Poor Laws in *Our Mutual Friend* was to appear alongside a powerful newspaper and parliamentary campaign. Two other contemporary topics of great significance affect the novel: financial speculation, and the debates about teachers and education which led to the Newcastle Commission and the controversial Revised Code (see 2.1). Financial speculation was the subject of much critical comment in the newspapers, *The Economist* and other publications, and Dickens's satire on the world of the Veneerings, the Lammles and Fledgeby was supported in *All the Year Round* by a series of articles by M. R. L. Meason, the majority of which were collected in 1865 as *The Bubbles of Finance*. Education generally, and the teaching profession in particular, was hotly debated in Parliament and in newspapers and periodicals. *Our Mutual Friend* thus shares with *Bleak House, Hard Times* and *Little Dorrit* a profound critical commitment to the issues of the day. Unlike those novels, however, it does not focus on a central symbolic institution, such as Chancery, Gradgrindism or the Circumlocution Office and the Marshalsea, though that may have been Dickens's idea for *Our Mutual Friend* in 1855, when Podsnappery loomed large enough to provide a possible title. Instead, he dispersed the characters and events across the grotesque and curiously promising landscape of dust-heaps, riverside, backstreets and outer suburbs of the city, as well as the Thames at Henley, to create the combination of 'drollery with romance' he sought.

With the exception of Sheridan Knowles, the three literary figures who lie behind Dickens's achievement are Shakespeare, Carlyle and Thomas Hood. Of Shakespeare's plays, *Hamlet* and *Macbeth* are the most frequently influential, particularly certain well-known scenes and lines. For these the reader is referred to the notes and index. It is striking that an article in *All the Year Round* used the example of Shakespeare to defend the novelist against the cry of 'Sensation!' in terms that strongly suggest a passage in *Our Mutual Friend* (see notes to book 1, chapter 11). This was probably felt to be a telling argument in the Shakespeare Tercentenary year (1864). Carlyle's importance for Dickens is well known. *Latter-Day Pamphlets* may have weakened Carlyle's standing with many literary figures, but the notes in these pages confirm what other commentators have suggested, that Carlyle's influence over Dickens remained strong. Indeed, the imagery of dung-heaps and scavenging in *Latter-Day Pamphlets* makes it the closest of Carlyle's writings to *Our Mutual Friend*. Two of Hood's narrative poems contribute to *Our Mutual Friend*: his immensely successful version of the story of the schoolteacher murderer Eugene Aram, *The Dream of Eugene Aram*, influences Dickens's presentation of Bradley, and his satiric 'Miss Kilmansegg and Her Precious Leg' affects the characterization of a gold-hungry society.

There remains the question of the extent of the influence on Dickens of Mayhew's *London Labour and the London Poor*, which was published in a four-volume edition in 1861–2. The *Book of Memoranda* gives clear evidence that Dickens's decision to make fictional use of both dust-heaps and riverside scavengers precedes the four-volume edition of Mayhew. Much of Mayhew's work, of course, was published in one form or another in the 1850s, but the reader of *Household Words* and *All the Year Round* will be aware that dust-heaps and all manner of ways of retrieving and using waste are a curious preoccupation of those journals (see Metz, 1979–80), as are, to a lesser extent, riverside life and scavenging. It is possible, though, that the publication in 1861–2 of Mayhew's complete work, revealing, as it did, a whole world of sad lives and curious occupations centred on the salvage and selling of waste, acted as a catalyst which enabled Dickens to bring together his ideas in 1862. The frequent citations from Mayhew in the notes that follow are, however, in most cases, intended to illustrate the world from which Dickens drew his fiction, not to suggest that they were the source of his knowledge of it.

A NOTE ON THE TEXT

The text of *Our Mutual Friend* used for this study is the two-volume edition of 1865, the first edition. The manuscript and work plans of the novel are in the Pierpont Morgan Library, New York. A complete set of proofs, parts of which are corrected by Dickens, is in the Berg Collection, New York Public Library.

Like the manuscripts of Dickens's other late novels, the manuscript of *Our Mutual Friend* is heavily corrected. Dickens also made substantial cuts and many minor changes at proof stage. In preparation for this volume, the manuscript and corrected proofs have been collated with the first edition. It has not been possible in the notes that follow to include more than a selection of the significant changes made in the manuscript and the proofs. For a complete collation of Dickens's work on *Our Mutual Friend*, we must await the publication of the Clarendon edition.

HOW TO USE THE NOTES

To help the reader locate in the novel the word or phrase quoted in an entry, the notes are presented in this way: the opening phrase of the paragraph which includes the entry is quoted as a guide and printed in italics; the entry itself appears in bold-face type. This system should also help the reader who turns from the novel in search of a note on a particular word or phrase.

Documentation within the notes is kept to a minimum by the use of an abbreviated form of referencing. Works of literature are referred to by their parts: *Vanity Fair* 12; *Past and Present* 3.2; *The Faerie Queene* 2.12.17.14–16; 'The Idiot Boy' 8–10. Frequently cited works of criticism and other secondary sources are referred to by author, part (where relevant) and page: '(Collins 171–2)', '(Mayhew 3.106–7)'. References to infrequently cited sources add the date of publication: '(Sala, 1859, 23)'. Complete details are given in the Select Bibliography.

The articles quoted from *Household Words* and *All the Year Round* always antedate or are contemporary with the composition of the novel unless the reference indicates otherwise.

The notes indicate the divisions of the novel in its first published form as a series of nineteen monthly parts (the final part a double number), published from May 1864 to November 1865.

The Work Plans

The notes include transcripts of the sheets of memoranda on which Dickens sketched out his ideas for each monthly number. He folded each sheet once to make two pages, and he referred to the sheets as 'Mems'. In the present volume they are referred to as 'work plans'. To distinguish the pages from each other, the left page is described as the 'number plan' and the right page as the 'chapter plan'. In the notes which follow, the work plans are located among the notes to the first chapter of each monthly number.

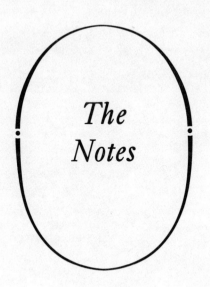

The
Notes

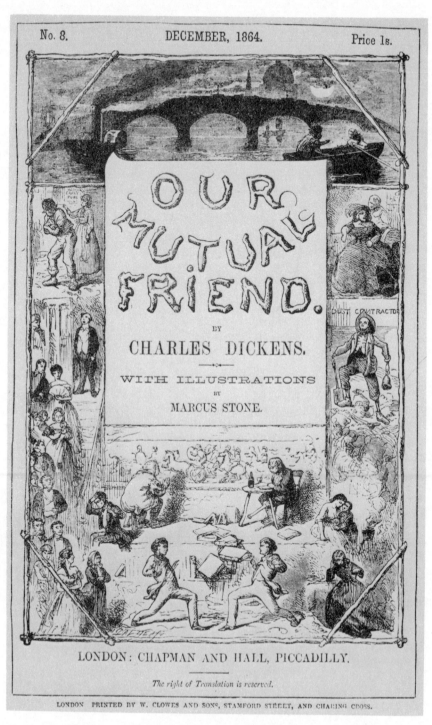

1   The cover of the monthly parts of *Our Mutual Friend*, by Marcus Stone

OUR MUTUAL FRIEND

Dickens made a list of 'General Titles' in his *Book of Memoranda* which includes: 'The Grindstone', 'Rokesmith's Forge', 'The Cinder Heap', 'Broken Crockery', 'Dust', 'The Young Person', 'Co' and 'Our Mutual Friend' (6). A slip inserted at the opening page of the first monthly part of the novel reads: '* * * *The Reader will understand the use of the popular phrase* OUR MUTUAL FRIEND, *as the title of this book, on arriving at the Ninth Chapter* (*page* 84).' There Boffin tells the Wilfers three times that Rokesmith is 'Our Mutual Friend'. Generally, Dickens used the phrase as a somewhat pompous cliché; for instance, in *The Chimes*, the 'Poor Man's Friend' Sir Joseph Bowley says: 'My lady, the Alderman is so obliging as to remind me that he has had "the distinguished honour" – he is very good – of meeting me at the house of our mutual friend Deedles, the banker' (2). The lack of mutuality in modern society was one of Carlyle's themes: in *Past and Present* (1843) he had complained that 'Our life is not a mutual helpfulness; but rather cloaked under due laws-of-war, named "fair competition" and so forth, it is a mutual hostility' (3.2). Prior to publication, the novel was advertised at the end of an *AYR* article which described the exorbitant interest rates of a Mutual, General, Universal, Benevolent, and Prudent Life and Loan Insurance Society (13.168).

SIR JAMES EMERSON TENNENT [Dedication]

Sir James Emerson Tennent (1804–69) was a distinguished traveller, politician and author. A philhellene who knew Byron in Greece, he became a Member of Parliament for Belfast in 1832 and was for most of his career a liberal conservative. He supported Grey in the struggle for the Reform Bill and Peel over the abolition of the Corn Laws. He was knighted in 1845, and from 1845 to 1850 he was the civil secretary to the colonial government of Ceylon. He was permanent secretary to the Poor Law Board from 1852 and secretary to the Board of Trade from the same year. He retired in 1867 and was created a baronet.

His *Ceylon: An Account of the Island, Physical, Historical, and Topographical*, 2 volumes (1859), is a masterly and fascinating account. Articles about Ceylon in *AYR* draw on the work.

Tennent came to know Forster in their days as law students at University College in the late 1820s. Forster included the Tennents in a list of Dickens's friends in 1848, describing them as 'very old friends of us both'; Dickens met them on his Italian trip of 1853. In his attack on the Poor Laws in book 3, chapter 8, Dickens remarked that the circumstances of the poor did not appear in 'the Returns of the Board of Trade'. It seems likely that Tennent's attitude to Poor Law administration coincided with his own.

BOOK THE FIRST.
THE CUP AND THE LIP.

The proverb is 'There is many a slip between the cup and the lip'. The titles of each of the novel's four books are parts of proverbs.

Book 1, Chapter 1   First monthly number
                                                    May 1864

ON THE LOOK OUT.

In these times of ours

In these times of ours, though concerning the exact year there is no need to be precise]   The opening words recall the original title for *HT*: *Hard Times, for These Times*. Allusions within the novel suggest it is set in the early 1860s. The events of the novel take place over three and a quarter years. The time-scheme can be established by way of the following references:

1.1	'an autumn evening'	Year 1
1.10	'greenhouse plants' for the Lammles' wedding	
1.12	'nipping spring'	Year 2
1.17	'the blooming summer days'	
2.1	'Autumn . . . full half a year had come and gone since the bird of prey lay dead': Gaffer died in the spring (1.14)	
2.12	'Not . . . a summer evening . . . a cold shrewd windy evening'	
2.16	'the first anniversary of the happy marriage of Mr. and Mrs. Lammle'	
3.1	'a foggy day in London'	
3.9	'the bright wintry scene'	
4.1	'an evening in the summer time'	Year 3
4.4	Bella tells John that she is pregnant	
4.12	'the ship upon the ocean . . . brought a baby-Bella' and it is again 'a winter evening'	Year 4
4.15	'One winter day'	

a boat of dirty and disreputable appearance]   Mayhew described the boats of the dredgermen:

There is ... always the appearance of labour about the boat, like a ship returning after a long voyage, daubed and filthy, and looking sadly in need of thorough cleansing. The grappling irons are over the bow, resting on a coil of rope; while the other end of the boat is filled with coals, bones, and old rope, mixed with the mud of the river. (2.149)

between Southwark Bridge which is of iron, and London Bridge which is of stone] New London Bridge, built of granite, replaced the ancient and picturesque Old London Bridge, with its two rows of houses, in 1831; in modern times it was removed to Arizona. Southwark Bridge, the 'Iron Bridge' of *LD*, was opened as a tollbridge by a public company in 1819. The distance between the two was just over a quarter of a mile.

The figures in this boat

a strong man ... and a dark girl ... sufficiently like him to be recognizable as his daughter.] Mayhew also described the typical dredgerman:

A short stout figure, with a face soiled and blackened with perspiration, and surmounted by a tarred sou'-wester, the body habited in a soiled check shirt, with the sleeves turned up above the elbows, and exhibiting a pair of sunburnt brawny arms. (2.149)

The girl rowed, pulling a pair of sculls very easily] Lady Tippins imagines Lizzie to be a 'horrid female waterman' (4.'The Last') such as is described in the *HW* article 'Powder Dick and his Train': 'His wife plies the oars – a tall, bony, ay, and strong-boned woman – quick of action, quicker of imprecation and vituperation, who on a disputed copper would not scruple to paint your eyes as black as Erebus with the fire out' (7.238).

his boat had no cushion for a sitter, no paint, no inscription ... and he could not be a waterman] Watermen carried passengers on the river. By an Act of Parliament of 1827 they were required to license their boats, and paint on them their names and the number of persons they were authorized to carry. In the eighteenth century there were as many as forty thousand watermen, but by the 1860s the introduction of steamers and the opening of new bridges had greatly reduced the trade, and many watermen were driven to scavenging for a living. Mayhew remarked that 'The dredgerman and his boat may be immediately distinguished from all others; there is nothing similar to them on the river. The sharp cutwater fore and aft, and short rounded appearance of the vessel, marks it out at once from the skiff or wherry of the waterman' (2.149).

his boat was too crazy and too small to take in cargo for delivery, and he could not be a lighterman or river-carrier] 'The river lightermen (as the watermen style them all, no matter what the craft) are ... so far a distinct class, that they convey goods only, and not passengers' (Mayhew 3.332).

17

Open between the bridges

        <u>It in <tow> tow</u>

<u>The Veneerings.</u> (who <u>is</u> their oldest friend?)

      at their dinner party. lay the ground carefully. Weary servant

        Late Mr <Harmon> Harmon

          <u>Lead up for old servant. Next N?</u>

'Man's Drowned.'

    Work in two witnesses by name: For end of story:

        Ship's steward – Potterson

                Job Potterson

      Passenger   Mr Jacob Kibble

Work in the girl who was to have been married and made
rich.

        4 Books.

        I – The Cup and the Lip

        II – Birds of a Feather

        III – a Long Lane

        IV – a Turning

Chapter I

On the Look-out

The man in his boat, watching the tide. The Gaffer

Gaffer

His daughter rowing – Jenny – Lizzie.

Taking the body in <tow> tow   Gaffer Hexam

<The rej> His rejected partner, who has   Hexam

'Robbed a live man!'

Riderhood

  this fellow's name

Chapter II

The Man from Somewhere

The entirely new people.

Everything new – Grandfather new, if they had one

    Dinner Party. Twemlow. Podsnap. Lady Tippins

Alfred Lightwood? also Eugene. Languid story of Harmon

Mortimer   the Dust Contractor

Chapter III

Another Man

Hexam's son charley Hexam's house, and the bills on the wall. old mill.

  Police Station.   Body 'Not much worse than Lady Tippins'   also 'Eugene'

  Mr. Julius <Hand> Handford   So Harmon Murder comes to be forgotten

Chapter IV

The R. Wilfer Family

Rumty. Majestic and monotonous female for his wife.

Two daughters. Bella Wilfer

Lavinia

cherubic husband – & allegorical wife

Mr. John Rokesmith.

Allied to the bottom of the river

business-like usage]   Gaffer is a dredgerman, so called because of the dredging-nets used to recover articles from the river bottom. He is a professional river-scavenger: 'They pick up a living, nobody knows how, out of the mud and soppy timbers, as men will pick up livings from every refuse; as a teeming population and an advanced population only can have such livings to be picked up'('Powder Dick and his Train', *HW* 7.236). There were about a hundred dredgermen operating on the river between Putney and Gravesend. Scavenging often slipped into petty theft from barges and other vessels: for instance, coal was often knocked off barges so it could later be ' "picked out of the river alongside" ' (Mayhew 2.149). Finding corpses was a small but sensationally interesting part of the activity (which Dickens mentions in *BH* 57 and *GE* 44). Mayhew recorded:

> The dredgers ... are the men who find almost all the bodies of persons drowned. If there be a reward offered for the recovery of a body, numbers of the dredgers will at once endeavour to obtain it, while if there be no reward, there is at least the inquest money to be had — beside other chances. What these chances are may be inferred from the well-known fact that no body recovered by a dredgerman ever happens to have any money about it, when brought to shore.

' "I never finds anythink on the bodies," ' a dredgerman told him: ' "Lor bless you! people don't have anythink in their pockets when they gits drowned, they are not such fools as all that" ' (2.149, 150).

'Keep her out, Lizzie

Lizzie]   In the MS, Lizzie appears as 'Jenny' throughout the first number, usually corrected.

The red light was gone

at the paddles of the river steamboats]   Steamboats, propelled by paddle rather than by screw, were introduced on the Thames in 1814. By the mid-century there was a large volume of traffic.

the filthy water]   In London the river was badly polluted by sewage and industrial effluent:

> The river it was yellow mud,
> With putrid colours varied,
> And every kind of filthy thing
> Upon the tide was carried. (*Punch* 29.84)

Dickens had called it a 'deadly sewer' in *LD* (1.3). Attempts in the late 1850s to clean the river with disinfectants had not been successful, but by the 1860s work had begun on an effective sewage system for the metropolis.

The girl turned her face towards him

a certain likeness to a roused bird of prey.]   Gaffer is the foremost bird of prey in the novel. Dickens may have remembered Jonson, *Volpone* (1606):

> vulture, kite,
> Raven, and gor-crow, all my birds of prey,
> That thinke me turning carcasse, now they come
> (1.2.88–90)

In *Past and Present*, Carlyle complained of a 'Scavenger Age'; in the 1840s he considered writing a volume with the title 'The Scavenger Age'; and in his *Latter-Day Pamphlets* (1850) he gave to his Mammonite the prayer 'Soul, take thy care, it is all *well* that thou art a vulture-soul' (Qualls, 1978).

'As if it wasn't your living!

meat and drink to you!']   An idiomatic term in common speech which appears in Romans 14.17: 'For the kingdom of God is not meat and drink; but righteousness, and peace, and joy in the Holy Ghost.'

'In luck again, Gaffer?'

Gaffer]   A term of respect for an elderly man, or one skilled in his trade; here with a suggestion of gaffing, as for bodies.

'He's had touches enough not to want no more

like the wulturs, pardner, and scent 'em out.']   Charles Waterton defended this mistaken idea in an essay 'On the Faculty of Scent in the Vulture' in his *Essays on Natural History* (1838), which Dickens had in his library.

'No. Has a dead man any use for money?

Has a dead man any use for money?]   This speech recalls Falstaff on honour in *1 Henry IV*: 'What is honour? A word. What is in that word? Honour. What is that honour? Air. A trim reckoning! Who hath it? He that died o' Wednesday. Doth he feel it? No. Doth he hear it? No' (5.1.130–4). Gaffer's self-justification is close to the views of the dredgermen, but for this scene, and for others involving Lizzie and Gaffer, Dickens drew on James Sheridan Knowles's play *The Daughter* (1837). See pages 42, 63 and 64. In the play Robert, the father of the heroine, is one of a community of wreckers on the Cornish coast. Their activities include robbing the bodies of drowned men. The play opens with this dialogue:

Philip.	Our craft is scandaliz'd! We strip the dead!
	But what of that? The dead but want a grave!
	We give it them; we take what they can spare.
Ambrose.	You're right; we do no more!

Philip.   As to the rights
              Of the living, whom they leave behind, let men
              Look to their own! If not, why let it go!
              Is it for us to stand the drenching rain!
              Wade to our necks into the sea! perhaps
              Take boat and pull among the breakers, at
              The peril, every moment, of our lives,
              For their behoof, while they lie snug in bed;
              Loll o'er their fires, or sit around their feasts?
              Methinks there's reason in the wrecker's trade!
Ambrose.   There is. He risks, and toils, for what he gets.
Philip.   But then he does no mischief to the dead,
              More than the waves have done!

The play's villain, Norris, is shunned by the heroine's father, Robert:

Norris.   Why shun me then?
Robert.   I like thee not.
Norris.   'Two of a trade!' Is't so?
          Well! I'm the luckiest wrecker of you all.
          I cannot help it!   (2.3)

Norris makes his 'good luck' as Riderhood accuses Gaffer of doing (1.6). He also arranges matters so that suspicion of a murder he has committed falls on the heroine's father. Norris's accomplice is called Wolf.

Book 1, Chapter 2

THE MAN FROM SOMEWHERE.

Mr. and Mrs. Veneering

Mr. and Mrs. Veneering were bran-new people]   In his *Book of Memoranda* Dickens made the note:

> The perfectly New people. Everything new about them. If *they* presented a
> father and mother, it seems as if THEY must be bran new, like the furniture and
> the Carriages, shining with Varnish, and just home from the manufacturer's. (20)

'Gilbert Glossin' is the name of a character in Scott's *Guy Mannering* (1815), and 'Vineer' is the name of a furnisher who provides the bran-new furnishings for a financier in Thackeray's *The Newcomes* (1853–5). 'Bran-new' was standard usage: for instance, in *DS* there is a 'bran-new Tavern' (6). Knowles (1985) has shown that the veneering and varnishing of cheap furniture was a recent development, and that a series of articles in Fraser's Magazine (1850–1) entitled 'The Age of Veneer' influenced Dickens's presentation of wealthy society in *OMF*.

Though the wealthy upstart is a traditional literary type, there may have been a distant original for Veneering among the financiers of the 1860s. A series of *AYR* articles by M. R. L. Meason in 1864–5 extends and substantiates the satire on financial speculation in *OMF* (see Select Bibliography). In one of the articles a Mr Grass is introduced as:

> a typical man of a class which ten years ago did not exist in England. He had made a very large fortune entirely by speculations in shares; and, having started without fifty pounds of capital, a stranger and a sojourner in the land, was now one of the magnates of fashion (in a certain set, of course), and a member of the first assembly of gentlemen in the world.

Grass's home is

> in one of the new quarters, of a new district, in a new part of London. The house, of course, was new, and everything in it was new ... the furniture looked, if possible, newer than anything I had yet seen, and the walls were covered from top to bottom with pictures which smelt of varnish.

There is even a 'bran-new marble clock on the chimney-piece'. Of course, Meason was adopting Dickens's terms, not vice versa. Grass is a German by birth who, beginning as a toyshop-keeper, 'changed his family designation and set up for a highly respectable Briton' (14.370). Meason probably intended to suggest the career of Albert Gottheimer, a German Jew born in Dublin in 1830, who began as a partner in a foreign 'fancy' business and became one of the leading financiers of the day. Gottheimer took the name of Albert Grant, Grant being the family name of the earls of Seaforth, the heads of the Clan of Grant. Veneering's Christian name is Hamilton, the name of another ancient Scottish family. Grant became MP for Kidderminster in 1865 and later Baron Grant (contemporaries thought it a '*barren grant*'). Gottheimer first came to public attention in the spring of 1859 when he put out a prospectus for a Mercantile Discount Company Ltd. His manner of conducting this company is described by a modern historian as 'dangerous' and an 'effrontery' (King, 1936, 224). The Mercantile Discount Company collapsed in 1859 but, in 1863, Gottheimer reappeared, under the name of Grant, to float the Crédit Foncier and Mobilier of England, and subsequently to become involved in the affairs of the finance house Overend, Gurney, the collapse of which brought about the crisis of 1866. (See pages 156 and 280.)

a bran-new quarter of London.]   Later named as Stucconia (1.10).

come home in matting from the Pantechnicon]   The word Pantechnicon ('Pertaining to all the arts') was used as the name of a large warehouse-cum-bazaar in Motcomb Street, off Belgrave Square.

There was an innocent piece

a livery stable-yard in Duke Street, Saint James's]   A livery stable was a place where horses were kept for the owner, and fed and groomed at a fixed charge; there was a large stable-yard (Mason's) off Duke Street. Duke Street is a small street in the fashionable West End. Edward Gibbon summed it up in 1772: 'Vile street good quarter.'

The name of this article was Twemlow]   Dickens made lists of names for characters in his *Book of Memoranda*. They include the names of a number of the characters introduced in this chapter: Twemlow, Snigsworth, Podsnap, Tippins, Lammle and Lightword (Lightwood).

But, it was not this which steeped

Saint James's Square.]   St James's was the most fashionable square in London.

Twemlow had first known Veneering at his club]   Gentlemen's clubs played an important part in Victorian social and political life. Membership was normally restricted to those known to and approved of by existing members. The most important clubs had their premises around St James's and Pall Mall.

a Member, an Engineer, a Payer-off of the National Debt, a Poem on Shakespeare, a Grievance, and a Public Office]   The Member is a Member of Parliament. The Engineer, like the Contractor introduced in book 3, chapter 17, is probably connected with the booming railway construction of the period. The National Debt, 'eminently a fighting debt', had risen from half a million pounds at the time of the Revolution of 1688 to over twelve million in 1863; the endless debate about whether to pay off the debt or not is described in *AYR* (11.557–64). The alteration in the MS of 'a poet' to 'a Poem on Shakespeare' makes an allusion to the poems written in honour of Shakespeare for the Tercentenary (1864). These are lines from Martin Tupper's 'Shakespeare. An Ode for his Three-Hundredth Birthday':

> O Paragon unthought before,
> O miracle of selftaught lore . . .
> O gentle, happy, modest mind,
> O genial, cheerful, frank and kind,
> Not even could domestic strife
> Sour the sweetness of thy life.

An *AYR* article that describes the official celebrations at Stratford mentions a poem that begins 'Come let us Tercentenerate' (11, 21 May 1864, 350). At the Circumlocution Office in *LD* there are 'people with grievances, people who wanted to prevent grievances, people who wanted to redress grievances' (1.10).

Thus it had come about

to soften any man's brain]   'Softening of the brain' was a common expression for loss of memory and mental power.

This evening the Veneerings give a banquet.

Four pigeon-breasted retainers in plain clothes stand in line in the hall.] The servants' posture is emphasized by their white boiled shirts and waistcoats set against black coats. They are in 'plain clothes' rather than in livery.

as who should say, 'Here is another wretched creature come to dinner; such is life!'] The phrase 'as who should say' is common in Shakespeare: for instance, 'And, speaking it, he wishtly look'd on me,/As who should say "I would thou wert the man"' (*Richard II* 5.4.7–8). The Analytical's words suggest passages of biblical gloom such as Romans 7.24: 'O wretched man that I am! who shall deliver me from the body of this death?'

Mrs. Veneering welcomes her sweet Mr. Twemlow.

Mr. Boots and Mr. Brewer] 'Boots' was the term for the youngest officer in a mess; also for a servant, generally a youth, responsible for cleaning boots. In *GE* Herbert Pocket remarks: 'I don't know why it should be a crack thing to be a brewer; but it is indisputable that while you cannot possibly be genteel and bake, you may be as genteel as never was and brew' (22).

A too, too smiling large man

A too, too smiling large man] An echo of Hamlet's words: 'O, that this too too solid flesh would melt,/Thaw, and resolve itself into a dew!' (1.2.129–30).

When the first shock fell upon him

his neat little shoes and his neat little silk stockings of a bygone fashion] Twemlow is wearing breeches or short pantaloons. His 'neat little shoes' are dress shoes or pumps. Like his high collar, cravat and ruffled wristbands, these items are in the style of the 1820s.

'Let me,' says the large man

in his fatal freshness he seems to find perpetual verdure and eternal youth in the phrase] Dickens balances the witty 'fatal freshness' against the poetical clichés; Wordsworth used the phrase 'perpetual verdure' in 'To the River Derwent' (8).

It is questionable whether any man

set up the shirt-front of the young Antinous] Antinous is a traditional type of male beauty: the young favourite of the Emperor Hadrian, he drowned himself in the Nile, probably from melancholy; the Emperor honoured his memory, and many statues of him were produced. He is usually represented with full locks, large melancholy eyes, and a broad and swelling breast.

Thus the melancholy retainer

'Come down and be poisoned, ye unhappy children of men!']   'Children of men' is the biblical phrase for the descendants of Cain and, after the Deluge, for the wicked and impious generally: 'Thou turnest man to destruction; and sayest, Return, ye children of men' (Psalms 90.3).

Twemlow, having no lady assigned him

Twemlow, having no lady assigned him]   When dinner was announced the host offered his arm to the lady most senior in social rank and led the way into the dining-room. The other guests, strictly in order of precedence, followed in procession, the hostess bringing up the rear with the senior gentleman.

Revived by soup, Twemlow discourses

the Court Circular]   The Court Circular records the daily activities of the royal family. It was compiled by the court and printed by the newspapers: 'Down with the *Court Circular* – that engine and propagator of Snobbishness!' (Thackeray, *The Book of Snobs*, 1846–7, 4).

a gloomy Analytical Chemist]   The Analytical Chemist recalls a character created by the versatile comic actor Charles Mathews (1776–1835), whose work Dickens admired. The character was a 'Mr Alum',

> the well-known writing Chemist . . . a sort of poisoner of the pantry, who, with his eternal 'Beware, that's poisonous! I've analyzed it, I've tried it, and I know it' – frightens every one's appetite away, and nearly starves all who are fools enough to attend him. (*Selections from Mr. Mathews' Celebrated Memorandum Book*, 1825, 6; noted by Davis, 1964)

Alum was based on Friederich Accum (1769–1838), the analytical chemist whose *Treatise on Adulterations of Food and Culinary Poisons* (1820) first drew public attention to the facts of food adulteration. He believed that 'In reference to the deterioration of almost all the necessaries and comforts of existence, it may be justly observed, in a civil as well as a religious sense, that "*in the midst of life we are in death*" ' (30). At the end of his preface he quoted 2 Kings 4.40: 'there is death in the pot'. Despite an anonymous publication in 1830, *Deadly Adulteration and Slow Poisoning Unmasked; or, Disease and Death in the Pot and Bottle*, widespread interest in food adulteration had to be re-created in the 1850s, when a series of articles in the *Lancet* between 1851 and 1854 and a number of further studies renewed concern. The first Adulteration of Foods Act was passed in 1860 but it was a bitter disappointment to radical reformers. Metz (1979) has drawn attention to a series of *HW* articles about food adulteration with titles like 'Death in the Teapot' (2.277), 'Death in the Bread-Basket' (2.323) and 'Death in the Sugar Plum' (2.426–7). Articles in *AYR* continued the theme: 'The Modern Alchemist' (8.380–4); 'Pull Devil, Pull Baker' (11.569–73), about the adulteration of bread;

and a comic fantasy, 'How Professor Gaster Lectured a Ghost' (7.107–11), which brings together dinner-parties, overindulgence in food and champagne, indigestion, food adulteration, chemical analysis, and talking skeletons in anticipation of some elements in *OMF*. Lady Tippins is said to make 'a series of experiments on her digestive functions' so daring they 'might benefit the human race'; the less hardy Twemlow suffers from permanent indigestion.

The great looking-glass above the sideboard

in gold and eke in silver]   Dickens frequently makes facetious use of the archaism 'eke': Mr Tulkinghorn in *BH* is 'an old-fashioned old gentleman, attorney-at-law, and eke solicitor' (2).

The Heralds' College found out a Crusading ancestor for Veneering] The popular revival of interest in the Middle Ages and in chivalry encouraged the revival of heraldry, even among families of obscure origin. Countless families employed genealogists and lawyers to establish their often dubious descent from an ancient title so that they could be granted the right to bear a coat of arms by the College of Arms, or Heralds' College. Dickens himself adopted, without any authority, what in a letter he called 'my father's crest: a lion couchant, bearing in his dexter paw a Maltese cross' (5 April 1869, *Nonesuch* 3.717).

a caravan of camels take charge of the fruits and flowers]   Egyptian motifs and styles were an important influence on Victorian decorative arts. Elaborate objects for the dining-table, such as candelabras, wine-coolers, centre-pieces and vases, often took the form of sphinxes, obelisks, camels, crocodiles and pyramids.

Reflects Veneering; forty . . . a kind of sufficiently well-looking veiled-prophet, not prophesying.]   The allusion is to Thomas Moore's popular narrative poem *Lalla Rookh* (1817). Mokanna is 'The Veiled Prophet of Khorassan':

> O'er his features hung
> The Veil, the Silver Veil, which he had flung
> In mercy there, to hide from mortal sight
> His dazzling brow, till man could bear his light. (9–12)

His followers are deceived: Mokanna is evil and has a hellish countenance.

two little light-coloured wiry wings, one on either side of his else bald head]   A comic suggestion of the seraphim and cherubim of painting, depicted by their heads only and as having one, two or three pairs of wings.

fine woman for Professor Owen, quantity of bone]   Sir Richard Owen (1804–92), known in the press as 'Old Bones', was a friend of Dickens and a leading naturalist of the time. He was the first Hunterian Professor of Comparative Anatomy and Physiology at the Royal College of Surgeons and later head of the natural history section at the British Museum. A *HW* article, 'Done to a Jelly' (indexed as 'Bone Soup'), reported Owen's lectures on the theme that the 'seemingly most worthless parts of animal bodies, are turned to uses of the most unexpected kind by the inventive skill and science of man' (9.438).

susceptible to east wind]   In *BH* Jarndyce attributes all his unhappy moments to the proverbially unpleasant east wind. In *OMF* it blows on the night and morning of Gaffer's death (1.12–14).

First-Gentleman-in-Europe collar and cravat]   The First Gentleman was the Prince Regent, later George IV. The collar of the shirt was worn upright; the two points projected to the cheeks and were kept in place by a neck-cloth, in the form of either a cravat or a stock. The collar and cravat were an important part of the dress of the Regency dandy.

a dyed Long Walk up the top of her head, as a convenient public approach to the bunch of false hair]   Lady Tippins's parting is so straight it resembles the road from Windsor Castle through the park, three miles long and perfectly straight, which was known as the 'Long Walk' (Hill).

a certain 'Mortimer']   The name Alfred is deleted and replaced by Mortimer a number of times in the MS of this chapter. Mortimer is a name of Norman origin.

Reflects Eugene]   The name means 'well born'.

the champagne chalice]   The *ch* in 'champagne' was pronounced as in 'chalice' at this time. The 'chalice' is the cup used to administer the Eucharist; the solemn Analytical has the appearance of an officiating clergyman.

two other stuffed Buffers interposed between the rest of the company and possible accidents.]   The word 'Buffer' is not capitalized in the MS. 'Buffer' suggests stupidity, also the buffers which absorb shock (the earliest use in relation to railways in *OED* is dated 1862).

The Veneering dinners are excellent dinners

this hardy old cruiser has last touched at the North Pole]   An allusion to the attempts to discover the fate of Sir John Franklin's Arctic expedition of 1845, about which there were many *HW* and *AYR* articles; one article describes some of the cruisers – *Resolute, Intrepid, Pioneer* and *Assistance* – being fitted out (*HW* 1.181).

'Give you my honor I never heard

any man from Jamaica, except the man who was a brother]   A Wedgwood cameo issued in 1768 showed a Negro in chains and bore the inscription 'Am I not a man and a brother?' The little medallions were mounted as hatpins, buttons and rings, and in many other ways. The motto was later adopted by the Anti-Slavery Society and was so overworked that it became a joke.

28

'Except,' Eugene strikes in

except our friend who long lived on rice pudding and isinglass . . . and a leg of mutton somehow ended in daygo.'] A garbled version of a nursery rhyme that first appears in 1822:

> There was an old man of Tobago
> Who lived on rice, gruel, and sago;
>   Till, much to his bliss,
>   His physician said this –
> To a leg, sir, of mutton you may go.

'Isinglass', made from fish bladders, was the most approved form of gelatine for cooking purposes.

'Now, my dear Mrs. Veneering

a rough Cymon] In Dryden's *Cymon and Ipheginia* (1699), from a tale by Boccaccio, the son of a Cyprian lord is described as

> Fair, Tall, his Limbs with due Proportion join'd
> But of a heavy, dull, degenerate Mind . . .
> A clownish Mien, a Voice with rustick sound,
> And stupid Eyes, that ever lov'd the Ground. (52–3, 56–7)

When Cymon sees Ipheginia love acts as a civilizing influence on him. In one of Dickens's comic tales, 'The Tuggses at Ramsgate', the hero changes his name from Simon to Cymon when he inherits some money (*SB*).

'I banish the falsh wretch

my Cupidon (my name for my Ledger, my dear)] The Book of Cupid, or of Love, on the model of the *Decameron* or the *Satyricon. Cupidon* is also the French for 'beau', 'gallant': Byron said Count D'Orsay had 'all the airs of a *Cupidon dechaîné'*.

'Upon my life,' says Mortimer languidly

languidly] Mortimer adopts the languid drawl affected by well-to-do young men of leisure. Compare Harthouse in *HT*.

to have the eyes of Europe upon me to this extent] Dickens elsewhere referred to the newspaper phrase 'the eyes of Europe'; for instance, in a speech to the Birmingham and Midland Institute: 'I have had it in my mind, first, to commend the short motto, in two words, "Courage, Persevere" . . . Not because the eyes of Europe are upon them . . . but because it is good and right of itself' (*Speeches* 405).

fixing him with a local habitation]   Theseus's words in *A Midsummer Night's Dream*:

> And as imagination bodies forth
> The forms of things unknown, the poet's pen
> Turns them to shapes, and gives to airy nothing
> A local habitation and a name. (5.1.14–17)

Eugene suggests 'Day and Martin's.'

Day and Martin's]   Day & Martin's was a blacking manufactory in High Holborn: the firm's name was a slang term for cheap port. Dickens makes the same joke in *OT*, chapter 25.

'The man,' Mortimer goes on, addressing Eugene

a tremendous old rascal who made his money by Dust.']   Mayhew gave an account of the dust business (2.166–7). The various London parishes contracted with individual entrepreneurs – the dust contractors – for the clearance of dust-bins and other rubbish. Formerly, dust had been of considerable commercial value and the contractors had paid a yearly sum for the right to collect it; subsequently, the demand fell off and the parishes had to pay the contractors to remove it. The contractor employed a gang of men directly, or indirectly through subcontractors, whom he equipped with shovels, baskets, carts and horses. The dust was removed to some local ground owned by the contractor where it was heaped. There it was sifted, usually by women labourers who worked long hours for the lowest of wages. This is a description of the scene at Dodd's yard (the canal is the Regent's Canal):

> Flanking one side of the yard were a score or so of upreared dustcarts, and on the other side, extending almost from the outer gate to the water's brink, were great mounds of ordinary dustbin muck; and in the midst of the mounds – literally, so that in many cases part only of their bodies were visible – were thirty or forty women and girls. In view of the canal, the surface covered with big yellow slabs of ice – with a rasping northwind blowing continuously through the yard, and with frost and snow everywhere to be seen, there sat the 'hill-women,' girls of sixteen and old dames of sixty, each holding before her a sieve as large as the top of a small loo-table, in which she dexterously caught the huge shovelfull supplies of the 'feeder'. ('Dust Ho!', *Penny Illustrated Paper*, 27 January 1866, 62)

A *HW* article, 'Dust; or Ugliness Redeemed', by R. H. Horne (1.379–84) combined information with romance about the dust business. The scene is 'a huge Dust-heap of a dirty black colour – being, in fact, one of those immense mounds of cinders, ashes, and other emptyings from dust-holes and bins, which have conferred celebrity on certain suburban neighbourhoods'. The yard is by a canal so it is probably Dodd's. An aged man and woman, Gaffer Doubleyear and Peg

LONDON LIFE, NO. 9,—DODD'S DUST-YARD.—SEE NƎXT PAGE.

2   The dust-heaps at Dodd's yard. From the *Penny Illustrated Paper*, 27 January 1866

Dotting, and a little cripple boy, Jem Clinker, are described at work on the heap. Each has kept alive his or her fancy and is able to imagine things of great value or beauty in the dust. Jem discovers a miniature and a parchment. Horne commented:

> These Dust-heaps are a wonderful compound of things. A banker's cheque for a considerable sum was found in one of them ... But banker's cheques, or gold and silver articles, are the least valuable of their ingredients. Among other things, a variety of useful chemicals are extracted. Their chief value, however, is for the making of bricks. (382)

At this point a young gentleman is discovered to have thrown himself in the nearby canal. They rescue him and bring him to life by burying him in the warm ashes. He awakes and says: 'I know where I am, now. I remember this great dark hill of ashes – like Death's kingdom, full of all sorts of strange things, and put to many uses' (384). The parchment Jem found turns out to be the title deed to the young gentleman's fortune. He rewards Jem and his two old friends by buying them a cottage: 'what they most desired was to have a cottage in the neighbour-hood of the Dust-heap, built large enough for all three to live together, and keep a cow' (384). The young gentleman marries the contractor's daughter. The contractor offers a dowry of £20,000 or the dust-heap. The couple take the money, but the heap 'was subsequently sold for forty thousand pounds, and was exported to Russia to rebuild Moscow' (384).

Dickens's relations with the dust contractor Henry Dodd are described on page 57. His work with Miss Burdett Coutts had involved him in dealings with another dust contractor. As Fielding (1965) has shown, Miss Burdett Coutts bought a large tract of land in Bethnal Green from a dust contractor on which to build workmen's flats. The project was discussed in 1852 but work only began in 1859 and the flats were not opened until 1862: 'The explanation of the delay is the dust-heap: for although Miss Burdett Coutts became the owner of the land she was, for some reason, unable to evict her principal tenant who was given seven years to find an alternative place to carry on his business' (117). In 1854, in a letter to Miss Burdett Coutts, Dickens referred to dust contractors as the type of those who used their influence to oppress the poor: 'a worthless Government which is afraid of every little interest and trembles before the vote of every dust contractor, will never do those things for them [working men] or pay the least sincere attention to them, until they are made election questions' (26 October, *Letters: Coutts* 273).

The growth of industry and urbanization made images of dust, cinder and dung-heaps compelling. In his *Latter-Day Pamphlets* (1850) Carlyle called for 'Abler men in Downing Street, abler men to govern us: yes, that, sure enough, would remove the dung-mountains, however high they are' ('Downing Street'). In Charles Reade's novel *Hard Cash*, serialized as 'Very Hard Cash' in *AYR* in 1863–4, the villainous speculator Richard Hardie supposes a vital receipt to have been carried to a 'monstrous heap of ashes on the London road': 'he resolved to buy security ... and quietly purchased that mountain, the refuse of all Barkington. But he felt so ill-used, he paid for it in his own notes [his bank has no capital]: by this means the treaty reverted to the primitive form of barter – ashes for rags' (23). Another character talks of 'the intellectual dust-heap of an oppressed nation' (3).

'Red velveteens and a bell?'

'Red velveteens and a bell?' . . . **'And a ladder and basket]** A coloured plate of 1829 shows a dustman wearing red breeches, a brown coat, blue waist-coat, blue and white striped stockings, blue checked shirt, white apron, and a fan-tail cap covering a red cap. He is carrying a large bell (Cunnington and Lucas, 1968, 278). Mayhew noted:

> These men used, before the passing of the late Street Act, to ring a dull-sounding bell so as to give notice to housekeepers of their approach, but now they merely cry, in a hoarse unmusical voice, 'Dust oy-eh!' Two men accompany the cart, which is furnished with a short ladder and two shovels and baskets. (2.175)

'And a ladder and basket

the growling old vagabond threw up his own mountain range, like an old volcano, and its geological formation was Dust.] Geology was con-troversial because it could be used to undermine a literal belief in the Scriptures. Mayhew remarked that the dust-heaps 'frequently . . . cover a large extent of ground in the fields, and there the dust is piled up to a great height in a conical heap . . . having much the appearance of a volcanic mountain' (2.171). An article in *AYR*, 'Fallen from the Clouds', described how volcanoes produce clouds of ashes and dust that covers huge areas (8.250–6). Another, 'Latest News from the Dead', reported on the excavation of the ancient sites of Pompeii and Herculaneum, cities buried under mountains of 'mud, ashes, and pumice-stones': 'There is a regular organization of labour, and about three hundred persons, many of them girls and women, are employed in removing the crust formed eighteen centuries ago by eruption from the mountain' (9.474). In ancient times it was believed that the active force of volcanoes was the giants who had risen against the gods and were now imprisoned in the earth.

Coal-dust, vegetable-dust, bone-dust, crockery dust, rough dust, and sifted dust, – all manner of Dust.'] Vegetable and animal matter, which was called 'soft-ware', was sold as manure. Dead cats were sold for their fur. Among articles of 'hard-ware' were bones, sent to the soap-boiler; rags, used to make paper; bits of tin, brass and lead; glass, sold to the glass shop; and jewellery and coins, which were liable to be regarded as the sifter's perquisites. Each dust-heap was thoroughly sifted; bits of coal collected were sold; the large cinders were sold for braziers; the next sort of cinders, 'called the *breeze*, because it is left after the wind has blown the finer cinders through an upright sieve', was sold to brick-makers (*HW* 1.380). The nightmen, who emptied cesspools, were usually also dustmen, scavengers or chimney-sweeps, and until 1848, when the practice was

33

prevented by the Nuisances Removal and Diseases Prevention Act, night-soil was dumped in the dust-yards: 'the cesspool matter was "shot" in a night-yard, generally also a dust-yard. These were the yards of the parish contractors, and were situated in Maiden-Lane, Paddington, &c., &c' (Mayhew 2.449; cited by Sucksmith, 1973). It will readily be appreciated that dust-yards stank, though Dickens does not mention the fact.

Many *HW* articles concern ways in which reclaimed waste can be put to use: for example, 'Penny Wisdom' (6.97–101), 'Important Rubbish' (11.376–9), 'A Way to Clean a River' (18.79–82) and 'Dirty Cleanliness' (18.121–3). In *AYR* tribute is paid to a local 'master in the art of turning to the purposes of life the riches of the gutter and dust-bin' (1.515); 'What's the Use of That?' (8.184–7) describes some inventive uses of waste; 'Bone-Making' (8.209–11) reveals that the very bones of pigs are built up from the waste matter on which they feed; and 'Artificial Fertility' (13.157–64) outlines the uses to which reclaimed London sewage might be put (see Metz, 1979–80).

The words 'all manner of Dust' suggest the biblical phrases 'all manner of', 'manner of man', 'manner of men'. That all comes to dust is both a biblical and a classical observation.

'The moral being – I believe

'The moral being]   Wordsworth used the phrase 'moral being' in 'Tintern Abbey' (111).

that popular character whom the novelists and versifiers call Another]   Examples abound; one such occurs in 'Alice Grey' by William Mee:

> She's all my fancy painted her,
> She's lovely, she's divine;
> But her heart it is Another's
> She never can be mine. (quoted by Hill)

'The pecuniary resources of Another

the Registrar of the District]   An Act of 1836 had established a modern system of registration. The Registrar-General had a staff at Somerset House and 624 district officers, each of whom was issued with 'an official book, all ruled ready for the purpose'; 'printed forms are abundantly supplied' (*HW* 2.236).

'We must now return

'We must now return, as the novelists say, and as we all wish they wouldn't]   Dickens occasionally made fun of conventional narrator's phrases: 'years roll on' ('The Boarding-House', 1, *SB*); 'we will draw a veil' ('Horatio Sparkins', *SB*); 'let me not anticipate' (*Dr Marigold's Prescriptions*, 1). This particular phrase is satirized in one of the *AYR* 'Small-Beer Chronicles' about 'The Legitimate Novel': 'And there was another little trial. "We must now return to Lenora." Or, "the exigencies of our story now require that we should return to Lenora." . . . And we didn't want to return to Lenora' (9.312).

cheaply educating at Brussels]   Continental education was inexpensive and hence quite common at this time; Dickens sent four of his boys to school in Boulogne. Some children, unwanted at home, remained at school during the holidays.

At this juncture, shuffling is heard

unseen tapper]   A witty allusion to the contemporary interest in spiritualism and mediums: at seances, 'spirits' signalled their presence by bumpings and rappings on the table which, to all appearances, the medium could not effect. Many *HW* and *AYR* articles debunk the mediums.

'His will is found

He directs himself to be buried with certain eccentric ceremonies and precautions against his coming to life]   Old Harmon may have had a fear of the 'resurrection men', who, like Jerry Cruncher in *TTC*, stole bodies from grave-yards and sold them to students of anatomy. Alternatively, there may be a recollection of the *Memoirs of Grimaldi*, which Dickens edited in 1837. Grimaldi's father had a fear of being buried alive: 'he left express directions in his will that, before his coffin should be fastened down, his head should be severed from his body, and the operation was actually performed in the presence of several persons' (ed. Findlater, 1968, 32).

and that's all – except – 'and this ends the story]   A misreading introduced in the proofs. The MS reads: 'and that's all. Except – and this ends the story –" '.

Mr. Podsnap inquires what would become

residuary legatee.]   One to whom the residue of an estate is left. The MS continues: 'Mr. and Mrs. Veneering have exchanged a look of some intensity observed by none but themselves, and Mrs. Veneering has just'. This is not a conspiratorial look (Shea, 1968), but a look of embarrassment: Lady Tippins is asleep at table, and Mrs Veneering wishes to lead the ladies upstairs.

Mrs. Veneering has just succeeded

shunting a train of plates and dishes]   'The railway system has introduced into general parlance, if it has not created, many new terms which are worthy additions to the vocabulary. "Stoke," "shunt," "siding," &c., are all perfectly legitimate words' ('Deprivations of English', *AYR* 10.181).

35

Mortimer, in spite of all the arts

a glass of Madeira]　An *AYR* article reported that owing to a vine disease on the island of Madeira the genuine wine had become a rarity and had trebled in price: 'Of course the whole world will continue to drink pretended Madeira ... thanks to our enterprising wine-manufacturing merchants' (12.151).

'Falser man than Don Juan; why don't you take the note from the Commendatore?']　Lady Tippins alludes to Mozart's opera *Don Giovanni* (1787). The Analytical's 'ghostly manner' has reminded her of the famous concluding scene when the statue of the Commendatore – whom Don Juan had killed – arrives at a dinner, to which Don Juan mockingly invited it, takes the false lover's hand, and drags him down to hell.

Book 1, Chapter 3

ANOTHER MAN.

As the disappearing skirts

the bran-new pilgrims on the wall, going to Canterbury]　Not the beautiful scene painted and engraved by William Blake, but the immensely successful 'Canterbury Pilgrims Setting Forth from the Tabard Inn', painted in 1806–7 by Thomas Stothard, RA (1755–1834), etched by Luigi Schiavonetti and others, and finished by James Heath, ARA, which was published in 1817 (Hill). 'For many years the engraving from Stothard's picture was one of the most popular of mural adornments, and the "Canterbury Pilgrims" were a household word to many people who had never seen a volume of "the Well of English undefiled"' (Coxhead, 1906, 23). Dickens's home at Gad's Hill was on the road to Canterbury.

'You wouldn't ask, sir

Pharaoh's multitude, that were drowned in the Red Sea ... Lazarus]　Exodus 14.26–30 and John 11. Charley has been taught to read out of the Bible (2.1) and these stories, in which he takes a professional interest, are new to him.

Eugene vouchsafed no answer

once boys together at a public school]　Dickens's public schoolboys are not on the whole distinguished for energy or resolution: for instance, Richard Carstone in *BH*, Henry Gowan in *LD*, and Sydney Carton in *TTC*. On the other hand, Tartar and Crisparkle in *MED* are public-school products, and there is Dr Strong's idyllic school in *DC*. At the urging of Miss Burdett Coutts, Dickens had sent his own son, Charley, to Eton (Collins, 1964, 24–5, 32–3, 119).

'Let me see,' said Mortimer

the honourable roll of solicitors of the High Court of Chancery, and attorneys at Common Law]   The Courts of Common Law were concerned with cases of theft, murder and other misdemeanours. Cases involving disputes about legacies, trusts, etc., would be submitted to the Court of Chancery where they would be decided on the principles of Equity rather than on the rules of Common Law.

'And I,' said Eugene, 'have been "called"

have been "called" seven years, and have had no business at all]   The phrase is 'called to the Bar', that is, admitted as a barrister, but Eugene is imply-ing that he has felt no 'calling', no sense of vocation. The rank of barrister was conferred by the four Inns of Court (Inner Temple, Middle Temple, Lincoln's Inn, Gray's Inn). The would-be barrister enrolled as a student at an Inn and after a period applied for a 'call to the Bar'. The briefless (or caseless) barrister was an established type:

> Every day is a week long to him. The year is one long vacation . . . he has a clerk, and a boy, and all-shamming business . . . As it takes a life-time to get hold of a brief, he wonders how many centuries it will require to make him Attorney-General; and then, what portion of eternity must elapse before he becomes a judge. (Laman Blanchard in *Heads of the People*, 1841, 293)

Eugene and Mortimer are of the type of young man that Meason indicated was drifting into dubious careers in speculation at this time: 'We were both – Wilson and myself – barristers, but barristers without briefs, and with no money to speak of . . . Failing every other resource, we determined to start a joint-stock company' (14.368); 'I belong to that numerous class of English gentleman, who, not being brought up to any particular calling or profession, can do little or nothing towards earning even dry bread, far less bread and cheese . . . "Why not turn speculator?" said my friend Vernon of the Guards, one night in the smoking-room of his club' (14.57). ' "Why should I not be a promoter?" ' another young man asks himself (13.485).

There are four of us

one black hole called a set of chambers]   Chambers are rooms or sets of offices used by lawyers. They were notoriously unpleasant: 'A well-ordained workhouse or prison is much better provided with appliances of health, comfort, and cleanliness, than . . . a learned Inn' (Thackeray, *Pendennis*, 1848–50, 29).

the fourth of a clerk – Cassim Baba, in the robber's cave]   Cassim is the rich brother of Ali in 'Ali Baba and the Forty Thieves', one of the tales in the *Arabian Nights*. Cassim attempts to steal the robbers' gold from their cave, but forgets the phrase that opens the cave's rock door and is discovered and quartered by the robbers.

37

'Then idiots talk,' said Eugene

of Energy.] The eighth chapter of Samuel Smiles's immensely successful *Self-Help* (1859), entitled 'Energy and Courage', suggests the conventional view: 'Energy enables a man to force his way through . . . energy of will may be defined to be the very central power of character in a man – in a word, it is the Man himself.'

'Precisely my view of the case

But show me a good opportunity . . . and I'll show you energy.'] Dickens has this note in his *Book of Memoranda*: ' "If they were great things, I, the untrustworthy man in little things, would do them earnestly" – but O No, I wouldn't!' (21).

The wheels rolled on, and rolled down

down by the Monument and by the Tower, and by the Docks; down by Ratcliffe, and by Rotherhithe] Their route takes them past the Monument, built to commemorate the Great Fire of London of 1666, which is near the end of London Bridge; along Eastcheap and into Tower Hill, passing behind the Tower of London; along East Smithfield and Ratcliffe Highway behind St Katharine Docks and the London Dock to join the river again at Narrow Street in Limehouse. Ratcliffe was the location of some of the worst slums – known as Rookeries – in London. Rotherhithe is actually on the south side of the river. The journey is a downward one socially (from the fashionable and wealthy West End to the impoverished East End) as well as in actuality; the East End is at a lower elevation, a significant contemporary fact: 'Mortality in the Metropolis seems regulated by a variety of circumstances, the principal being the elevation of each district above the level of the river Thames' (*HW* 1.331–2).

down by where accumulated scum of humanity seemed to be washed from higher grounds, like so much moral sewage] What has been described as a 'curious and disturbing correspondence' existed between the language used of the sanitary condition and that used of the human condition: ' "Residuum" was the offal, excrement, and other waste that constituted the sanitary problem; and it was also a name applied to the lowest layer of society, the class that was thought to constitute the major social problem' (Himmlefarb, 1970–1, 320). The 1860s saw the establishment of an efficient system of sewage for the metropolis: in a letter to W. F. de Cerjat, Dickens called this 'great system of drainage' a 'really fine work' (30 November 1865, *Nonesuch* 3.445).

The low building had the look of having once been a mill.

having once been a mill.] The area of Millwall, otherwise called the Isle of Dogs, which is adjacent to Limehouse, owed its name to the windmills standing along the river wall on its west side. There were seven: Brown's; three Smith's;

Baker's; Churn's, later called Tommy Tinker's; and Ward's, later called Theobald's. 'Some of these mills are well remembered even now. The foundations of two or three may yet be traced; and in fact one of them without its sails stills exists' (Cowper, 1853, 19).

a common lamp ... smoked and flared in the neck of a stone bottle] This is an oil-lamp. Gas was not available to the poorer classes at this time: their light came, rather expensively, from wax, oil, tallow and (from the later 1850s) paraffin. The Veneerings' home flares with gaslight; the newly wealthy Boffins have gas in the Bower; the Wilfer home and Venus's shop are lit by cheap tallow candles.

'You're Mortimer Lightwood Esquire

Mortimer Lightwood] The name Lightword appears in the *Book of Memoranda*. The MS is unclear, but Dickens may have written 'Lightword' the first three times the name is used here.

Taking up the bottle with the lamp in it

a paper on the wall, with the police heading, BODY FOUND.] Two notes in the *Book of Memoranda* show the development of the idea for this part of the novel:

> Found Drowned. The descriptive bill upon the wall, by the waterside. (*Done in Our Mutual*)

> A 'long shore' man – woman – child – or family. <Query Found>. connect the Found Drowned Bill with this? (8)

Dickens wrote 'FOUND DROWNED' for 'BODY FOUND' in the MS and 'another FOUND DROWNED placard' for 'another similar placard' below. He had referred to them as 'Found Drowned' bills in earlier novels: in *BH*, 'Against the mouldering wall by which they stood, there was a bill on which I could discern the words, "FOUND DROWNED" ' (57); and, in *LD*, Clennam passes 'a narrow alley leading to the river, where a wretched little bill, FOUND DROWNED, was weeping on the wet wall' (1.3).

'This is my friend,' Mortimer Lightwood interposed

'Mr. Eugene Wrayburn.'] 'Wrayburn' appears in the MS as a correction of 'Scannon' the first three times the name is used.

'I am lost!' replied the man

'I am lost!' replied the man, in a hurried and an eager manner.] Dickens entered in his *Book of Memoranda*:

> LEADING INCIDENT FOR A STORY. A man – young and eccentric? – feigns to be

dead, and *is* dead to all intents and purposes external to himself, and <xx> for years retains that singular view of life and character. *Done Rokesmith* (19)

A little winding through some muddy alleys

a Police Station] Limehouse police station was not built until 1879. In the 1860s the nearest police station was at Newby Place, Poplar. Dickens's admiration for the New Police, and particularly for the detective force, is expressed in a series of articles he and W. H. Wills wrote for *HW* and in the portrayal of Inspector Bucket in *BH*.

as if he were in a monastery on the top of a mountain, and no howling fury of a drunken woman were banging herself against a cell-door] The imperturbability of the British policeman rapidly became part of the British mythology (Collins, 1962, 203). In *BH* the police station is 'very quiet altogether, except for some beating and calling out at distant doors underground, to which nobody paid any attention' (57). Dickens's *HW* article 'On Duty with Inspector Field' (*RP*) mentions 'a raving drunken woman in the cells, who has screeched her voice away, and has hardly power enough left to declare, even with the passionate help of her feet and arms, that she is the daughter of a British officer, and, strike her blind and dead, but she'll write a letter to the Queen'. Dickens had visited the monastery at the Great St Bernard Pass; it appears in *LD*, book 2, chapter 1.

'A bull's-eye,' said the Night-Inspector

'A bull's-eye] A kind of lantern with a protruding glass lens used by the police.

'Now, gentlemen.'] The MS and proofs continue:

In the same abstracted and scholarly way, he was leading them across the cool clean-paved yard studded with strong doors, when the fact that there was a banging and shrieking going on somewhere seemed to occur to him. He stepped to the door that was banged at, drew back a slide, and disclosed – as if it were in a rather large box for water-colours – a distorted bloated face, bounding up and down and backwards, and forwards, and incessantly yelling for that liver.

'This is her game, gentlemen,' said the contemplative scholar, 'about twice a week. And she'll keep it up without stopping, half the night, if not the whole of it. Ah! she's a pretty spectacle of a woman!' and so drew the slide close again (she frantically spitting out of it), as if she were an unconscious Subject in a dissecting room.

Mr. Inspector dipped a pen

Exchequer Coffee House, Palace Yard, Westminster.] The Exchequer Coffee House at Westminster Hall gate was a hotel and coffee house which had existed for 130 years.

The Abbot replied with reticence

that superstition about bodies bleeding when touched by the hand of the right person]   A traditional belief: in *Richard III* Anne cries out when Richard approaches her husband's corpse: 'O, gentlemen, see, see! Dead Henry's wounds/Open their congeal'd mouths and bleed afresh' (1.2.55–6). In *LD* Mrs Clennam warns her son: 'if . . . you were to come into this darkened room to look upon me lying dead, my body should bleed, if I could make it, when you came near me' (1.5).

There being nothing more to be done

a red-curtained tavern]   Red curtains were traditional for public houses.

'One of the gentlemen, the one who didn't speak

And I was afraid he might know what my face meant.]   The MS and proofs continue:

> 'What did it mean?'
> 'It meant,' said the girl, looking round her, 'that it seems to be following me. Made fast to me and following me, as it was made fast to the boat and followed that.'
> 'But you didn't look at it. You know you never do.'
> 'No, no,' said the girl with a shiver.
> 'Well then; how can you be followed by you don't know what?'
> 'I only know I am,' returned the girl, with wonder in her dark eyes at the unimaginative question, 'and it's the worst kind of following there is.'

I was all in a tremble]   Despite her background, and unlike her father, Lizzie does not deviate from standard English, with the exception of a few homely phrases. Though he has the advantage of a little education, Charley also speaks more roughly than his sister.

when you owned to father you could write a little.']   In his *Book of Memoranda* Dickens made the note: 'The uneducated father (or uncle?) in fustian, and the educated boy in spectacles. Whom Leech and I saw at Chatham' (6). This suggests Pip and Magwitch in *GE* as well as Charley and Gaffer. Mayhew commented that 'The dredgers, as a class, may be said to be altogether uneducated'. One man told him: ' "Larnin's no use to a dredger, he hasn't got no time to read; and if he had, why it wouldn't tell him where the holes and furrows is at the bottom of the river" ' (2.148–9).

'That's gas, that is,' said the boy

'That's gas, that is . . . coming out of a bit of a forest that's been under the mud that was under the water in the days of Noah's Ark.]   The story of

41

Noah is told in Genesis 6–9. Charley's observation reflects Victorian reconciliations of geology and Genesis. Dickens may have intended to imply that Charley's knowledge is not useful to him: in a letter praising Miss Burdett Coutts for promoting the study of Common Things he commented on the uselessness of 'a knowledge of Watersheds and Pre Adamite vegetation' to the 'labouring man' (11 July 1856, *Letters: Coutts* 321).

'Well! There am I, continuing with father

I have not the influence I want to have]   In Knowles's *The Daughter*, Marian (the daughter of the title) attempts to persuade her father not to rob the dead.

'Ha, ha! Fortune-telling not know

'Pupil-teacher.']   The pupil teacher system was instituted by the pioneer educationalist Kay-Shuttleworth in 1846. It provided a five-year apprenticeship for young people from 13 to 18 years of age. In return for five and a half hours of teaching a day, the pupil teacher received seven and a half hours of instruction a week. Charley currently attends a ragged school (see p. 127). To become a pupil teacher he would have to read with fluency; write neatly, with correct spelling and punctuation, a simple prose narrative; do sums in the first four rules of arithmetic, simple and compound, and know the tables of weights and measures; point out the parts of speech in a simple sentence; have an elementary knowledge of geography; repeat the catechism (at a Church of England school) and show a knowledge of the outline of Scriptural history; and teach a junior class to the inspector's satisfaction. The life was hard: 'The strain upon pupil teachers, the younger ones in particular, was heavy, and this was one of the darkest aspects of the system' (Rich, 1933, 120, 142). The instruction the pupil teacher received placed an emphasis on the mechanical acquisition of a large number of facts. Matthew Arnold, a supporter of the system, discussed this problem in his *Reports on Elementary Schools, 1852–82* (1889).

Under the system, masters received payment for the instruction of pupil teachers at the rate of £5 for one, £9 for two, £12 for three, and £3 each for any further students. This payment was revoked by the Revised Code of 1861 (see p. 134, so men like Bradley Headstone had their incomes cut by large sums. During the controversy about education at that time the pupil teachers were much criticized:

> Why, conceit is the very nursling – the necessarily attendant evil, perhaps, yet the besetting sin – of the pupil-teacher system. A lad of 13 taken from an illiterate home is placed all day and every day in authority over a set of boys who are to hear the law from his mouth; and returns at night from his official duties to his home, where his little learning makes him the wonder of the circle. (letter to *The Times*, 17 July 1863, 6)

In the parliamentary debates the following passage from a report on the pupil teachers was quoted:

many of them only become eye-servants, inflated with self-importance, over-bearing towards the younger children, contemptuous towards their social equals, highminded towards their parents, brothers, and sisters, and other relatives; very dreary out of school, and forward and deficient in outward tokens of respect towards their betters. (*The Times*, 6 May 1863, 5)

'You come to be a pupil-teacher

it has divided you from father, and from me.'] What has been characterized as a stratification of the working class was particularly acute in areas like Limehouse where the better-off workers and artisans, who felt divided by a new respectability from their relatively impoverished fellows, were moving out leaving a population 'containing an artificially high number of people chronically unhealthy, unemployable, "unlucky," dispirited'. See pages 176–7. Lizzie's attitude to the pilfering to which Gaffer is reduced and her desire to raise Charley represent a stratification within the Hexam family. A not untypical road up for a pretty girl from the slums was by 'the higher harlotry or as a private mistress. If she were successful, her income could give her younger brothers and sisters an education' (Sinclair, 1950, 247–8).

It being now past midnight

at the Six Jolly Fellowship-Porters . . . a Coroner's Jury.] The practice of holding inquests at public houses was criticized in *HW* (1.109–13) and by Dickens himself in *BH*, chapter 11.

The case was made interesting to the public

a rapturous admirer subscribing himself 'A friend to Burial' (perhaps an undertaker), sent eighteen postage stamps, and five 'Now Sir's to the editor of the Times.] Dickens was not a friend to burial or, at least, to undertakers: see Jenny Wren's remarks in book 4, chapter 9. When Dickens's character Mr Booley wrote to the newspapers he took 'the liberty of endeavouring to give this communication an air of novelty, by omitting the words "Now, Sir," which are generally supposed to be essential to all letters written to Editors for publication' ('A Card from Mr. Booley', *MP*).

This Proclamation rendered

you get a woman and a fish apart, or a Mermaid in combination.] An allusion to the opening of Horace, *Ars poetica*: 'If a painter chose to join a human head to the neck of a horse, and to spread feathers of many a hue over limbs picked up now here now there, so that what at the top is a lovely woman ends below in a black and ugly fish, could you, my friends, if favoured with a private view, refrain from laughing?' (Loeb translation).

Book 1, Chapter 4

THE R. WILFER FAMILY.

Reginald Wilfer is a name

Reginald Wilfer is a name with a rather grand sound]   The name Reginald means 'powerful judgement', though Dickens may have thought it meant 'kingly'.

the De Wilfers who came over with the Conqueror.]   In the MS: 'the De Wilfers who < of course > came over with the Conqueror < and the De Bores in general >'. The Norman gentry acquired their land and social position after the victory over the Saxons at Hastings (1066). The same chivalric revival which led men like Veneering to acquire a coat of arms encouraged other families, often without any genealogical evidence, to intimate the Norman origins of their own lineage by adding 'de' to their surname.

But, the Reginald Wilfer family

subsisted on the Docks, the Excise Office, and the Custom House]   That is, in minor clerical posts relating to the great shipping activity along the Thames. Dickens's father was in a clerical post in the Navy Pay Office at Somerset House when he was arrested for debt in 1824.

pantaloons]   Applied to trousers generally.

If the conventional Cherub

In short, he was the conventional cherub, after the supposititious shoot just mentioned]   Play on 'shoot' as the word for a sudden thought and for the offspring of a family (a 'shoot' of the family tree).

He was shy, and unwilling

the neighbourhood surrounding Mincing Lane]   Mincing Lane was at the centre of an area where dealings in produce were transacted: 'Here is the great market for tea, sugar, spices and colonial produce generally. The street is wholly occupied by merchants and brokers congregated in offices and chambers, some of the new blocks of buildings being of great size and height, and of considerable architectural pretension' (Wheatley and Cunningham 2.546).

bestowed upon him by a gentleman of convivial habits . . . as the beginning of a social chorus . . . which had led this gentleman to the Temple of Fame]   Harmonic meetings, such as that described in *PP* chapter 20, preceded the development of the full-scale English music-hall. They were held in public houses or what were called song and supper rooms. There were both instrumental and vocal music, and hot meals were served till the early hours of the morning. The host often acted as chairman. Dickens parodies the smart manner of the places.

He was clerk in the drug-house

the drug-house of Chicksey, Veneering, and Stobbles]   According to a *HW* article the dealers in drugs, perfumes and dyes formed 'a little-known world of their own' in Mincing Lane. The article describes the excited behaviour of the drug-brokers: 'Any Thursday morning, between the hours of ten and eleven, and at every alternate doorway, may be observed catalogues of various drugs and dyes that are to be on sale at noon, gibbetted against the door-posts. Mincing Lane men will be seen rushing madly along the pavement, as if a fire had just broken out.' The business was highly speculative: 'When I expressed my astonishment that men of such undoubted substance as I saw there, should condescend to haggle, like any hucksters, at an odd farthing, I was told that ... at certain seasons, some paltry odd farthing had realized or lost fortunes' (5.273, 275). The sale of opium was an everyday part of the drug trade (see p. 83) and there was a regular trade to supply drugs for the adulteration of food and drink, such as the *cocculus indicus* berries and bittern (calcined sulphate of iron) used by unscrupulous brewers, and the alum used in bread.

a quantity of plate-glass window and French-polished mahogany partition, and a gleaming and enormous door-plate.]   Plate-glass windows were first employed for business premises in the 1820s. Montague Tigg adopts this kind of showy façade for the fraudulent Anglo-Bengalee Assurance Company in *MC* (27). Some contemporaries looked gloomily on the conspicuous building of business premises in the decade preceding *OMF*: 'commodious premises', 'handsomely fitted', 'of fabled Eastern magnificence', adorned with 'mahogany, glass, and fretwork' and 'highly-burnished door-panels', all demonstrated 'the greatest misfortune of the age – a love of show, that may lead eventually to excessive expenditure' (Evans, 1864, 8–12).

R. Wilfer locked up his desk

his peg-top]   Peg-tops were pear-shape wooden spinning-tops, favourite boys' toys.

Between Battle Bridge and that part of the Holloway district in which he dwelt, was a tract of suburban Sahara]   The dust-heaps in *OMF* are at Belle Isle; according to Boffin, the Wilfer residence is 'not above a mile or so' away, which suggests a situation somewhere in Lower Holloway, between Camden Road and Holloway Road. Wilfer passes through Agar's Town and lower Camden Town. Agar's Town was a slum district which 'crawled out of the mud between Euston Road (as it now is) and the Regent's Park canal about 1810, and was obliterated by St Pancras station fifty years later' (Best, 1973, 49). It is described in the *HW* article 'A Suburban Connemara' as consisting of a few hovels and filthy, muddy roads deep in rubbish of every kind. There were no sewers, and many buildings were left unfinished (2.562–5). There were dust-heaps at its southern end at Battle Bridge, and, further north,

> was what was termed La Belle Isle, a dreary and unsavoury locality, abandoned to mountains of refuse from the metropolitan dust-bins, strewn with decaying vegetables and foul-smelling fragments of what had once been fish, or occupied by knackers'-yards and manure-making, bone-boiling, and soap-manufacturing works, and smoke-belching potteries and brick-kilns.
>
> (Thornbury and Walford, 5.368)

The Midland Railway was brought into its London terminus (St Pancras) in 1866.

dogs were fought] 'These fights take place on the sly . . . A few men are let into the secret, and they attend to bet upon the winner, the police being carefully kept from the spot' (Mayhew 1.15).

Mrs. Wilfer was, of course, a tall woman

a pair of gloves worn within doors] The wearing of gloves was considered genteel. In *GE*, for instance, Miss Skiffins retains 'her green gloves during the evening as an outward and visible sign that there was company' (37).

'Yes,' said Mrs. Wilfer, 'the man came himself

another LADIES' SCHOOL door-plate] Dickens's own mother exerted herself at the time of the family financial crisis by having a 'large brass plate' with the words 'MRS. DICKENS'S ESTABLISHMENT' attached to the front door. Young Charles delivered circulars, but ' "nobody ever came to school" ' (Forster 1.23). The detail of the door-plate is mentioned in 'Shops and their Tenants' in *SB*, and in *DC*, chapter 11, Mrs Micawber makes a similar attempt to start a school. The *HW* article about Agar's Town mentions a 'garden . . . exhibiting a board inscribed with the words "Ladies' School", [that] had become a pond of thick green water' (2.564).

'The milkman said he knew

with severe monotony, as if she were reading an Act of Parliament aloud.] A *HW* article described the reading of private Acts in Parliament: 'All this goes on in the most monotonous sing-song, varied only by the loud key in which upon each occasion the title of the bill and the name of the mover are pronounced' (9.90).

'And poor Lavinia, perhaps, my dear?'

Lavinia] There is a Lavinia in the *Aeneid* and in *Titus Andronicus*, but the name probably owed its popularity to James Thomson's introduction of the love-story of Palemon and Lavinia into his poem 'Autumn' in *The Seasons* (1730). In 'Sentiment' in *SB* the daughter of a Member of Parliament is called Lavinia Brook Dingwall; Lavinia Spenlow is one of Dora's aunts in *DC*.

'No, R. W. Lavinia has not known the trial

Bella in her black dress]   Full mourning normally lasted twelve months, and was then followed by periods of second mourning, ordinary mourning and finally half-mourning, in which dresses of white, grey or lilac trimmed with black were introduced. Within nine months Bella is 'No longer in mourning' and is 'dressed in as pretty colours as she could muster' (1.16).

lay your head upon your pillow and say, "Poor Lavinia!" ']   Dickens gave this cliché to his Member for Verbosity in his *HW* article 'Our Honourable Friend':

> 'I do NOT, gentlemen, I am free to confess, envy the feelings of that man whose mind is so constituted as that he can hold such language to me, and yet lay his head upon his pillow, claiming to be a native of that land,
>
> > Whose march is o'er the mountain-wave,
> > Whose home is on the deep!, (*RP*)

'You are a chit and a little idiot

everything cut and dried beforehand, like orange chips. Talk of orange flowers indeed!]   Orange chips are pieces of dried orange-peel. The custom for brides to carry orange-blossom at their wedding was introduced into England from France in the early part of the century.

'The gentleman, R. W.,' said Mrs. Wilfer

your apartments]   'The curate's lodgings – apartments his landlady would call them' (Mary Mitford, *Our Village*, 1824, 1).

'– Why then I – might lose it.'

'– Why then I – might lose it.']   Harmon's furniture might be taken by the Wilfers' creditors. MS and proofs continue: 'It had cost the gentleman a great effort to get to this point through a want of words, and an apparent wandering of his thoughts. He now sat silent, with his hat to his mouth, and his eyes on the floor.'

The gentleman listened to her

brought writing materials to complete the business.]   These words begin four pages of 'Overmatter of No. 1 of the New Serial', as it is headed in the proofs.

Having overwritten, Dickens was forced to make substantial cuts in the remainder of the chapter.

He sat, still and silent, while the landlord wrote.]   This sentence replaces a long passage in MS and in the proofs:

> Then he took his purse from his pocket, and laid it on the table. He had either very quick ears or very quick eyes, for he instantly detected some very slight – some almost imperceptible – communication between the sisters in reference to the fashion of the purse, which was rare and curious.
>
> 'Yes. It is made of a foreign grass,' he said, raising his eyes for the second time to Bella's face, as she stood at the fender, looking over her shoulder. 'You see what it is. It's – it's nothing.' And crushed it up, and put it in his pocket.
>
> Not only that, but when he afterwards took eight sovereigns from this same purse, to pay in earnest of the agreement, he took them out of it, in his pocket; which was difficult to do, and caused him to tell them on the table one by one, very slowly. Bella looked at this proceeding with her pretty face made very characteristic by its earnest attention. Thus, in her different way, she bestowed as marked an attention on him as he had previously bestowed on her.
>
> The agreement being by this time ready

When the agreement was ready

like some cherubic scribe, in what is conventionally called a doubtful, which means a not at all doubtful, Old Master]   In *PI* and elsewhere Dickens expressed scepticism about the merits of paintings and frescoes traditionally regarded as great (such as the Correggio frescoes in the Duomo in Parma, or the frescoes by Giulio Romano in Mantua), and about attributions: 'few very great masters can possibly have painted, in the compass of their lives, one-half of the pictures that bear their names' ('By Verona . . .': *PI*). In *LD* Mr Meagles unwittingly acquires some fake masterpieces on his travels (1.16). An *AYR* article of 1863, 'The Shop-Side of Art', described a case of what it suggested was the widespread imposition of fake old masters on wealthy but undiscerning collectors (10.374–9).

When it came to Bella's turn

they looked at one another.]   Altered in the proofs from 'they looked at one another and his eyes were the first to turn away'.

'Signing my name? Yes, certainly.

But I am your landlord's daughter, sir.']   MS and proofs continue:

> Showing no consciousness of her supercilious rejection of the idea that she had taken any trouble for *him*, Mr. Rokesmith examined her signature with his downcast eyes, and dipped the pen in the ink.
>
> 'Excuse me, Mr. Wilfer. Do I add "spinster" here?'

'My daughter Bella,' Mrs. Wilfer promptly proclaimed, in her fillet and gloves, from her corner, 'is not married yet. But I *have* married daughters and they are br-r-right examples!'

'I would not have asked the question,' said Mr. Rokesmith, writing in the word, 'but that the young lady's black dress—'

'There!' was the suppressed exclamation of Miss Bella to Miss Lavinia, 'What did I say of this ridiculous mourning? Everybody notices it.'

In formal contracts, unmarried women are required to write 'spinster' after their signature.

'To see him unable for his life

to look anybody in the face!' said Bella.] In MS and proofs Bella continues: 'to see him clutch that purse when it was noticed, to see his evasive manner and his listening way, as if he constantly expected to hear the air rent with a shout of "Stop him!" There never was such an exhibition.'

'I hate our landlord!' said Bella.

'I hate our landlord!' said Bella.] MS and proofs continue:

'Hate him, my dear?'

'It's a very hard thing indeed,' said Bella, 'that we no sooner get a little money than that arbitrary Monster comes and gobbles it up.'

'Well; but my dear, if we had no landlord of our own, we couldn't be landlord to other people, and shouldn't get the money.'

'I don't see that,' retorted Bella.

'My dear, we have no house of our own—'

'Very well; then we ought to have,' said Bella.

However, as it was brown

Scotch ale] Less bitter and more potent than English beer.

'Impossible to say, my dear.

'Impossible to say, my dear.] MS and proofs continue:

'Do you think he meant me well, or ill, pa?'

'I think he must have meant well – to you, my dear.'

'Oh! Is that as much as to say that he meant anything but well to his son, in ordering him to marry me? Is that the compliment, pa?'

'My dear, it is impossible to say what the whims of a rich, secluded, suspicious old man mean. I can't undertake to find a meaning for them; it would require a much better head than mine so to do.'

As that was all the rum and water

she cherubically escorted, like some severe saint in a painting, or merely human matron allegorically treated.]   Saints accompanied by cherubs are frequently depicted in baroque painting. The 'merely human matron' is perhaps Marie de' Medici, wife of Henry IV of France, whose career is portrayed in Rubens's great series of allegorical paintings, commissioned in 1621, and hung in the Louvre.

Lavvy declining equally to repeat

suspicious lodgers.]   Altered in the proofs from the MS: 'murderous lodgers'.

Book 1, Chapter 5   Second monthly number
June 1864

BOFFIN'S BOWER.

In the MS the chapter title is altered from 'Harmony Jail'.

Over against a London house

a corner house not far from Cavendish Square]   In the fashionable West End, 'likely enough in one of those long genteel streets – Wimpole Street or Harley Street – which were Dickens's pet aversion' (Fitzgerald, 1895, 241–2). Victorians regarded Georgian architecture in London streets with distaste: Disraeli, for instance, remarked on 'your Gloucester Places, and Baker Streets, and Harley Streets, and Wimpole Streets, and all those flat, dull, spiritless streets, resembling each other like a large family of plain children' (*Tancred*, 1847, 2.10); Tennyson described Wimpole Street as a 'long unlovely street' in *In Memoriam* (1850, 7). Mr Dombey lives in 'a corner house' in a 'dark, dreadfully genteel street' in this area (*DS* 3).

a man with a wooden leg]   Crude surgery and the Napoleonic Wars meant that wooden legs were not an uncommon sight in Dickens's lifetime, though the bull-necked and wooden-legged school porter described in *DC* (5) may have been the origin of his interest in men so equipped. Hatchway, a comic character in a favourite novel of his childhood, Smollett's *Peregrine Pickle* (1751), has a wooden leg. 'Old Tom' Beazeley, in Marryat's *Jacob Faithful* (1834), a novel of riverside life, is a Trafalgar veteran with two wooden legs who shares with Wegg the characteristic of altering the words of the songs he sings to fit the occasion:

> They who through a spying-glass,
> View the minutes as they pass,
> Make the sun a gloomy mass,
>   But the fault's their own, Tom. (14)

There may be a debt to Thomas Hood's poem 'Miss Kilmansegg and Her Precious Leg' (1840), a satire which has the refrain 'Gold! Gold! Gold! Gold!' Miss Kilmansegg is a rich young beauty who, after a riding accident, wears a leg made of gold:

> A wooden leg! what, a sort of peg,
>   For your common Jockeys and Jennies! . . .
> . . . nothing would move Miss Kilmansegg!
> She could – she would have a Golden Leg,
>   If it cost ten thousand guineas! (761–2, 765–8)

See also pages 70, 88 and 113–14.

Street singers were often physically disabled: for instance, Billy, the blind fiddler, who sang one song falsetto; Sam Horsey, the legless 'go-cart Billy', known to pass the day around Holborn, Fleet Street and the Strand; and Blind Joseph, the flute-player.

the unfolded clothes-horse displayed a choice collection of halfpenny ballads and became a screen]   The street ballad trade centred on the Seven Dials district (see 'Seven Dials', *SB*) and the printing presses of Catnach and Pitts. There, 'five or six well-known bards who get their living by writing for Seven Dials, and then chanting their own strains to the people' rapidly produced ballads on contemporary events, often with as little attention to the requirements of rhythm as Wegg; for instance, a song on Palmerston's death has the lines: 'He was born in October, seventeen eighty-four, / That good able statesman who now is no more'; and a near-accident is commemorated in this manner:

> O see that father how he stands so calm
> The Boy on his shoulder, the girl under his arm,
> Don't let him die, that father good and brave
> The Boat has reach'd them, Oh! thank God they're saved.
>   (*Quarterly Review* 122, 1867, 392–5)

Wegg belongs to the class of ballad-sellers known as 'pinners-up', 'men and women . . . who sell songs which they have "pinned" to a sort of screen or large board, or have attached them in any convenient way, to a blank wall' (Mayhew 1.272). The ballads were on broadsheets having one or more songs, often with a crude woodcut illustration. The ballad-sellers usually bought their songs from presses such as Catnach and Pitts for about 2*d* or 2½*d* a dozen, making 200–300 per cent on outlay, or even more if they cut the sheets or sold halfpenny songs at one penny, as was the practice. A pinner-up would make about £60 a year, from £18 outlay.

Lady Tippins? at the marriage of mature young lady & do gentleman
Twemlow?   D°
Veneerings?   D°
Progress of that artful match?   ⌉ Yes – to their contract
          between mature young gentleman |
          and mature young lady   ⌋
on the Dust-ground? Certainly

Harmony Jail
          or Boffin's Bower

Cut adrift
Cast out
Turned out
Under suspicion
Parting Company

This chapter (too long for the N°) transferred to N° 3. In its stead
                              Chapter VII
          In Which Mr Wegg looks after himself
Picture of the queer St Giles's business
                    with Imaginary man

Chapter V
Boffin's Bower

S. Wegg at his stall.

    Soloman? Silas? Yes. 'Our House'

        Seems to have taken his wooden leg naturally

So, Mr Boffin

        Teddy Boffin?

            Nicodemus. 'Noddy Boffin'

Lead up to Boffin's Bower

        and to 'declining and falling off the Rooshan Empire.'

Mrs Boffin a High-Flyer at Fashion.   This to go through the Work

In a hat and feathers.

Chapter VI
Cut adrift.

The Six Jolly Fellowship Porters. Description | Bow |

    Miss Potterson

        Miss Abbey

            She, the Sister of the ship's steward.

The man from the 1st chapter. Riderhood.

    Boy departs to seek his fortune.   'Unnat'ral young beggur!'

Chapter VII
A marriage contract

Veneerings again.

        Mr and Mrs Lammle.

        Having taken one another in, will now

take in every one else.

He had established his right

by imperceptible prescription.] 'It is customary for a street-seller who wants to "pitch" in a new locality to solicit the leave of the housekeeper, opposite whose premises he desires to place his stall. Such leave obtained, no other course is necessary' (Mayhew 1.99). Wegg has omitted this form.

Shelterless fragments of straw got up revolving storms] 'In some parts of the suburbs on windy days London is a perfect dust-mill, and although the dust may be allayed by the agency of water-carts . . . it is not often thoroughly allayed, and is a source of considerable loss, labour, and annoyance' (Mayhew 2.188).

On the front of his sale-board

small text] A term for the carefully written script for the textbook, as distinct from the less formal cursive style (Hill).

Silas Wegg] The names Silas Blodget and Wegg appear in the lists of names in Dickens's *Book of Memoranda*.

Over the house itself

a piece of fat black water-pipe . . . had rather the air of a leech on the house that had 'taken' wonderfully] Leeches were still used medically to let 'excess' blood; ' "taken" ' was jargon: leeches 'never "took" on Mrs. Miggot, the laundress' (*UT* 14).

two iron extinguishers] Iron cones attached to the front of a house in which footmen formerly smothered the torches used to escort guests from their carriages into the house.

Assuredly, this stall

a little wooden measure which had no discernible inside, and was considered to represent the penn'orth appointed by Magna Charta] In the MS not 'by Magna Charta' but 'by the British Constitution'. Magna Carta, one of the foundations of English liberty, embodies the concessions granted by King John to the barons at Runnymede in 1215. This is what was called a 'slang' measure: the bottom was taken out of a wooden measure and put in again a half-inch or so higher up.

Whether from too much east wind

a watchman's rattle] An instrument, used to give alarm, with a tongue that vibrated noisily over a ratchet wheel when it was whirled.

if his development received no untimely check] An allusion to the theory of development, a pseudo-scientific anticipation of the theory of evolution, advanced by Robert Chambers in his *Vestiges of the Natural History of Creation* (1844). The work was widely read and frequently reprinted. Until its theories were superseded by those of Darwin, Chamber's *Vestiges* deeply influenced the ideas of many eminent Victorian thinkers. Dickens had praised the *Vestiges* for making scientific discoveries interesting to the general public in his review of Robert Hunt's *The Poetry of Science* (1848) (*MP*).

Mr. Wegg was an observant person

shady preliminary meditation at church]   'A child enquired of us, the other day, why a gentleman always said his first prayer in church, in the crown of his hat' ('A Few Conventionalities', *MP*).

The words referred to a broad, round-shouldered

a broad, round-shouldered, one-sided old fellow in mourning] Dickens's instructions to the illustrator Marcus Stone indicate his intentions with Boffin: 'I want Boffin's oddity, without being at all blinked, to be an oddity of a very honest kind, that people will like' (23 February 1864, *Nonesuch* 3.380). His conception seems to owe something to the street ballad 'The Literary Dustman', which was printed by both Catnach and Pitts sometime in the 1830s:

> Some folks may boast of sense, egad!
>   Vot holds a lofty station;
> But tho' a dustman, I have had
>   A lib'ral *hedication.*
> And tho' I never went to school,
>   Like many of my betters,
> A turnpike-man, vot varnt no fool,
>   He larnt me all my letters.
>
> They calls me Adam Bell, 'tis clear
>   As Adam vos the fust man, –
> And by a co-in-side-aunce queer,
>   Vy I'm the fust of Dustmen,
>   Vy I'm the fust of Dustmen!
>
> At sartin schools they makes boys write,
>   Their alphabet on sand, sirs,
> So, I thought dust would do as well,
>   And larnt it out of hand, sirs;
> Took in the 'Penny Magazine,'
>   And Johnson's *Dixonary.*
> And all the Peri-o-di-cals,
>   To make me *literary.*   They calls, &c.

My dawning genus fust did peep,
    Near Battle bridge 'tis plain, sirs,
You recollect the cinder heap,
    Vot stood in Gray's-Inn-lane, sirs?
'Twas there I studied pic-turesque,
    While I my bread vos yearnin';
And there inhalin' the fresh breeze,
    I *sifted out my larnin'*!   They calls, &c.

Then Mrs. Bell 'twixt you and I,
    Vould melt a heart of stone, sirs,
To hear her pussy's wittals cry
    In such a barrow-tone, sirs;
My darters all take arter her,
    In grace and figure easy;
They larns to sing, and as they're fat,
    I has 'em taught by *Grisi*!   They calls, &c.

Ve dines at four, and arter that,
    I smokes a mild Awanna;
Or gives a lesson to the lad,
    Upon the grand *pianna*.
Or with the gals valk a *quod-rille*.
    Or takes a cup of coff-ee;
Or, if I feels fatig'd or ill,
    I lounges on the *sophy*.   They calls, &c.

Or arter dinner read a page
    Of Valter Scott, or Byron;
Or Mr. *Shikspur*, on the stage,
    Subjects none can tire on.
At night we toddles to the play,
    But not to gallery attic;
Drury-Lane's the time o' day,
    And quite *aristocratic*!   They calls, &c.

I means to buy my eldest son
    A commission in the Lancers,
And make my darters every one,
    Accomplished Hopra dancers.
Great sculptors all conwarse wi' me,
    And call my taste diwine, sirs,
King George's *statty* at King's Cross,
    Vas built from my design, sirs!   They calls, &c.

And ven I'm made a member on,
    For that I means to try, sirs,
Mr. Gully fought his way,

And verefore shou'dn't I, sirs?
Yes, when I sits in Parli'ment,
     In old Sin Stephen's College,
I means to take, 'tis my intent,
     The 'taxes off o' knowledge.'

They calls me Adam Bell, 'tis true,
     'Cause Adam was the fust man,
I'm sure it's very plain to you,
     I'm a *litterary dustman.*

In 1858 the dust contractor and brickmaker Henry Dodd, who contracted for the dust of the districts of St Luke's and Clerkenwell, offered the Royal General Theatrical Fund a gift of five acres of land. Dickens was one of the trustees of the Fund, and in a speech of 21 July proposed the gift be accepted, but difficulties arose over stipulations the donor wished to make and a meeting of 12 January 1859 rejected the offer: 'Dickens held aloof, but he is later said to have told Mark Lemon "that he never had occasion to repent but of two things, one being his conduct to Mr. Dodd". He is said to have introduced him into *Our Mutual Friend* as Mr. Boffin, the Golden Dustman' (Fielding, in *Speeches* 277).

'Here you are again,' repeated Mr. Wegg

Are you in the Funns]   To be 'in the Funds' was to have plenty of money. 'The Funds' was the general term for money lent to the government.

'But there's another chance

'Do you like the name of Nicodemus? Think it over. Nick, or Noddy.']   The name is corrected from 'Teddy' the first few times it is given in the MS. In the Bible, Nicodemus (the name means 'master of the people') was a Pharisee who made a secret visit to Christ and was converted. Christ spoke to him of spiritual conversion through baptism (John 3.5).

The wooden Wegg looked at him

being unacquainted with the tune, I run it over to him?']   Street ballads were written and sung to tunes already popular; song-sheets often had the words 'To be sung to the tune of ———— ————' printed at the head. Balladmongers also sang lists of their wares to passers-by.

' "A literary man – with a *wooden leg*

' "A literary man – *with* a wooden leg – and all Print is open to him!"']   In Marryat's *Jacob Faithful*, the Domine (Dobbs, the schoolmaster) reacts in a similar way to 'Old Tom' Beazeley: 'The Domine gradually turned round, and when old Tom had finished, exclaimed, "Truly it did delight mine ear, and from such – and," continued the Domine, looking down upon old Tom – "without legs too!" ' (11).

'Indeed, sir?' Mr. Wegg returned

'Education neglected?']   The phrase probably owed its currency to Thomas De Quincey, *Letters to a Young Man Whose Education Has Been Neglected* (1823).

'Man alive, don't I tell you?

it's too late for me to begin shovelling and sifting at alphabeds]   The malapropism suggests an allusion to the Madras system of education invented by Andrew Bell (1753–1832) in 1789, which utilized sand-tracing instead of writing in books or on slates. See the second stanza of 'The Literary Dustman'.

a gorging Lord-Mayor's-Show of wollumes]   At the annual Lord Mayor's Show (9 November) the elected mayor rides through the city in a gilt coach, accompanied by cavalry and a procession of allegorical floats (see Dickens's satirical 'Mr. Booley's View of the Last Lord Mayor's Show', *MP*). Boffin associates the show with the notoriously lavish mayoral dinners.

'I don't,' said Boffin, in a free-handed manner

I live over Maiden-Lane way – out Holloway direction]   Boffin later amends this to 'about a odd mile, or say and a quarter if you like, up Maiden Lane, Battle Bridge'. Battle Bridge was at the point where the Pentonville Road joined King's Cross. Maiden Lane was the old name for York Road (the old name is remembered in Maiden Lane Bridge, where the road crosses the Regent's Canal). About a mile up York Road was Belle Isle Shoot, the site of a famous London dust-yard.

two long 'uns and a short 'un]   A technique of counting derived from scoring by marking dashes, like the 'long chalk scores' that record customers' debts in the Three Jolly Bargemen in *GE* (10).

'I thought you might have know'd him

'His name is Decline-And-Fall-Off-The-Rooshan-Empire.']   In his *Book of Memoranda* Dickens made the note:

> Gibbon's Decline and Fall. The two characters, one reporting to the other as he reads. Both getting confused as to whether it is not all going on now! (21)

Edward Gibbon's *The History of the Decline and Fall of the Roman Empire* was first published in six volumes between 1776 and 1788. In his library at Gad's Hill, Dickens had an edition of 1825, like Boffin's, in eight volumes. Despite the relative success of the Crimean War (1854–6), the British continued to mistrust the ambitions of the gigantic and illiberal Russian Empire.

'I haven't been not to say

'Beside that cottage door, Mr. Boffin]   A version of a stanza from 'The Soldier's Tear' by George Alexander Lee, words by T. H. Bayly:

> Beside that cottage porch,
>   A girl was on her knees,
> She held aloft a snowy scarf
>   Which flutter'd in the breeze;
> She breath'd a pray'r for him,
>   A pray'r he could not hear,
> But he paus'd to bless her as she knelt,
>   And wip'd away a tear.

Heavy MS deletions indicate that this song was not Dickens's original choice. Though the Pitts and Catnach broadsheets include sentimental songs of this type, the bulk of the street ballads proper were comic or narrative songs: Wegg's genteel effusions would have been as familiar in middle-class homes as in Seven Dials.

The Bower was as difficult to find

as Fair Rosamond's without the clue.]   The story of Fair Rosamond, the paramour of Henry II, appears in *CHE*:

> It relates how the King doted on Fair Rosamond, who was the loveliest girl in all the world; and how he had a beautiful Tower built for her in a Park at Woodstock; and how it was erected in a labyrinth, and could only be found by a clue of silk. How the bad Queen Eleanor, becoming jealous of Fair Rosamond, found out the secret of the clue, and one day, appeared before her, with a dagger and a cup of poison, and left her to the choice between those two deaths.(12)

Pushing the gate

two lines of broken crockery set in ashes.]   Dickens considered 'Broken Crockery' as a title for the novel (*Book of Memoranda* 6).

an undress garment of short white smock-frock.]   'Undress' as opposed to the formal 'full dress'. Smock-frocks were loose-fitting garments, like the artist's smock (which derives from them), worn by farmers and labourers. Dustmen sometimes wore them for work.

a low evening-dress of sable satin]   Mrs Boffin's desire to go in for fashion is reminiscent of the ambitions of the wife of the newly rich coal-dealer, Nicholas Tulrumble, in Dickens's early piece 'The Mudfog Papers' (*SB*).

It was the queerest of rooms

a flowery carpet on the floor]   This is against the principle Dickens satirized in *HT*: ' "You don't walk upon flowers in fact; you cannot be allowed to walk upon flowers in carpets." ' The object of Dickens's satire was the newly established Department of Practical Art which had declared the gaily patterned Brussels carpets typical of the Victorian home to be in bad taste.

the heavy frames of its old-fashioned windows . . . seemed to indicate that it had once been a house of some mark standing alone in the country.]   In the eighteenth century this area was open country with farmhouses, inns and manor-houses of the chief manors; even at the end of the century it was 'almost exclusively pastoral' (Thornbury and Walford 5.340).

'So now, Wegg,' said Mr. Boffin

It's a spot to find out the merits of]   The Bower is set in a dusty parody of a garden landscaped in the eighteenth-century style, complete with serpentine walk, a view and an arbour.

Canine Provision Trade]   A commercial genteelism for a 'knacker's' or horse-slaughterer's yard. Live horses were purchased and slaughtered by the use of pole-axe and cane. The flesh and bones were chopped and boiled for cats' and dogs' meat (Mayhew 1.181–2). Adam Bell's wife in 'The Literary Dustman' engages in the trade (stanza 4). An *AYR* article, 'Jack's Castle Up the Lane', complained that such trades were carried on 'in baneful proximity to an overcrowded city'; near the upper end of the lane was 'the famed "Belle-isle" – beautiful island – suggestive to a London ear of dust-heaps and dustmen' (3.574–6).

'Thank you, Mr. Boffin, I think I will

Mr. Wegg did not say what organ, but spoke with a cheerful generality.]   The word 'organ' was at this time used not only of the vital parts of the body, but also, in phrenology, as a term for the supposed regions of the brain.

Then, Mr. Wegg, in a dry unflinching way

entered on his task]   At this sitting Wegg reads four of Gibbon's long chapters, about a hundred pages. The achievements of the Emperors Augustus, Hadrian, Trajan and the two Antonines, Titus Antonius Pius and Marcus Aurelius Antonius, are discussed in the general survey of the Empire in the first three chapters. Polybius, the Greek historian, is not mentioned in this part of the work. The reign of the Emperor Commodus (Gibbon's chapter 4), the son of Marcus Aurelius, was distinguished by cruelty and corruption. The 'character' that Commodus fought as 735 times was that of Paulus, a celebrated secutor (a type of gladiator, armed with helmet, sword and buckler). The Emperor's human victims – for this was not merely a 'wild-beast show' – were armed only with leaden weapons. Commodus killed the hundred lions in the character of the 'Roman Hercules', using a bow. He was a skilful hunter, but there was little risk to his person. Of course, all this slaughter did not take place on one occasion. Commodus was poisoned by his concubine Marcia, and then strangled by a wrestler. He was succeeded by Pertinax. The 'beastly' Emperor Vitellius is mentioned in chapter 3. Gibbon's footnote remarks that Vitellius 'consumed in mere eating at least six millions of our money, in about seven months. It is not easy to express his vices with dignity, or even decency. Tacitus fairly calls him a hog.' He is the improving subject of Dr Blimber's dinner-time conversation in *DS* (12).

burnt pens . . . which acted as a restorative]   Though by the 1860s steel pens were in use, Dickens always used a quill pen. Ladies who fainted were sometimes restored to consciousness with the aid of a burnt feather held under the nose.

'Commodious,' gasped Mr. Boffin, staring at the moon

to an old bird like myself these are scarers.]   Scarers, usually small boys, were employed to chase birds away from crops in fields.

'I didn't think this morning there was half so many Scarers in Print.] Perhaps an ironic allusion to the debate about the so-called 'sensation novel'; see pages 91 and 96. The works of historians like Gibbon, and those Wegg later reads – Rollin, Josephus and Plutarch – were a substantial part of the 'improving' reading in many young Victorians' education.

Book 1, Chapter 6

CUT ADRIFT.

The Six Jolly Fellowship-Porters

The Six Jolly Fellowship-Porters]   The Fellowship-Porters has long been identified with the Grapes, once the Bunch of Grapes, which still stands in Narrow Street. Young (1935) argued that the original was the Two Brewers, which stood about a hundred yards east of the Grapes and, like the Fellowship-Porters, at the top of a causeway (known as Duke Shore Stairs); the Two Brewers was more the shape and size of the Fellowship-Porters and impended further over the water than does the Grapes. It was demolished around 1905. Fellowship Porters were members of the Fellowship of Billingsgate Porters, also known as the Fellowship of Corn, Salt and Coal Porters. Fellowships were an inferior form of guilds for the least-skilled labourers. Porters worked in permanent gangs of from four to sixteen men (Stern, 1960). Dickens used the phrase 'jolly porters' of the Cheerybles' employees in *NN*, chapter 37, and the village pub in *GE* is called the Three Jolly Bargemen.

The wood forming the chimney-pieces

The wood forming the chimney-pieces]   Because the Great Fire of 1666 did not extend to the east of London, there were many old wooden buildings in the area.

The bar of the Six Jolly Fellowship-Porters

a bar to soften the human breast.]   Perhaps an echo of Congreve, *The Mourning Bride* (1697): 'Musick has Charms to sooth a savage Breast' (1.1). The description of the interior of the Fellowship-Porters recalls Dickens's delighted account of Eel Pie House on Twickenham Island in a letter to Leigh Hunt. He mentioned: 'the little pile of clean spittoons in one nook near the fireplace, looking like a collection of petrified three-cornered hats once worn by the dead-and-gone old codgers who used to sit and smoke there'. In the bar was

> the window seat on which the landlady sits o' fine evenings, where the lemons hang in a grove each in its own particular net, where 'the cheese' is kept, with great store of biscuits hard by in a wicker basket – where those wonderful bottles are, that hold cordials. You know 'em? great masses of grapes painted on 'em in green, blue and yellow, and the semblance of an extraordinary knot of ribbon supporting the emblem of a label. (12 May 1840, *Letters* 2.67)

not much larger than a hackney-coach]   'There are still about half a dozen hackney-coaches of the "good old" build . . . but these are attached entirely to the metropolitan railway stations, and are only made use of by Paterfamilias with much luggage and many infants on his return from the annual sea-side visit' (*AYR* 9.485).

This haven was divided from the rough world]   Nineteenth-century editions of *King Lear* (following Q3) gave 'rough world' for 'tough world': 'He hates him/That would upon the rack of this rough world/Stretch him out longer' (5.3.312–14).

For the rest, both the tap

sugar-loaf hats]   Conical hats, rounded or flat at the top, worn during Tudor and Stuart times.

mulled your ale]   Ale is mulled by sweetening and spicing, then heating; it was sometimes thickened with the beaten yolk of an egg.

Purl]   A mixture of hot beer and gin, sometimes with ginger and sugar added. It was popularly a warming morning drink. Mayhew mentions that purl was particularly sold along the river; there were even purl-boats.

Flip]   A mixture of beer and spirit, into which was beaten an egg, sweetened with sugar, and heated with a hot iron.

Dog's Nose]   Beer and gin or ale and rum: in *PP* it is said to be 'compounded of warm porter, moist sugar, gin, and nutmeg' (33).

its alluring name: Cosy]   The word 'snug' is used of the smallest room in an inn or a pub; a 'cosy seat' is a canopied corner seat for two.

'Now, you mind, you Riderhood

Riderhood]   In Knowles's *The Daughter*, Norris's accomplice is called Wolf. Riderhood suggests the wolf in 'Little Red Riding-Hood', though the name also appears among those Dickens copied into his *Book of Memoranda*.

Gaffer was not there, but a pretty strong muster

Miss Abbey's pupils ... exhibited ... the greatest docility.]   Though there were rough and disreputable waterside public houses, they were not typical of East End public houses:

> Go into any of these houses – the ordinary public-house at the corner of any ordinary East End street – there, standing at the counter, or seated on the benches against wall or partition, will be perhaps half-a-dozen people, men and women, chatting together over their beer ... behind the bar will be a decent middle-aged woman, something above her customers in class, very neatly dressed, respecting herself and respected by them. The whole scene comfortable, quiet, and orderly. (Booth 1.113–14)

a glazed hat]   Hats with smooth shiny surfaces, produced by a coating substance, especially worn by sailors, like Captain Cuttle in *DS*.

'You Bob Glibbery,' said Miss Abbey

Bob Glibbery]   CD misprints the name as 'Gliddery'. Dickens listed the name Glibbery in his *Book of Memoranda*.

No supper did Miss Potterson take

hot Port Negus]   A mixture of port and hot water, sweetened with sugar and flavoured, named after the inventor, Colonel Francis Negus (d.1732).

'By the time of Miss Abbey's closing

Father at Chiswick]   Chiswick is about thirteen and a half miles from Limehouse by river. The Thames makes a great curve there and washes three sides of the parish. Because of an island the place was avoided by steamers.

'Now listen, Charley dear.

Go straight to the school]   In the early 1840s the ragged school at Field Lane 'rented a wretched house' with a 'few common beds' for 'the most constant and deserving scholars'. Ten years later, the dormitory was 'like an extensive coach-house', well lit, well heated and aired, and with a supply of water. The boys slept in 'wooden troughs, or shallow boxes' with 'one coarse rug' ('A Sleep to Startle Us', *MP*).

'There's a drop of brandy

a drop of brandy . . . this bit of meat.]   Gaffer eats better than the Wilfers do. Mrs Beeton gave the price of broiling steak as 1*s* or 1*s* 2*d* a pound.

If the river was to get frozen, there would be a deal of distress]   The last occasion on which the river had been fully frozen over in London was for five days in February 1814. There were severe winters in both 1860 and 1861. In 1860 the *Annual Register* reported that, though the Thames nowhere froze over, 'all traffic, whether by steam-boats or barges, was stopped' (199). The following year

> The sufferings of the poor in all parts were extreme . . . In the eastern parts of London, in particular, the destitution was terrible. The dock labourers and wharfmen were thrown for weeks out of employment by the stoppage of traffic on the river . . . they rose now with the frightful certainty that the food for the day they could not earn. (1861, 2)

An *AYR* article, 'The Frozen-Out Poor Law', discussed the administration of the Poor Law during that terrible winter and argued that the only alleviation for 'certain poor parishes, such as those along the Thames by Ratcliffe and Wapping' was the 'equalization of poor rates', or centralization (4.448).

'Ah! there's always enough of that

'distress is forever going about, like sut in the air]   Coal was the fuel widely used in London since 1600, but it produced more soot and black smoke than any other fuel. An authority on air pollution quoted by Mayhew described the problem of metropolitan smoke and spoke of 'those black portions of soot that everyone is familiar with' (2.339, 341).

'Father, don't! I can't bear to see you

I can't bear to see you striking with it.]   In *The Daughter*, Marian, who has gone to the scene of the wreck to persuade her father not to rob the dead, sees the villain, Norris, stab a half-drowned man. Owing to the darkness of the night she thinks it is her father, whom she has seen bending over the prostrate figure moments before. She faints at the sight of the blow and later cannot bear to look at her father when he approaches her (2.4, 3.2).

'Have we got a pest in the house?

a pest]　The word 'pest' was used of any deadly epidemic disease, but especially of the plague.

Book 1, Chapter 7

MR. WEGG LOOKS AFTER HIMSELF.

Dickens overwrote the original chapter 7 (now chapter 10) and had to find a new subject to complete the number:

> While I was considering what it should be, Marcus who has done an excellent cover, came to tell me of an extraordinary trade he had found out, through one of his painting requirements. I immediately went with him to Saint Giles's to look at the place, and found – what you will see. (25 February 1864, *Nonesuch* 3.380)

Marcus Stone described what happened:

> One evening in the early spring of 1863, I went to dine at the Office of 'All the Year Round'. We were going to the theatre opposite to see Fichter, he was then at work on the first number of Our Mutual Friend. He told me he had a personage who had just appeared upon the scene who was to have some eccentric calling, and that he could not find the calling that would suit him. I had that same day been to see a certain Willis who lived in Seven Dials, who was an articulator of skeletons, a stuffer of birds, and dealer in bottled monsters. I had some pigeons to paint in a picture and he had been recommended to me, to provide, kill, and set up for me, the poor birds, who were to be sacrificed that I might have better sitters. I suggested Mr. Willis, or rather his occupation, as an idea that might be suggestive. 'It is the very thing that I want he said it couldn't be better.' The next day I took him to Seven Dials. Willis, who was a brisk, active, cheerful, little man, was not at home, and we found the shop in charge of an assistant who was at work on the bones of a foot. He was a despondent melancholy youth. We examined the contents of the shop and made a sketch of it. This was the origin of Mr Venus, in whom I afterwards recognized much of Mr Willis's melancholy deputy. (autograph note in the Suzannet Collection in the Dickens House)

Kitton (1897) records that the shop was at 42 St Andrew Street, off Holborn Circus.

'If I get on with him as I expect

'it wouldn't become me to leave it here. It wouldn't be respectable.'] In the late eighteenth and early nineteenth century there were not enough human bodies available for dissection. Relatives and friends objected to bodies of their kin being dissected. Only bodies of murderers could be used, and they were too few: hence there arose the activities of the body snatchers, or 'resurrection men', like Jerry Cruncher in *TTC*. The Anatomy Acts of the 1830s regulated the situation, but there was still a shortage of bodies for anatomical research (Keith, 1957). A *HW* article, 'Use and Abuse of the Dead', discussed the scandal of work-house masters and undertakers 'jobbing' in the corpses of paupers (17.361–4). It would not become a ' "genteel person" ' to provide a part of such society.

Aware of a working-jeweller population

a working-jeweller population taking sanctuary about the church in Clerkenwell] In his *Book of Memoranda* Dickens made the note 'The working Jewellers of Clerkenwell – Dutch? (11). In the mid-nineteenth century the staple industries of the parish of Clerkenwell were watch- and clock-making, gold-beating, diamond-cutting, and the manufacture of jewellery. Many foreigners lived in the area, chiefly employed as workers in diamonds and other precious stones. The church is St John's, in St John's Square.

the delights of a coat of invisibility] In the nursery tale 'Jack the Giantkiller' Jack destroys the giants with the help of a coat that makes him invisible.

Not, however, towards the 'shops'

making their hands so rich, that the enriched water in which they wash them is bought for the refiners] This was the practice in Clerkenwell: 'so carefully is any loss guarded against that even the water in which the workmen wash their hands is made to yield up what gold it may contain' (Duckworth in Booth 6.8).

not towards these ... but towards the poorer shops] Percy Fitzgerald remarked that the locality described in the rest of this paragraph is 'not at all like Clerkenwell, where watch dealers and fancy goodsmen mainly flourish. We can recognize such a place much nearer to the West End ... St. Andrews Street, one of the streets leading to the Seven Dials, where dealers in birds, rabbits, etc., abound' (1895, 243). Dickens's description of 'Seven Dials' in *SB* confirms the suggestion. Walford called the area 'the great haunt of bird and bird-cage sellers, also of the sellers of rabbits, cats, dogs, &c. ... Cheap picture-frame makers also abound here' (Thornbury and Walford 3.205). Brokers dealt in second-hand furniture and apparel.

two preserved frogs fighting a small-sword duel.] On Dickens's writing-desk there was a French bronze group representing a duel with swords, fought by a couple of very fat toads, one of them (characterized by that particular buoyancy which belongs to corpulence) in the act of making a prodigious lunge forward, which the other receives in the very middle of his digestive apparatus. (Forster 3.186n)

An *AYR* article described the many arrangements of stuffed frogs created by the French taxidermist M. Verreaux, among which were 'a couple of terrific duel-scenes' (5.154). Queen Victoria thought some German stuffed frogs at the Great Exhibition of 1851 'really marvellous'.

The face looking up is a sallow face

a sallow face with weak eyes]   Venus's eyes are strained by close work in bad light; they would also be affected by the corrosive sublimates and arsenical soap used by taxidermists. But the disappointed lover traditionally has weak eyes: in *NN* Mr Crummles's company has 'a slim young gentleman with weak eyes, who played the low-spirited lovers and sang tenor songs' (23).

The little counter being so short

musty, leathery, feathery, cellary, gluey, gummy]   The smells of dry, decaying objects, and of the substances used by taxidermists in preservation and setting up: cement, gum paste, flour paste, solution of gum arabic, paper paste and red varnish were among them (Brown, 1836, ch. 7).

It being one of Mr. Wegg's guiding rules

a pretty little dead bird ... and a long stiff wire piercing its breast.] When a bird was to be mounted, the skin was removed and a false body of tow or similar substance was made upon a wire pointed at its upper end. This false body was then inserted, the pointed end of the wire going up the neck and through the skull, emerging through the beak. Other wires were thrust through the butts of the wings and the soles of the feet. The specimen would be spoiled if the breast was pierced: an incision was usually made under the wing on the side most damaged.

As if it were Cock Robin]   The nursery rhyme, first recorded in 1742:

> Who killed Cock Robin?
> I, said the Sparrow
> With my bow and arrow,
> I killed Cock Robin.

> Who saw him die?
> I, said the fly,
> With my little eye,
> I saw him die.

Mr. Wegg, as an artful man

a Hindoo baby in a bottle, curved up with his big head tucked under him] In the 'large gloomy room' of Mr Stargazer in Dickens's one-act farce *The Lamplighter* (1838) there are, among other strange objects, a 'large phial' containing a 'male infant with three heads' and a skeleton, articulated by the 'genius' Mr Mooney (3). Dickens probably drew on his knowledge of the interiors of the apothecaries' shops of earlier times, and may have known of the 'Museum of Anatomy and Curiosities' established in Fleet Street by Benjamin Rackstraw which flourished in the eighteenth century. Among the objects on display were fish, birds, shells, skeletons, a mummy, and a variety of preserved foetuses, human and animal abortions, and placentas, as well as preserved female reproductive organs and a penis injected to the state of erection (Altick, 1978, 55). See page 231. He would also have been familiar with the Hunterian Museum at the Royal College of Surgeons in Lincoln's Inn Fields. His friend Professor Owen (see p. 27) was, from 1836, the first Hunterian Professor of Comparative Anatomy and Physiology, and one of his duties was to deliver twenty-four annual lectures illustrative of the Hunterian collection. A *HW* article described some of the contents of the museum: 'besides remarkable instances of normal structure', there were the skeletons or other remains of 'many curious freaks of nature', including giants, dwarfs, 'extinct monsters', a Bengalese boy with two heads, and two mummified women (2.281). Curiosities in glass bottles were also often displayed in taverns, coffee houses and at popular exhibitions.

'With ribs (I grant you) always.

I can't keep to nature, and be miscellaneous with ribs] Venus is correct: there is too great a variation in the length of ribs.

'An easy wager, when we run so much

we run so much into foreign!] The shortage of bodies was limited to England and America. On the European mainland objection was not raised to dissection of bodies of people whose burial was paid for by the state, provided a religious service was heard (Keith, 1957).

'There!' he whimpers. 'There's animation!

'There's animation! On a twig, making up his mind to hop!] Dickens owned the 1852 edition of Charles Waterton's *Wanderings in South America* (1825) and may have remembered the enthusiastic section 'On Preserving Birds':

> Then you will place your eagle, in attitude commanding, the same as Nelson stood in, in the day of battle, on the Victory's quarter-deck. Your pie will seem crafty, and just ready to take flight, as though fearful of being surprised in some mischievous plunder. Your sparrow will retain its wonted pertness, by means of

placing his tail a little elevated, and giving a moderate arch to the neck. Your vulture will show his sluggish habits, by having his body nearly parallel to the earth...

Your dove will be in artless, fearless innocence; looking mildly at you, with its neck, not too much stretched, as if uneasy in its situation; or drawn too close into the shoulders, like one wishing to avoid a discovery; but in moderate, perpendicular length... And the breast ought to be conspicuous, and have this attention paid to it; for when a young lady is sweet and gentle in her manners; kind and affable to those around her; when her eyes stand in tears of pity for the woes of others, and she puts a small portion of what Providence has blessed her with into the hand of imploring poverty and hunger, then we say, she has the breast of a turtle-dove. (308–9)

'Oh dear me, dear me!' sighs Mr. Venus

A Wice. Tools. Bones, warious.]   Captain Thomas Brown (1836) listed the tools of the taxidermist: a box of scalpels; a pair of scissors; two or three pointed forceps; two flat pincers, or pliers; a round pincer for turning wire; a cutting pincer for wire; a hammer, two files; a triangular file; brass awls, etc. The bottled preparations would include corrosive sublimates, solution of pearl ashes, and arsenical compositions. According to the *HW* article 'Dust; or Ugliness Redeemed', cats could be found in dust-heaps. There were English babies, a Negro baby and a Chinese baby in the Hunterian Museum. Hutter (1983) gives an advertisement from the *Lancet* (5 September 1835) in which one A. Alexandre announces that he has fitted up a new museum, and just received the first importation of osteology for the forthcoming season, consisting of

> Five Adult Articulated Skeletons.
> Ditto Unarticulated ditto.
> Separated Skulls, in boxes, warranted perfect.
> Skulls divided in sections showing the Internal Ear.
> Entire Skulls at all prices.
> Foetus Skeletons and Skulls.
> Female Pelvis, with Ligaments.
> Midwifery Apparatus connected with the Foetus.
> Female Pelvis covered with Leather.
> Foetus Skeletons covered with ditto.

That's the general panoramic view.']   A panorama was a picture of a landscape or other scene unrolled or unfolded so as to pass before the spectator and show the various parts in succession and, in some cases, to give the illusion of travel. Scenes such as views of Edinburgh, the Queen's coronation and the Mississippi river were exhibited in London. One such place of exhibition was called the 'Panorama'.

'Well,' replies Venus, blowing his tea

his head and face peering out of the darkness, over the smoke of it, as if he were modernizing the old original rise in his family] An allusion to the birth of the goddess Venus from the foam of the sea near the island of Cythera. A running title in CD reads: 'VENUS RISES FROM THE COUNTER'. In Hood's poem 'Miss Kilmansegg and Her Precious Leg' there is a lapdog who is referred to as ' "Wenus" ' (2127). The two pieces of the statue of the Venus de Milo, found in 1820, were assembled and exhibited at the Louvre from 1821. A much publicized copy was displayed in the Greek Court of the Crystal Palace exhibition (Hutter, 1983, 151).

'Mr. Wegg, I know it ain't.

I've gone on improving myself in my knowledge of Anatomy] Such application was necessary for an 'Articulator of human bones' and for a taxidermist: 'Their studies should be commenced by a deep attention to drawing, modelling, anatomy, and chemistry, while they, at the same time, proceed with the practical part of their art' (Brown, 1836, 3).

'And so a man climbs to the top

surrounded by the lovely trophies of my art] 'But, if you wish to excel in the art, if you wish to be in ornithology, what Angelo was in sculpture, you must apply to profound study, and your own genius to assist you' (Waterton 308).

Book 1, Chapter 8   Third monthly number
                                                       July 1864

MR. BOFFIN IN CONSULTATION.

Whosoever had gone out

Whosoever had gone out of Fleet Street into the Temple] An echo of the opening of the Athanasian Creed in the Book of Common Prayer, 'Whosoever will be saved', and perhaps also of Matthew 23.16: 'Woe unto you, ye blind guides, which say, Whosoever shall swear by the temple, it is nothing; but whosoever shall swear by the gold of the temple, he is a debtor!' The Temple is a liberty or precinct between Fleet Street and the Thames, so called for the Knights Templars who made their habitation there in the twelfth century. The Inner and Middle Temples are Inns of Court. The Inner Temple was entered through Inner Temple Lane by a gateway beneath 17 Fleet Street. Lightwood's chambers are on the west side of the lane where Goldsmith's Building (built 1861) now stands. Temple Church (St Mary's), a notable building of Norman origin, has a sunken church-yard with ancient tombs.

a dismal boy]   In his *Book of Memoranda* Dickens noted the idea of 'The office-boy for ever looking out of the window, who never has anything to do. *Done in Our Mutual*' (5).

common-law clerk, conveyancing clerk, chancery clerk]   Common law is law grounded on custom, 'unwritten' or 'judge-made' law. Conveyancing is to do with the transfer of land and property. Dickens had commented on the variety of lawyers' clerks in *PP*, chapter 31.

Mr. Boffin having been several times

much regretting the death of the amiable Pertinax]   Pertinax briefly succeeded Commodus and met his death at the hands of the Praetorian guards; Gibbon concluded his fourth chapter by regretting 'the transient blessings of a reign, the memory of which could serve only to aggravate their approaching misfortunes'.

By which he probably meant

the Directory]   The first London directory had been published in 1677. Since 1801 the Post Office had produced a *London Directory*.

The boy virtually replied

a Briton who never never never]   The refrain of 'Rule Britannia!', which first appeared in *Alfred: A Masque* (1740) by James Thomson and David Mallet (music by Dr Arne): 'Rule, Britannia, rule the waves;/Britons never will be slaves.'

Then Mr. Boffin, with his stick

his stick at his ear, like a Familiar Spirit]   Witches and wizards were supposed to have 'familiars', lower demons left them by the devil, which often took the form of a cat or a dog.

an empty blue bag]   Junior barristers and solicitors carried their documents in blue bags.

a box of wafers]   Small coloured discs of flour and gum or of gelatine used for sealing papers or letters or for taking the impress of a seal.

Work out the story towards:
    Mr and Mrs Boffin's showing their disinterestedness
    Taking Bella Wilfer to live with them
    and Rokesmith's becoming Secretary

    Get all the affairs square, and the Boffin's square
        clear the ground, behind and before.

    Glimpse of Wrayburn.

Chapter VIII
Mr Boffin in consultation

at Mortimer Lightwood's chambers.

The Bees   History young Blight

Mr and Mrs Boffin always the poor children's friends. quite defying the rich old man.

Lead up gradually to their taking 'Our House.'

Rokesmith and Boffin come together.

Chapter IX
Mr and Mrs Boffin in consultation

Their plans.

Fashion:

and orphan to be adopted:

and Bella

Sketch of Curate

and wife

At the Wilfers'

Rokesmith and Mrs. Boffin come together.

Chapter X
A Marriage Contract

This chapter transferred bodily from No. 2

Mr. Lightwood explained that he came

the proctor's] Proctors conducted their clients' business in courts administering civil or common law.

Mr. Lightwood, without explaining

standing in the books of the Governor and Company of the Bank of England] The words 'For the Governor and Company of the Bank of England' date from the incorporation of the Bank in 1694 and appear on every English banknote. In a world of financial speculation Boffin's money is secure: the phrase 'as safe as the Bank of England' was proverbial.

'And what is particularly eligible

no estates to manage] 'Land is a luxury, and of all luxuries the most costly' as Trollope observed in *The Way We Live Now* (1875, 6). Eugene calls his family estate the ' "Family Embarrassments" ' (1.12). In the period after the repeal of the Corn Law Acts (1844) agricultural investment yielded little pecuniary return.

no rents to return so much per cent upon in bad times] In bad years of crop failure or low prices, it was the practice for landlords to return a certain percentage of the rents received from tenant farmers. On 2 July 1862, Dickens wrote to Frederick Ouvry:

> I don't care to have land, because I don't understand it, and because that sort of proprietorship is not in my way, and seems to me to put a public man of my notoriety – with a good-natured reputation – at a disadvantage with tenants. (*Nonesuch* 3.299)

no voters to become parboiled in hot water with] Should the landlord wish to influence the local election or run for Parliament himself; perhaps with a suggestion of the embarrassment of bribery or of bribery detected.

no agents to take the cream off the milk] Agents were appointed to manage estates in the absence of their owners.

under a fatal spell . . . to mention the Rocky Mountains] The Rockies had been in the news because masses of American settlers were moving westwards and particularly because of the Gold Rush of 1849.

'And speaking of satisfactory

the moment when he's lifting . . . the cup and sarser to his lips.] A homely version of the proverb that provides the title for book 1. A MS passage is omitted here:

> to his lips. Similar to Pertintacks.'
> Mr. Lightwood repeated in amazement. 'To—?'
> 'Pertintacks,' said Mr. Boffin. 'What declined and falled after Commodious.

And a parlous [?] state of things in the Empire ensues! What's to come of it? Them guards don't know what they want, you know! The only thing I see clear as yet is, that there's nothing more calc'lated to produce rows, than a mob of violent chaps that don't know what they want, and that will have it. Don't you see?' said Mr. Boffin, rather dwelling on this historical discovery. 'They don't know what they want, and they will have it.'

Mr. Lightwood passed his hand across his forehead and looked at his client with an air of extreme desolation.

'Humsumever,' said Mr. Boffin, 'that's not the poor dear boy.

she wore . . . a black straw]   As worn by women sifters on a dust-mound: 'Their coarse dirty cotton gowns were tucked up behind them, their arms were bared above their elbows, their black bonnets crushed and battered like those of fish-women' (Mayhew 2.171–2).

Mr. Lightwood murmured 'Vigorous Saxon

'**Vigorous Saxon spirit – Mrs. Boffin's ancestors – bowmen – Agincourt and Cressy.'**]   The English victories over the French at Agincourt (1415) and Crécy (1346) were in large part due to archers, drawn from the common people, which is to say the Saxons, rather than the Normans. Mortimer speaks as one of the Normans. The independence and vigour of the Saxons was a popular Victorian idea: in *CHE* Dickens celebrated the 'English-Saxon character' as 'the greatest character among the nations of the earth' (3).

'My dear Mr. Boffin

everything wears to rags]   A traditional observation: in the *HW* article 'A Paper-Mill' by Dickens and Mark Lemon, there is the comment: 'enough to consider, at present, what a grave of dress this rag-store is; what a lesson of vanity it preaches . . . all dwindle down to this, and bring their littleness or greatness in fractional proportions here. As it is with the worn, it shall be with the wearers' (1.530).

'I won't go so far

there's some things that I never found among the dust.]   A passage in the MS and in the proofs is omitted:

among the dust.'

'Manufactured articles, Mr. Boffin?'

'No, Mr. Lightwood, articles not to be made, nor weighed, nor measured, nor bought, nor sold. Excuse me, I am a much older man than you, sir. Don't make light of what's good and true, or you'll come to find it heavy. Bold speaking, you'll say,' resuming his usual good-humoured manner, 'for a man who's no scholar; but you're a scholar yourself, and you'll overlook the liberty.

the gentleman in the uncomfortable neckcloth]   In *SB* Dickens described 'a number of very self-important looking personages, in stiff neckcloths, and black gowns with white fur collars, whom we set down at once as proctors'.

'Doctors' Commons,' observed Lightwood.

Doctors' Commons]   Doctors' Commons was a college of Doctors of Civil Law, situated in Great Knightrider Street, south of St Paul's churchyard, in the south-west corner of which was an arched gateway. In *SB* Dickens described Doctors' Commons as 'familiar by name to everybody, as the place where they grant marriage-licences to love-sick couples, and divorces to unfaithful ones; register the wills of people who have any property to leave, and punish hasty gentlemen who call ladies by unpleasant names' ('Doctors' Commons'). Here were the Principal Registry of the Court of the Probate, where wills were deposited, and the Prerogative Court, wherein wills and testaments were proved. As a young man, Dickens spent nearly two years as a reporter for one of the offices in Doctors' Commons.

'Too dry for you, eh?

Look at the bees.']   In his *Book of Memoranda* Dickens made the note:

> How do I know that I, a man, am to learn from Insects – unless it is to learn how little my littlenesses are? All that botheration in the hive about the queen Bee, may be, in little, me and the ∧ court ∧ circular. (21)

In a letter of 1 October 1864 he wrote: 'I don't like Bees as a subject: having had my honey turned into Gall by Bee Masters in The Times' (*Nonesuch* 3.399). The best-known expression of the model industry of the bees is the lines from Isaac Watts's 'Against Idleness and Mischief' in his *Divine Songs for Children* (1715): 'How doth the little busy bee/Improve each shining hour'. Skimpole complains of the bees in *BH*, chapter 8.

'As a two-footed creature

the camel . . . is an excessively temperate person. . . . fitted up with a convenient cool cellar]   The allusion is to those who recommend a temperance they do not themselves practise: in *Sunday under Three Heads* (*RP*) Dickens had complained that the enforcement of Sabbath observance would still allow the 'sumptuous dinner and the rich wines' of the rich but would deny the poor man his 'pint of beer and . . . plate of meat' (2). At the time of *OMF* there was a debate over whether beer should be provided in newly established working men's dining-places (see the *AYR* article, 'Temperate Temperance', 9.188–9).

'Exactly. And may I represent to you

Tuft-hunting]   Meanly or obsequiously courting the acquaintance of persons of rank or title; in university slang a titled undergraduate was a 'tuft'.

'Ye-es,' returned Eugene, disparagingly

And am I never to have change of air]   MS and proofs read: 'And am I never to get out of town'.

'If you will allow me to walk

Clifford's Inn]   Clifford's Inn is an Inn of Chancery. It is situated behind St Dunstan's Church, Fleet Street. There was a terrace and raised garden.

('Now,' thought Mr. Boffin, 'if he proposes

a game at skittles, or meets a country gentleman just come into property, or produces any article of jewellery]   Mayhew described these cheats:

> This is a peculiar class of unprincipled men, who play tricks with cards, skittles, &c. &c., and lay wagers with the view of cheating those strangers who may have the misfortune to be in their company . . . They generally dress well, and in various styles, some are attired as gentlemen, others as country farmers . . . They frequent Fleet Street. (4.385)

The skittles cheats were known as 'magsmen' or 'sharpers'; those who pretended to have found valuable articles were known as 'fawney' or 'ring droppers'.

carrying his stick in his arms much as Punch carries his]   In the popular Punch and Judy shows Punch uses his stick to fight his wife, a policeman, Death and finally the devil himself.

Book 1, Chapter 9

MR. AND MRS. BOFFIN IN CONSULTATION.

Betaking himself straight homeward

(in a walking dress of black velvet and feathers, like a mourning coach-horse)]   In fact, Mrs Boffin is wearing evening dress. In the elaborate formal funerals of the time, coach-horses were decorated with tall black plumes: the undertaker Mr Mould in *MC* offers 'to be perfectly profuse in feathers' (19).

'People have to pay to see Wax-Work

'People have to pay to see Wax-Work]   In *OCS* Mrs Jarley charges sixpence entry to her travelling waxwork exhibition. The most famous of the many waxwork exhibitions in London, Madame Tussaud's, in Baker Street, was established in 1802.

'Lor-a-mussy!' exclaimed Mrs. Boffin

'Lor-a-mussy!'] A corruption of 'Lord have mercy'.

a light yellow chariot and pair] Mrs Boffin wants a town chariot or coupé, a light cut-down coach of graceful lines. Yellow was a fashionable colour for carriages (the Podsnaps have a 'custard-coloured phaeton', 1.11): 'For bright sunny days the straw or sulphur yellow is very brilliant and beautiful; but for the autumn haze, the rich deep orange hue conveys the most agreeable sensations' (Adams, 1837, 210–11).

silver boxes to the wheels] Iron boxes were fitted over the axle ends. All the ironwork was 'covered with brass or silver in highly-ornamented carriages' (Adams, 1837, 136).

'Yes!' cried the delighted creature.

a footman up behind, with a bar across, to keep his legs from being poled!] The footman or footmen rode on a step attached to the back of the carriage body. The bar protected them from the carriage poles of vehicles behind.

a coachman up in front, sinking down into a seat big enough for three of him, all covered with upholstery in green and white!] 'The coachman's seat ... is covered by the hammer-cloth, the colour of which sometimes harmonizes with and sometimes forms an agreeable contrast to that of the paint ... The upper edge has a single row of broad lace round it; the lower edge is made somewhat to resemble an architectural basement, by three rows of broad lace, or two rows of lace and one of deep heavy fringe' (Adams, 1837, 153–4).

'Ne-ever once thought of the way

'What a thinking steam-ingein] Boffin's metaphor suggests his excited response to an important modern invention. James Watt invented his steam engine in 1763 and by the nineteenth century steam engines were adapted to ships (1802) and railways (1829) as well as put to a wide variety of industrial uses. *AYR* articles discuss the comparisons made by scientists between human energies and those of the steam engine (14.32–3).

These two ignorant and unpolished people

For, Evil often stops short of itself and dies with the doer of it; But Good, never.] A striking reversal of Mark Antony's famous lines in *Julius Caesar* (3.2.75–6): 'The evil that men do lives after them;/The good is oft interred with their bones.'

This consisted of a long hammer-headed

entombed by an honest jobbing tailor ... in a perfect Sepulchre of coat and gaiters, sealed with ponderous buttons.] To 'job' is both to do occasional odd pieces of work and to cheat, especially to misuse public office: Veneering is said to have 'over-jobbed his jobberies as legislator' (4.'The Last'). A 'great stone' was used as 'the door of the sepulchre' (Matthew 27.60).

Behind this domestic, Mr. and Mrs. Boffin

hailed it in stentorian tones] In Homer, Stentor is the Greek warrior 'whose voice was as powerful as fifty voices of other men'.

'Down with the dust] A traditional phrase, demanding the show of money: 'She cried, "Come, down, now, with your dust!" ' ('The Dust About the Gold Dust', *Comic Almanack*, 1840, 217).

At length the Bower district

The Reverend Frank Milvey's abode was a very modest abode] The poor curate was a recognized type:

> our poor Curate ... be it remembered, is 'Benedick, the married man,' – cherishing all the better feelings and refined affections of our nature, and mingling with them those high and enobling studies which are not of the 'earth, earthy;' ... aye, and ... too frequently with an income considerably less than what a wealthy merchant would deem a fitting remuneration for one of his junior clerks. (James Smythe in *Heads of the People*, 1841, 137)

An 1860 *AYR* article, 'The Wolf at the Church Door', discussed the fact that many town and country clergy were genuinely impoverished (4.177–80). A number of *HW* and *AYR* articles considered the problems and praised the efforts of the clergy in the poorer urban parishes, but in 1865, responding to the *AYR* article 'Through Lambeth to Vauxhall', Dickens complained to W. H. Wills that

> However estimable these Clergymen are, it is quite out of the question for us to go on spinning out dry catalogues of what they do ... From the time when we did What a London Curate Can Do if He Tries, it is but one perpetual drowsy repetition, generally with anything good in the original treatment left out. (29 January 1865, *Nonesuch* 3.413)

expensively educated] Anglican clergymen were normally graduates of Oxford or Cambridge universities.

teaching and translating from the classics] Many clergymen took pupils, as Crisparkle does in *MED*, or put their classical educations to other use by producing translations for series like Bohn's Classical Library.

'But, like the Kings and Queens

like the Kings and Queens in the Fairy Tales, I suppose you have wished for one?']   For instance, 'Sleeping Beauty', which begins: 'There was once upon a time a King and Queen, who were so sorry that they had no children.'

'No, don't say that,' assented Mr. Milvey

your District.']   A district was a section of a parish allotted to a lay 'visitor', usually a woman, working under the clergyman.

'Here's Mr. and Mrs. Boffin!' growled the hammer-headed

as if he were on view in a Menagerie]   The Regent's Park Zoo, opened in 1828, and known as 'the Menagerie', was a popular place of resort.

Mr. and Mrs. Boffin complying

three pairs of listening legs]   In his *Book of Memoranda*, Dickens noted the idea: ' "The family's Legs" ' (17).

After waiting some quarter of an hour

blindman's buff]   A game in which one player is blindfolded and tries to catch and identify the others.

'The avocations of R. W.

'The avocations of R. W. ... keep him fully engaged in the City]   Avocations are properly those employments which divert from the main occupation. The phrase 'in the City' has a vague grand sound: 'Nobody knew what he was, or where he went; but Mrs. Tibbs used to say with an air of great importance, that he was engaged in the City' ('The Boarding-House', 1 *SB*).

'Yes, do what your Ma says

Mrs. Wilfer sitting stiffly by, like a functionary presiding over an interview previous to an execution]   Describing the condemned cells in Newgate prison, Dickens mentioned the gates through which 'the prisoners are allowed to see their friends: a turnkey always remaining in the vacant space between, during the whole interview' ('A Visit to Newgate', *SB*).

Bella was nervous now

and would have been glad to recall her question.]   The MS continues:

'I gather,' said Mr. Rokesmith as they returned to the house, that these good

80

people are going to be your intimate friends. I hope so. I hope they may adopt you, as they have adopted the child who is to be named after—'

'The Dead,' said Bella, stealing an expressive look at him.

You thought it strange

But my interest remains.']   Another MS passage is omitted:

'I think it strange? Mr. Rokesmith will you mind my saying that I always think you strange?'

'That depends – Does it imply a doubt of me?'

'You know well, I think, that it implies many doubts.'

'Then I mind it very much.'

And now the worthy Mrs. Wilfer

as a lay-figure]   A jointed wooden figure of the body used by artists: in *BH* Chadband adjusts Jo 'like a lay-figure' to receive his sermon (25), and in *GE* Wopsle uses Pip as 'a dramatic lay-figure, to be contradicted and embraced and wept over' (15).

Book 1, Chapter 10

A MARRIAGE CONTRACT.

This chapter was the original chapter 7. Dickens wrote in pencil at the end of the MS of chapter 9: '*Marriage Contract last Chapter of No. 2, to be added here.*'

There is excitement

a spring-van is delivering its load of greenhouse plants]   MS and proofs read 'blooming plants', but in book 1, chapter 12, it is still 'nipping spring', and the 'blooming summer days' do not come till book 1, chapter 17. A spring van was a large van for goods delivery.

The mature young lady is a lady of property.

a lady of property. . . . a gentleman of property.]   In book 3, chapter 5, Boffin pretends to take his stand as a ' "man of property" '. Such phrases were long common usage, as Galsworthy's title, *A Man of Property* (1906), indicates.

He goes, in a condescending amateurish way, into the City, attends meetings of Directors, and has to do with traffic in Shares.]   'The number of new companies is an unceasing theme of remark,' *The Economist* commented in 1864. 'They fill the City articles; they swell the advertisement lists of all important papers. Most men are directors of some company or another' (349). Lammle affects to be one of the gentlemanly young men, like those in Trollope's *The Way We Live Now* (1875), who were drifting into directorships, exchanging the use of their names for easy money. 'Why not become one of your regular City fellows, and turn speculator?' asks such a figure in one of Meason's *AYR* articles: 'They have always lots of money, and don't seem to work very hard for it. Their chief business . . . seems to be to go into the city every day at about eleven o'clock with an umbrella, and walk back at about four' (14.57). In all probability, Lammle is more like another of Meason's characters 'whose only trade or calling was to become a director of anything that was offered him, for the sake of the two guineas a week it yielded him in fees' (*AYR* 12.496). He is an example of the 'third-class director – and his name is legion', who, 'for fee and reward', will do 'everything, and anything to secure position', and who ' "skedaddles" to the Continent' when a company collapses (Evans, 1864, 81–2).

As is well known to the wise in their generation]   Luke 16.8–9: 'And the Lord commended the unjust steward, because he had done wisely: for the children of this world are in their generation wiser than the children of light. And I say unto you, Make to yourselves friends of the mammon of unrighteousness; that, when ye fail, they may receive you into everlasting habitations.'

traffic in Shares is the one thing to have to do with in this world.]   There had been a major financial crisis in 1857 but confidence had quickly recovered and by the early 1860s there was a boom in company flotations that was not checked until, in 1866, the failure of the 'cornerstone' of the British financing system, the discount house of Overend, Gurney, precipitated another crisis. The boom was in part due to the establishment of limited liability by a succession of parliamentary Acts in the 1850s and 1860s, in particular the Partnership and the Limited Liability Acts (1855), and the Joint Stock Companies Act (1856): hence it is sometimes referred to as the 'limited liability mania'. As early as 1857 *The Economist* had said that 'one of the certain and foreseen dangers which would attend the introduction of the principle of limited liability, was that persons unconnected with business would be tempted to embark their capital in companies pretending to afford high profits, no trouble, and limited risks' (1065). Meason's *AYR* articles describe many of the aspects of the intense speculation of the early 1860s, in particular the risky and even dishonest way in which the business of some joint-stock banks and general credit companies was conducted.

Have no antecedents, no established character, no cultivation, no ideas, no manners; have Shares.]   These words could be applied to Merdle in *LD*, to Melmotte in Trollope's *The Way We Live Now*, and to a number of Meason's characters. In 1860 *The Economist* remarked that 'As the magnitude of our commerce increases, the difficulty of knowing the exact circumstances of those who carry it on increases also . . . "What can you know about a man who lives in London?" it used to be said. And now for this purpose, as for many others, the whole of England is fast becoming an extended London' (294). Limited liability also meant that

Parliament legally recognized a new form of business association in which the members might not know each other personally, need not necessarily work together, and could not 'be called upon to contribute to the debts and liabilities of the company beyond the nominal amount of shares they have bought and paid up for.' Thus, under the new legislation capital became, as one historian puts it, 'blind' and 'anonymous'. (Feltes, 1974, 359–60)

oscillate on mysterious business between London and Paris]   The London Stock Exchange and the Paris Bourse were the two great European centres of financial speculation (for the Bourse, see p. 83).

never originated anything, never produced anything?]   Many companies were floated simply to provide an opportunity to speculate in their shares: 'A company that is created that the shares may be immediately saleable, and for no other business, is a dangerous company,' *The Economist* declared in 1864. 'It does not begin a regular business because it expects to obtain the ordinary gains of regular business, it does not start because it expects to succeed as a *company*, but because certain projectors hope to puff the shares for a time, and before the crash sneak out and get quit of it. Such companies – and there are certainly some such – are pure engines of unmixed mischief. . . . More companies than usual are started now to entrap the unwary' (350).

Sufficient answer to all]   Matthew 6.34: 'Sufficient unto the day is the evil thereof.'

O mighty Shares! To set those blaring images so high]   MS and proofs read 'flaring images'. They ignite the 'torch for Hymen' that leads Sophronia to the altar. Share mania was frequently characterized as Mammon-worship or worship of graven images or of the Golden Calf.

as under the influence of henbane or opium]   Henbane is a narcotic plant particularly destructive to domestic fowls. There were no controls on the sale of opium until the Pharmacy Act of 1868, though there was a campaign in the 1860s to reduce the use of the drug, and two Bills were submitted to Parliament in 1864. At the time of *OMF*, opium was still an everyday part of the drug trade, and was consumed in a multitude of forms, among them powders, lozenges, children's syrups (like the famous 'Daffy's Elixir'), and, dissolved in alcohol, as laudanum (Berridge and Edwards, 1981, 24, 99).

'Relieve us of our money]   It was commonplace to speak of 'the speculative tendencies of our people' (*The Times*, 1 January 1863, 8). There was a 'general reluctance' in the period 'to keep even small tanks of capital stagnant. Everybody wanted it to circulate and fructify the ground' (Clapham, 1967, 371). The enthusiasm of investors was certainly exploited, but after the failure of Overend, Gurney, *The Times* argued that it was because investors had demanded high rates of return that companies had been forced into reckless practices: 'if the shareholders insisted on the profit they could not escape the peril' (10 May 1866, 8).

only we beseech ye take rank among the powers of the earth]   There are suggestions of biblical phrases : Jonah 1.14: 'Wherefore they cried unto the Lord, and said, We beseech thee, O Lord, we beseech thee'; and Ephesians 6.12: 'For we wrestle ... against principalities, against powers, against the rulers of the darkness of this world, against spiritual wickedness in high places'.

While the Loves and Graces

the Loves and Graces have been preparing this torch for Hymen] Hymen, the Greek and Roman god of marriage, was represented as a young man carrying a torch and veil. The three sister goddesses, the Graces, were regarded as bestowers of grace and charm. Loves are cupids, little gods of love.

Anastatia]   A name popular in Ireland, but not in England. It means 'who shall rise again'.

Sophronia Akershem]   Sophronia means 'of sound mind', and was often used in the instructive dialogues of the eighteenth century. The name Akershem is in the *Book of Memoranda*.

Alfred Lammle]   Lammle is one of the names Dickens listed in his *Book of Memoranda*. Alfred, the name of the great Saxon king, was a popular name. Dickens considered it for Lightwood.

went to school as a junior with Alfred?]   The word 'junior' is public-school usage. Twemlow is being naïve: it is unlikely that either Lammle or Veneering went to public school.

But, two or three weeks ago

received a highly-perfumed cocked-hat and monogram]   A 'cocked hat' was a short note, folded in on itself, resembling the paper hats made by children. Women sent them: in Thackeray's *Yellowplush Papers*, Deuceace receives ' "skoars of rose-coloured *billydoos*, folded up like cockhats, and smellin like barber's shops" ' ('Mr. Deuceace at Paris' 1).

Twemlow ought to know the dear friend Podsnap

executing a statuette of the Colossus at Rhodes.]   The gigantic statue of the god Helios that stood at the entrance of the harbour at Rhodes was one of the seven wonders of the ancient world. It was popularly believed to straddle the harbour mouth.

'My dear Mr. Podsnap, it's very foolish

Hamilton]   An aristocratic Scots name: there is a Duke of Hamilton.

So, it has come to pass

strewing flowers on the rosy hours]   Perhaps a recollection of words from the song 'Away with melancholy' (see notes to 2.6):

> Come on ye rosy hours,
> Gay smiling moments bring
> We'll strew the way with flowers
> And merrily merrily sing fal la.

The 'rosy hours' are 'beguiled' at the Wilfers' wedding anniversary (3.4).

And now Veneering shoots

St James's Church]   St James's, Piccadilly, otherwise known as St James's, Westminster, a large and richly ornamented Wren church. An ornamental arched entrance to the churchyard and a large vestry hall had been added in 1857. It was a favourite church for fashionable weddings.

the Reverend Blank Blank, assisted by the Reverend Dash Dash]   Of a wedding at St James's, G. A. Sala remarked: 'They are all so noble and distinguished, that one clergyman can't perform the ceremony, and extra parsons are provided like extra oil-lamps on a gala night at Cremorne' (*Twice round the Clock* 115).

Sackville Street, Piccadilly]   A street off Piccadilly that was said to be the longest street in London of any consequence without a turning out of it on either side. It was inhabited by a mixture of minor nobility, Members of Parliament, army officers, and medical men. There were solicitors' offices, and a number of tailors' shops.

Stucconia]   There was no suburb of this name, though certain localities were sometimes dismissively referred to as 'cities' or 'suburbs' of 'stucco'; a *HW* writer commented on 'the wild mania for building – the lath-and-plaster, stucco palace, Cockney-Corinthian frenzy' (4.259). Dickens probably intended Tyburnia, a part of Bayswater 'for the most part covered ... with large and costly mansions ... Like its more aristocratic rival *Belgravia*, its name, extent and boundaries are merely conventional, but are very well understood by the residents' (Wheatley and Cunningham 3.419). According to G. A. Sala, Tyburnia was inhabited by 'the nobility of yesterday, your mushroom aristocracy, millionaires, ex-lord mayors, and people of that sort' (*Gaslight and Daylight* 319).

So, Twemlow goes home to Duke Street

a plate of mutton broth with a chop in it]   Hill gives lines from R. H. Barham's *The Ingoldsby Legends* (1840–7):

85

> Is it Paris, or Kitchener, Reader, exhorts
> You, whenever your stomach's at all out of sorts,
> To try, if you find richer viands won't stop in it,
> A basin of good mutton broth with a chop in it.
> ('The Bagman's Dog')

and has galvanic starts all over him.] Luigi Galvani (1737–90) is said to have discovered the theory of animal electricity when he noticed that the leg of a skinned frog convulsed when touched by an electrified instrument. That in modern times life was merely 'galvanic' was one of Carlyle's observations.

Betimes next morning,

knighted in mistake for somebody else by His Majesty King George the Third, who ... was graciously pleased to observe, 'What, what, what? Who, who, who? Why, why, why?'] Fanny Burney recorded the crazy old king's mannerism in her diary: ' "Was there ever," cried he "such stuff as great part of Shakespeare? Only one must not say so? But what think you? – What? – Is there not sad stuff? What? – what?' (19 December 1785).

Bond Street] Then, as now, a fashionable shopping street.

you might scalp her, and peel her, and scrape her ... and yet not penetrate to the genuine article.] 'The genuine article' is a commercial phrase. Dickens's descriptions of the cosmetic preparations of old charmers probably derive from Lady Wishfort in Congreve's *The Way of the World* (1700, 3.1).

'Beyond an impression

he is to sit upon my knee and be seconded at some point ... like a principal at a prize-fight] 'I was picked up, and sat upon my second's knee, who whispered to me, as I spat the blood out of my mouth, "Take it coolly, and make sure when you hit" ' (Marryat, *Jacob Faithful*, 4). With the Heenan–Sayers fight (17 April 1860) prizefighting had recently made an illegal return to England.

But, hark!

looking rather like a spurious Mephistophiles and an unacknowledged member of that gentleman's family.] Mephistopheles is the evil spirit to whom Faust sold his soul. The devil is proverbially a gentleman.

never saw such velvet, say two thousand pounds as she stands, absolute jeweller's window, father must have been a pawnbroker] 'As she stands' is an auctioneer's phrase. Jewellers' windows were often lined with velvet. In *SB* Dickens observed: 'There are some pawnbrokers' shops of a very superior description ... the better sort of pawnbroker calls himself a silversmith, and decorates his shop with handsome trinkets and expensive jewellery' ('The Pawnbroker's Shop').

pokey]   Shabby, dowdy. In Thackeray, *The Newcomes*: 'The ladies were in their pokiest old head-gear and most dingy gowns' (57).

Ceremony performed, register signed

servants with favours]   'Favours' were ribbons, cockades and the like, worn at a wedding as a sign of goodwill. At Queen Victoria's wedding in 1840, 'Every lady exhibited a white favour' (*The Times*, 11 February 1840).

his hair curled, and his gloves buttoned on tight]   White kid gloves were worn at weddings. At David's wedding in *DC*: 'Mr. Dick ... has had his hair curled. Traddles ... and Mr. Dick have a general effect about them of being all gloves' (43).

a widowed female of the Medusa sort, in a stoney cap, glaring petrification]   Medusa was one of the three sisters of Greek mythology called the Gorgons. They had serpentine locks and whoever looked them in the face was instantly turned to stone.

an oilcake-fed style of business-gentleman]   Oilcake, made from compressed seeds, was used as fattening food for sheep or cattle.

Thir-ty Thou-sand Pou-nds!]   The *Book of Memoranda* records the idea of

People (Mem: B^{er}) realizing immense sums of money, imaginatively – speculatively – counting their chickens, before hatched. Inflaming each other's imaginations about great gains of money, and entering into a sort of intangible, impossible, competition as to who is the richer. (24)

In 'A Slight Depreciation of the Currency' (*MP*), Dickens recalled that

It was said by the wise and witty Sidney Smith, that many Englishmen appear to have a remarkable satisfaction in even speaking of large sums of money; and that when men of this stamp say of Mr. So-and-So, 'I am told he is worth TWO HUn-dred THOU-sand POUNDS,' there is a relish in their emphasis, an unctuous appetite and zest in their open-mouthed annunciation, which nothing but the one inspiring theme, Money, develops in them.

The Analytical, in course of time

doing the thing in the way of business]   MS and proof read: 'doing the thing in the way of speculation'.

In which state of affairs

the nuptial journey to the Isle of Wight]   The Isle of Wight was one of the discoveries of high society in the early Victorian period: a guidebook of 1840 described it as 'a place to which Fashion has "set her seal"'; it had, in consequence, become 'the annual resort of thousands'. Shanklin, on the east side of the island, became popular in about 1840; there was an excellent hotel; the railway reached it in 1862; and the esplanade was built about 1865. One of the features of the locality was 'the beautiful bay of Sandown ... with the sea rolling its massy waves over the pebbly beach' (Brettell, 1840, 1, 185).

the outer air teems with brass bands]   According to Mayhew, there were about 250 street bands in London, usually with four or more members (3.163).

the malignant star of the Analytical has pre-ordained]   'O malignant and ill-boding stars!' (*1 Henry VI* 4.5.6)

So, they all go up again

flushed with breakfast, as having taken scarlatina sociably]   Scarlatina is scarlet fever.

the combined unknowns do malignant things]   Altered from 'banded' to 'combined' at proof. 'Combination' was a word associated with trade unions at this time: in *HT* Mrs Sparsit feels that 'the united masters' should not 'allow of any such class-combinations' (2.1).

All is over, that is to say, for the time being

All is over, that is to say]   In his *Book of Memoranda*, Dickens noted:

> A poor <imp> imposter of a man marries a woman for her money; she marries *him* for *his* money; after marriage both find out their mistake, and enter *into* a league and covenant against folks in general.
>
> *Done Lammles* (19)

In Hood's 'Miss Kilmansegg and Her Precious Leg' there are golden dinners like those the Veneerings give and a golden wedding at St James's. The lavish wedding breakfast is followed by a disillusioning honeymoon on which the bride discovers that she has married a cruel and coarse adventurer.

So the happy pair

signed, sealed and delivered]   Originally a legal formula applied to deeds.

Book 1, Chapter 11   Fourth monthly number
                                                    August 1864

PODSNAPPERY.

Mr. Podsnap was well to do

Mr. Podsnap]   Dickens used aspects of his friend the critic and man of letters
John Forster for the character Forster himself called 'the vulgar canting Podsnap'
(Forster 3.344). Even in the early days of the friendship, in the late 1830s and
1840s, Dickens ridiculed the exaggerated and overbearing manner of Forster. By
the 1860s the two men had drifted apart and, though Dickens continued to ask
Forster's advice on important personal and professional matters, the advice was
always rejected. 'Forster became ... the baleful representative of middle-class
values which Dickens did not altogether despise but found impossible to practise'
(Davies, 1974, 151–2). Podsnappery may owe something to James Fitzjames
Stephen, the son of Sir James and brother of Leslie Stephen. Among his many
writings are studies of 'Gentlemen', 'Dignity' and 'National Character'. He
criticized Dickens in a number of articles in the *Saturday Review* and elsewhere:
'There was something inexpressibly repugnant to Fitzjames in the tone adopted
by the school of which he took Dickens and Douglas Jerrold to be representatives'
(Leslie Stephen, 1895, 155). Believing that Dickens's Circumlocution Office
satire in *LD* was aimed at Sir James Stephen and his circle, he had attacked
Dickens in the *Edinburgh Review* under the heading 'The License of Modern
Novelists' (106, 1857). Dickens responded with his 'Curious Misprint in the
Edinburgh Review' (*MP*).

Beginning with a good inheritance, he had married a good inheritance]
Forster had not begun with a good inheritance (his father was a butcher), but at
the age of 44 he had surprised his friends by marrying a wealthy widow and
proceeding to live in ostentatious magnificence (Davies).

in the Marine Insurance way]   Forster's brother, Christopher, was a partner
in Slack & Forster, Ship and Insurance Brokers, 29 Quayside, Newcastle-upon-
Tyne (Davies, 1974). Lloyd's, and marine insurance generally, had lost some of
their former importance since the end of the Napoleonic Wars, but business was
reviving, and a number of new joint-stock marine insurance companies were
formed in the 1860s.

He could never make out why everybody was not quite satisfied]
Dickens noted in his *Book of Memoranda*:

> The man whose vista is always stopped by the image of Himself. Looks down a
> Long walk, and can't see round himself, or over himself, or beyond himself. – Is

89

Take up Wrayburn
                        – and Lightwood?
                                            Yes. And bring out Eugene

Riderhood? Yes.
Podsnappery? Yes

Mem: The N? < overwritten and > overwritten
        and chapter divided into two, and
        carried on into N? V

Chapter XI

Podsnappery.

The whole Institution of Podsnappery, as embodied in its representation

man

    Not English

        all disagreeables put behind him.

           The blush on the cheek of the young person | Miss Podsnap |

               Podsnap plate

A set of quadrilles

    Mr and Mrs Lammle. Lay the ground.

Chapter XII

The sweat of an honest man's brow.

Cold spring evening – Wrayburn and Lightwood. Twilight

To them, Mr. Riderhood. To earn the reward 'by the sweat

    of his brow.'

    Mr Riderhood's testimony and its <u>corroborative Proofs</u>

                    all on alfred David

Chapter XIII

Tracking the Bird of Prey < brought down >

Watching all night.

    On the river in the early morning

        Kill Gaffer retributively. 'Many a slip' for

        Mr Riderhood.

<u>Bring on Eugene.</u> <u>Imply</u> some change between him and

    Lizzie Hexam. <u>Don't shew them together.</u>

always blocking up his own way. – Would be such a good thing for him, if he could knock himself down.

– And by denying a thing, supposes that he altogether puts it out of existence. (*Done in Podsnap*) (4)

Mr. Podsnap's world was not a very large world

Mr. Podsnap's world was not a very large world, morally; no, nor even geographically]　　The word 'world' was used to mean high, or fashionable, society:

> The great world – which, being interpreted,
> Meaneth the West or worst end of a city,
> And about twice two thousand people bred
> By no means to be very wise or witty.
>
> > (Byron, *Don Juan*, 11.45)

The limits of 'the world' are defined in *BR*: 'It was high noon in those quarters of the town in which "the world" condescended to dwell – the world being then, as now, of very limited dimensions and easily lodged' (23). In *BH* Lady Dedlock's 'fashionable world' is said to be 'not a large world' (2). In his attitude to other countries, Podsnap is like Mr Dombey, who believes that 'the earth was made for Dombey and Son to trade in' (*DS* 1), and Sapsea, in *MED*, who says: ' "If I have not gone to foreign countries, young man, foreign countries have come to me. They have come to me in the way of business" ' (4).

'Not English!']　　The Ancient Gentleman in Dickens's 'Threatening Letter to Thomas Hood' (*MP*) regards 'Science, Literature, Art' as 'quite un-English'; in *MED* 'when Mr. Sapsea has once declared anything to be Un-English, he considers that thing everlastingly sunk in the bottomless pit' (14). In 'The License of Modern Novelists', Fitzjames Stephen had declared that 'boundless luxury and insatiable thirst for amusement . . . have raised a class of writers who show strong sympathies for all that is most opposite to the very foundations of English life' (152). The *Spectator* believed that because Dickens's 'picture of domestic affections' was 'defective in simplicity and reserve' it was 'not really English' and tended 'to modify English family feeling in the direction of theatric tenderness' (1869, quoted in *Speeches* 393).

when, PRESTO! with a flourish of the arm]　　The conjuror's formula 'Hey presto, pass!' ('presto' meaning quickly). Dickens was a skilled amateur conjuror.

Literature; large print, respectfully descriptive of getting up at eight]　　The words 'large print' are added above the line in the MS. An *AYR* article made fun of 'The Legitimate Novel, in three fat octavos, with three hundred and twenty pages in each of the two first volumes, and three hundred and fifty at least in the last, and not many lines in any of the pages, and not many pages in any of the chapters!' (9.309–10). Another *AYR* article defended the use of dramatic events in fiction, against the 'loud cry of "Sensational!"', by reference to the example of Shakespeare. (For the contemporary debate about the 'Sensation Novel', see Stang, 1959, 153–8.) The writer argued that

> life has its tremendous passes of anguish and crime, as well as its little joys and little sorrows – its strange adventures and vicissitudes, as well as its daily progresses from Brixton to the Bank, and from the Bank back again to Brixton.

He asked:

> Why is it necessarily immoral to shadow forth the awful visitations of wrath and evil and punishment, or to depict those wonderful and unwonted accidents of fortune which are just as real as anything that happens between Brixton and the Bank, only of less frequent occurrence? ('The Sensational Williams', *AYR*, 13 February 1864, 11.14)

Fitzjames Stephen considered that 'One of the most obvious causes which makes novels unlike real life is the necessity under which they lie of being interesting', remarking sarcastically that 'A list of the killed, wounded and missing amongst Mr. Dickens's novels would read like an *Extraordinary Gazette*. An interesting child runs as much risk there as any of the troops who stormed the Redan' ('The Relation of Novels to Life', 1855, 174). An 1857 *HW* article, 'Something that Shakespeare Lost', consists of mock reviews of *Hamlet*, one of which dismisses the play as ' "a melodrama of the worst school" ' because of the number of deaths in the last act (15.49–52).

Painting and Sculpture; models and portraits representing Professors of getting up at eight]   Miss La Creevey in *NN* says there are 'smirking' and 'serious' portraits: 'Look at the Royal Academy. All those beautiful shiny portraits of gentlemen in black velvet waistcoats, with their fists doubled up on round tables or marble slabs, are serious, you know' (10). Dickens had many artist friends, but by the mid-1850s he had become disillusioned with the 'general absence of ideas' in English painting. Of the English exhibits at the Art Exposition in Paris in 1855 he remarked: 'There is a horrid respectability about most of the best of them – a little, finite, systematic routine in them, strangely expressive to me of the state of England itself' (October 1855, Forster 3.123).

Music; a respectable performance (without variations) on stringed and wind instruments]   The wordplay of '(without variations)' is not in the MS. The mid-nineteenth century is the least distinguished period in English musical history.

to those same vagrants the Arts]   The interlineation of 'same' in the MS creates the suggestion of an official proclamation. By a statute of 1572 wandering troupes of actors had been designated as 'rogues and vagabonds'; Dickens's allusion is to the state of the arts in Shakespeare's time. His own amateur company called themselves the Splendid Strollers.

These may be said to have been

the articles of faith]   Like the Thirty-Nine Articles of the Church of England.

its representative man]   The phrase 'representative man' had great potential for irony: it could mean the merely average man (or his parliamentary representative: see 2.3) or the types of great men Emerson had described in his *Representative Men* (1850). Dickens indicates the representative significance of a number of his characters in *OMF*.

There was a Miss Podsnap.

crushed by the mere dead-weight of Podsnappery.]   Dickens may have had Forster's wife in mind. Clarkson Stanfield described her after her marriage: 'the depreciation that has taken place in that woman is fearful! She has no blood Sir in her body – no color – no voice – is all scrunched and squeezed together – and seems to me in deep affliction' (quoted in Davies, 1974, 155).

A certain institution in Mr. Podsnap's mind

a blush into the cheek of the young person?]   Forster's first review, of the 1828 editions of *The Keepsake* and *The Anniversary*, complained that some passages 'would be apt to raise a blush on the cheek of a young English female becoming the pride of her purity' (Davies, 1974, 156); the 1837 Preface to *PP* promised that it contained nothing 'which would call a blush into the most delicate cheek'. There was always some concern for the young person's cheek in the early and middle Victorian period, but in the 1860s it was on the increase, partly because the rise of the shilling magazines extended the family reading of fiction. In an open letter of 1 November 1859 advertising the *Cornhill Magazine*, which was to publish the work of many important novelists, Thackeray announced that 'At our social table we shall suppose the ladies and children always present' (Tillotson, 1954, 57–73), Gill, 1971, 900). The phrase ' "young person" ' was respectable, but slighting: Mrs Podsnap referred to Bella as a ' "young person" ' in book 1, chapter 2, though Mortimer had called her ' "a young woman" '; Mrs Wilfer insists that her potential pupils are ' "not young persons. Two young ladies of the highest respectability" ' (1.4).

The Podsnaps lived in a shady angle

a shady angle adjoining Portman Square]   Immediately after his marriage Forster lived at 46 Montagu Square, which is just north of Portman Square (Davies, 1974). Portman Square is one of the largest and handsomest squares in London, though the houses lack architectural character.

walnut and rosewood tables . . . swarthy giants of looking-glasses]   The furniture of the time was usually made of dark wood: dark mahogany, with a reddish tinge (imparted by the use of brickdust), rosewood, black walnut and bog oak were used.

solemnly tooled through the Park ... in a great tall custard-coloured phaeton]   A phaeton was a four-wheeled open carriage, usually of light construction, drawn by a pair of horses, and generally with two seats facing forwards. It was fashionable to drive and ride in Hyde Park.

Said Mr. Podsnap to Mrs. Podsnap

Said Mr. Podsnap to Mrs. Podsnap]   This is a formula used in riddles.

So it came to pass

friends of their souls]   Thomas Moore begins an 'Anacreontique' with the lines 'Friend of my soul! this goblet sip,/'Twill chase away that pensive tear'.

her list]   Every hostess had her 'guest list' of people she considered worthy of acquaintance; here as well she kept a record of those to whom she 'owed' entertainment.

There were still other friends

invited to come and take a haunch of mutton vapour-bath]   It was the practice for a certain number of guests to be invited to dine, others to arrive after dinner. A vapour-bath was a steam-bath. The late arrivals at the Podsnaps' are like the guests in *DS* 'whose portion of the feast was limited to the smell thereof' (36), or like David Copperfield when he 'plunged into a vapour-bath of haunch of mutton' and 'divined' he was 'not the only guest' (25). The vapour-bath later receives a 'gamey infusion, and a few last touches of sweet and coffee': game was usually served in the third course, sweets and coffee followed.

Mr. and Mrs. Veneering, and Mr. and Mrs. Veneering's

a mushroom man]   The traditional phrase for a *parvenu*: 'these mushrompe gentlemen,/That shoot up in a night to place, and worship' (Jonson, *Every Man out of His Humour*, 1599, 1.2.162–3). In the relations between the Podsnaps' and the Veneerings' social worlds, Dickens reflects the developing distinction between 'respectable' and 'fashionable' society.

A corpulent straddling epergne]   The centre of the table was always decorated with an epergne or centrepiece, often ornamented with classical or allegorical figures bearing dishes of fruit and bonbons, or little cups and vases filled with ferns and flowers.

The majority of the guests

believing the whole European continent to be in mortal alliance against the young person] English mistrust of Continental morality was strengthened by a dislike of immoral French literature. *Punch* offered a 'Prospectus of a New Journal The Sensation Times' including 'A Sensation Novel itself, in which atrocities hitherto undreamed of, even by the most fashionable fictionists of Paris, will form a feature' (44, 1863, 193). Comparing the work of Dickens and Charles Reade to the French ' "literature of desperation" ', Fitzjames Stephen claimed that 'English life is too active, English spheres of action too wide, English freedom too deeply rooted to be endangered by a set of bacchanals, drunk with green tea, and not protected by petticoats' ('The License of Modern Novelists', 152).

As a delicate concession

then subsided into English.] Dickens made fun of Forster's French in a letter to Thomas Beard:

> you will be waylaid by three implacable Gauls who will lay hold of your great coat, and ask 'Est-ce que Monsieur ait quelque chose à declarer?' Hereupon you will blandly smile, and reply 'Rien' (therein not imitating Forster, who, the other day, not at all understanding the enquiry, said after a moment's reflection with the sweetness of some choice wind instrument 'Bon Jour!' and was immediately seized). (*Nonesuch* 2.488)

Forster's chauvinism is evident in his writings (see Davies, 1974).

'And Do You Find, Sir,' pursued Mr. Podsnap

The World's Metropolis] The phrase was often used of London. In a letter to Wilkie Collins, Dickens called London 'the Metropolis of the world, the Emporium of commerce, and free home of the Slave' (17 July 1859, *Nonesuch* 3.112); it is 'the capital of Europe' in *MHC*.

But the gentleman with the lumpy forehead

delivered himself of all that he found behind his lumps] An allusion to phrenology, the method of reading character from the contours of the skull, developed from Lavater by Franz Joseph Gall (1758–1828) and Johann Kaspar Spurzheim (1776–1832), and popularized in England by the brothers George and Andrew Combe. Different propensities, such as Veneration, Benevolence and Combativeness, were supposed to be located in different 'organs' or regions of the brain. Though Dickens frequently makes humorous play with phrenology, in a letter to Charles Lever he claimed to 'believe in it, in the main and broadly, as an essential part of the truth of physiognomy' (21 February 1860, *Nonesuch* 3.152).

'It merely referred,' Mr. Podsnap explained

We Englishmen are Very Proud of Our Constitution, Sir.] The national conceit confirmed itself by a sense of the superiority of the unwritten British constitution, embodied in the parliamentary system, over Continental systems of government. Dickens saw the adverse effect of this repeated invocation of 'that sensitive Constitution, the property of us Britons, the odd fortune of which sacred institution it is to be in exactly equal degrees croaked about, trembled for, and boasted of, whatever happens to anything, anywhere in the world' (*MED* 11). In his attack on Dickens's Circumlocution Office satire in *LD*, Fitzjames Stephen asserted that a belief in the British constitution was 'part of the training of a gentleman' (124). Dickens's satire meant, if it meant anything, 'that the result of the British constitution, of our boasted freedom of parliamentary representation, and of all we possess, is to give us the worst government on the face of the earth' (128). Dickens had a different perspective: in *BH* he had wondered about Jo's idea of 'that inestimable jewel to him (if he only knew it) the Constitution' (16).

Forster's historical writings lay great emphasis on the 'Constitution' and the 'Charter of the Land'. The introductory essay to his *The Debates on the Grand Remonstrance* (1860) celebrates Magna Carta as the link between the (mythical) 'Saxon Constitution' and the parliamentary struggle of the seventeenth century: 'There is not an English freeman living in the nineteenth century who does not owe his freedom to the "Great Charter" '(15). Forster's other major historical works, *The Arrest of the Five Members by Charles I* (1860) and *Sir John Eliot* (1864), are similarly concerned to vindicate the character and motives of the seventeenth-century Parliamentarians: in his view, they are the forefathers of the nineteenth-century middle-class liberals (see Davies, 1974, 154).

'Undoubtedly,' assented Mr. Podsnap; 'But So it is.

It was the Charter of the Land.] With great originality Podsnap quotes from the first stanza of 'Rule, Britannia!':

> When Britain first, at Heaven's command
>   Arose from out the azure main,
> This was the charter of the land,
>   And guardian angels sung this strain —
>   'Rule, Britannia, rule the waves;
> Britons never will be slaves.'

of such Other Countries as — as there may happen to be.] Podsnap means France, at this time under the rule of the Emperor Napoleon III.

there is in the Englishman a combination of qualities] Forster had written, in his well-known essay on Defoe, of the 'inflexible constancy, sturdy dogged resolution, unwearied perseverance, and obstinate contempt of danger and of tyranny [of] the great Middle-class English character' (Davies, 1974, 154). Fitzjames Stephen felt Dickens had not fairly represented 'those manly, disinterested, and energetic qualities which make up the character of an English gentleman' ('The License of Modern Novelists', 126).

And now the haunch of mutton vapour-bath

like partners at cards who played a game against All England.] The All-England XI was a cricket team, established as a business venture by William Clarke in 1846. They played a long programme of matches all over the country each summer.

'No, I'm sure you won't

a chimney-sweep on May-day.'] It was the tradition for sweeps to dance in the streets on 1 May, wearing colourful and fantastic costumes representing traditional characters like the 'green', 'my lady' and 'my lord'. In *SB* Dickens described a shabby attempt at the event by dustmen in Maiden Lane (dustmen often doubled as sweeps) ('The First of May').

'Upon my word, my love,' said Mrs. Lammle

I am dressed as a bride now, you see.] It was the practice for a bride to wear her wedding dress, though without the veil, to balls and dinners for a time after her marriage.

This was such an entirely new view

the Terpsichorean art] Terpsichore was the Muse who presided over dancing.

(in short sleeves)] The evening dresses of the period were low-cut to reveal the wearer's neck, shoulders and arms.

'But it is, and it always has been

Madame Sauteuse's, where I learnt to dance] The English have traditionally learnt dancing from French and Italian instructors. *Sauter* is French for 'to jump'; *sauteuse* was the popular word for a flea.

But the Ogre advanced under the pilotage

a blossomless tuneless 'set,' and sixteen disciples of Podsnappery went through the figures] The French quadrille was for two, four or any number of couples. Each pair of dancers remained *vis-à-vis* and danced only with each other, except for a variation in the fifth figure which involved a continuous change of partners. Dickens plays on the word 'set' as meaning the figures making up a quadrille and a slip or shoot for planting.

And now, the grand chain riveted

an archery meeting] Many young ladies became enthusiastic members of toxophilic societies in the 1860s; as *Punch* cartoons attest, open-air meetings and tournaments became fashionable events. The sport was thought to show off the female figure well.

At length the procession was dissolved

the violent arrival of a nutmeg] The aromatic nutmeg was an ingredient in punches and cups. They were served in large hemispherical bowls, sometimes with a similar-shaped lid. There is little but nutmeg in the Podsnaps' punch.

In the mean time

some half-dozen people had lately died in the streets, of starvation] Deaths in the streets from starvation were much in the news at the time. In London people were dying at a (reported) rate of about two a week: 'Scarce a day passes without there appearing in the papers, like a spot in the sun or a mote in the eye, a dismal little paragraph, headed "Death from Starvation" ' (*The Times*, 12 March 1864, 11). The cases were reported under headings like 'Apparently Dead in the Streets' (25 December 1863, 5). The reports make dismal reading: 'A shoe-maker, aged 60 years, died in a cab on the 6th of January from exhaustion from exposure to cold' (20 January 1864, 6); 'The son of a school-master, aged 12 years, died at De-Beauvoir-Square, West Hackney, from effusion to the chest from want of proper food' (25 February 1864, 12); 'A man, unknown, aged 55 years, was found dead on a dunghill in Shadwell, from "exposure and destitution" (Inquest)' (30 November 1864, 11). Dickens has the meek man raise the matter in the context of Podsnap's boasts about the wealth of the metropolis. Readers of *The Times* often made the same kind of ironic point: 'There is London, still,' wrote a correspondent in 1863, 'the "glory, jest and riddle of the world," ' – the grand central depôt of terrestrial wealth, and the head-quarters of chronic starvation' (1 December, 7). *The Times* itself thought it 'a sort of personal and social reproach that human beings should be starving and shivering into death within the boundaries of a rich metropolis' (11 May 1864, 9).

Podsnap is alluding to proposed amendments to the organization of facilities and the division of costs provided under the Poor Law Amendment Act of 1834 (a running title in CD reads: 'MR. PODSNAP ON THE POOR LAWS'). Under the 1834 Act the parish from which a pauper derived was responsible for his or her maintenance (though after 1846 a parish was responsible for a pauper who had resided there for five years, and after 1863 for one who had resided there for three years). This had two adverse effects on the paupers: on becoming destitute they were removed to the parish from which they derived, far from friends and from the prospect of renewed employment; and those who were called the 'casual poor', applicants for relief from a parish from which they did not derive, were actively discouraged by workhouse officials anxious to save the local ratepayers' money.

In respect of the Poor Laws, the cry of 'Centralization' was an attempt to obscure a system of financing which was grossly inequitable. With the growth of the industrial and commercial centres real massive centralization had taken place. Under the Act, country parishes, already depopulated, were responsible for men and women who worked in the cities, and who had helped, when employed, to provide the wealth of the city. There was the same inequity within the city itself. Men and women who worked in a wealthy city parish lived in a poorer one and it was the poorer one which had to rate its inhabitants for their maintenance when hardship reduced them to applying for relief. Naturally this had its effect on the hard-pressed officials of the poorer parishes, as an East End clergyman writing to *The Times* pointed out:

> I do not wish for a moment to palliate inhumanity in a Poor Law official, or in any other man, yet I cannot but admit that the officials . . . are very likely to be as careful of the ratepayers' money as possible, and that they sometimes – I do not say intentionally – refuse help when it ought not to be refused. When a man has to pay 4s. 2½d. poor-rate on every pound of rated value, it is highly probable that his liberality to the poor will not be very great. What many persons desire to see is an equalized rate over the whole of London. (17 March 1864, 7)

HW and *AYR* had taken up the subject in the late 1850s. An 1858 article, 'Parish Poor in London', complained that the ratepayers of a parish like St George's, Hanover Square (which paid seven pence in the pound poor rate, compared to the ten shillings in the pound paid by the East End parish of St Nicholas, Deptford), had 'thrown their burden, so to speak, over the parish wall' (*HW* 17.577). In 1859 'A Sum in Fair Division' called for 'the more even distribution of the poor-rate and the consequent suppression of the cruelties arising from the law of Settlement and Poor Removal' (*AYR* 1.44). In 1861 'A New Chamber of Horrors' detailed 'the deaths from "privation," "deaths from want of breast-milk," "deaths from neglect," "deaths from cold" – or, in plain unsavoury words, from utter starvation' (*AYR* 4.500). One of the chapters of *UT* published in *AYR* in 1860 made the same case, again singling out St George's, Hanover Square, as an example.

The newspaper debate about centralization continued throughout the early 1860s. Then, in February 1864, a Private Member's Bill was introduced in the House of Commons, ' "providing for a more equitable distribution of the charge on landed property for the relief of the sick and destitute" ' (*The Times*, 18 February, 6). It was withdrawn on the understanding that the government would take up the matter. The government brought the Poor Relief (Metropolis) Bill before the House in July: it was ' "proposed to lay on the property of the whole Metropolis the relief of these unhappy derelicts, who evidently belong to no one Union more than another" ' (*The Times*, 26 July, 9). The Bill was carried through Committee but was subject to two amendments, the first of which ensured that its operation was to continue only until March 1865. This amendment rendered the Act ineffective. The workhouses refused to build the wards required of them because the measure was temporary: 'This Act, though very well meant,' *The Times* concluded, 'has proved a signal failure.' A powerful leading article called for a full-scale inquiry like that of 1834 (24 December 1864, 7).

As reports of death by starvation continued through the winter of 1864–5, the matter was once again raised in the House of Commons. In February the government introduced the Union Chargeability Bill ' "to provide for the better distribution of the charge for the relief of the poor in Unions" '. It was proposed to charge the whole cost of relief on a common fund of the Union. Removals would be made from Union to Union not from parish to parish. As a result, there would be fewer removals; costs would be more equally distributed; and financial responsibility would rest more with the Guardians, who would be less likely to skimp on expenses than workhouse overseers. In addition, the proposed amendments ' "would destroy the temptation which now exists to drive the poor out of one parish into another by destroying their cottage accommodation, or by declining to build what is necessary for them" ' (*The Times*, 21 February 1865, 9). The Union Chargeability Act became law on 20 June 1865.

He was not aware (the meek man submitted

he certainly was more staggered by these terrible occurrences than he was by names, of howsoever so many syllables.]   In a speech to the Metropolitan Sanitary Association, Dickens suggested that the opposition to the Board of Health amounted to no more than 'a long word which I seem to have heard pronounced with a sort of violent relish on two or three previous occasions – *Centralization*' (10 May 1851, *Speeches* 130).

'You know what the population of London is

'You know what the population of London is]   'Twice or three times have we heard the lamentations and prophecies of a humane Jeremiah, mourner for the poor, cut short by a statistic fact,' wrote Carlyle in *Chartism* ('Statistics').

'And you know; at least I hope you know

Providence has declared that you shall have the poor always with you.]   As in Matthew 26.11: 'For ye have the poor always with you; but me ye have not always'; and in Deuteronomy 15.11: 'For the poor shall never cease out of the land; therefore I command thee, saying, Thou shalt open thine hand wide unto thy brother, to thy poor, and to thy needy, in thy land'.

'I must decline to pursue

I remove it from the face of the earth.]   In imitation of Providence: 'And the Lord said, I will destroy man whom I have created from the face of the earth . . .

every living substance that I have made will I destroy from off the face of the earth' (Genesis 6.7, 7.4).

Certain big, heavy vehicles

the Podsnap plate was put to bed.]   The butler's task: 'At bedtime he appears with candles; he locks up the plate, secures doors and windows, and sees that all the fires are safe' (Mrs Beeton).

Book 1, Chapter 12

THE SWEAT OF AN HONEST MAN'S BROW.

Mr. Mortimer Lightwood and Mr. Eugene Wrayburn

a bachelor cottage near Hampton]   Hampton, thirteen miles west of central London, was a favourite place for pleasure parties on the water and for anglers; it was the headquarters of the 'disciples of Izaak Walton', the Thames Angling Preservation Society.

float with the stream through the summer and the Long Vacation.] Summer vacation at the law courts was called the Long Vacation. In Thackeray's *Pendennis* those 'who represented the idle part of the little community' at the Temple were 'ferocious dandies, in rowing shirts' (29).

It was not summer yet

not gentle spring ethereally mild, as in Thomson's Seasons]   *The Seasons* (1726–30), the popular poem in four books by James Thomson. Dickens refers to the opening line of 'Spring' (1728): 'Come, gentle Spring, ethereal Mildness, come.'

nipping spring]   'It is a nipping and an eager air' (*Hamlet* 1.4.2).

there were no top-sawyers; every passenger was an under-sawyer] Hand-sawn timber was cut by being stood in or lain across a pit; the saw was operated by two men, the under-sawyer standing in the pit. 'Top-sawyer' was colloquial for top man.

That mysterious paper currency

electric wires]   The 'electric wires' are for the electric telegraph referred to in book 4, 'The Last'.

In Paris, where nothing is wasted . . . wonderful human ants creep out of holes and pick up every scrap]   A reference to the *chiffoniers* described in *PI*:

'there were, outside the Post-office Yard in Paris, before daybreak, extraordinary adventurers in heaps of rags, groping in the snowy streets with little rakes, in search of odds and ends' ('By Verona . . .'). See Marcus Stone's illustration to *PI*, 'The Chiffonier'.

sharp eyes and sharp stomachs reap even the west wind]   Hosea 8.7: 'For they have sown the wind, and they shall reap the whirlwind.'

The wind sawed, and the sawdust whirled.

repented of their early marriages, like men and women]   Dickens, of course, had himself repented of his marriage (made at the age of 24).

the colours of the rainbow were discernible, not in floral spring] Thomson's well-known description of a rainbow in 'Spring':

> the grand ethereal Bow
> Shoots up immense; and every Hue unfolds,
> In fair Proportion, running from the Red
> To where the Violet fades into the Sky. (204–7)

When the spring evenings are too long

a black shrill city, combining the qualities of a smoky house and a scolding wife]   As in Hotspur's comment on Glendower in *1 Henry IV*:

> O, he is as tedious
> As a tired horse, a railing wife;
> Worse than a smoky house. (3.1.159–61)

Observations of this kind derive from Proverbs 27.15: 'A continual dropping in a very rainy day and a contentious woman are alike.'

a beleaguered city, invested by the great Marsh Forces of Essex and Kent.]   The marshes on each side of the Thames between London and the sea. There is a suggestion of the Peasants' Revolt of 1381, when the men of Kent and Essex besieged the city.

'Not more than any other place

no Circuit to go.]   The district or division of the country through which judges, barristers and other functionaries travelled for the purpose of holding courts at various places. There were eight circuits in England and Wales.

'Yes, regarding my respected father

a glow of Wallsend.']   Coal of a certain quality and size, the name originating from the seam at the town of Wallsend, situated at the end of the Roman Wall in Northumberland.

'With some money, of course

M.R.F., which sounds military, and rather like the Duke of Wellington.'] Like C-in-C (Commander-in-Chief). Wellington, who died in 1852, led the British forces against Napoleon and subsequently became prime minister. MRF also sounds like MFH (Master of Fox Hounds), a highly respected position in county society.

Mortimer lighted the candles.

an old sodden fur cap] Fur caps, made from cat fur, and known as 'Bendigos', were worn in the East End into the 1880s. In *BH* Jo has a 'bit of a fur cap . . . which he picks as if it were some mangy bird he had caught' (25).

'Lawyer Lightwood,' ducking at him

by the sweat of my brow.] The popular adaptation of Genesis 3.19: 'In the sweat of thy face shalt thou eat bread, till thou return unto the ground; for out of it wast thou taken; for dust thou art, and unto dust shalt thou return.'

'I am not a swearer in of people

a swearer in of people] A notary public, a person authorized to draw up or attest contracts or similar documents.

The visitor, clearly anything but reliant

'Alfred David.'] An affidavit is a statement made in writing, confirmed by the maker's oath, and intended to be used as judicial proof.

'Lime 'us Hole.'

'Lime 'us Hole.'] On a map of 1792–9, Limehouse Hole appears as the name of both a long street running parallel to the river from Limehouse Dock to the Isle of Dogs and a short street running down to the riverside at what was subsequently the site of Limehouse Hole Pier.

'Haven't I said – I appeal

this here world-without-end-everlasting chair] A conflation of phrases from the Book of Common Prayer.

'He doesn't,' said Eugene. 'But neither

The firm are cut-throat Shepherds both] From cockney rhyming slang: shepherd's pie/spy. The spy Barsad in *TTC* is called a 'shepherd'.

The waterside character pulled his drowned cap

round by the Temple Church, across the Temple into Whitefriars]
They pass out of the Temple by the gate at the King's Bench Walk. Whitefriars
was a precinct, or liberty, bounded by the Temple walls, Fleet Street, Water Lane
and the river.

They said little else as they followed

an ugly Fate] He is called below an 'advancing Destiny': in Greek and Roman
mythology the Fates or Destinies were three goddesses.

The blast went by

**as if the streets were absorbed by the sky, and the night were all in the
air.]** A recollection of *Julius Caesar*, Act 1, scene 3: 'But never till to-night,
never till now,/Did I go through a tempest dropping fire' and 'this disturbed sky/
Is not to walk in' (9–10, 38–9).

Also, within doors, Mr. Inspector

his stock] The stiff, close-fitting neck-cloth, worn with the high-collared
coat of the police uniform.

'Very good,' said he, taking his hat

**taking his hat from its peg, and putting a pair of handcuffs in his pocket as
if they were his gloves.]** The comparison depends on the fact that a tall black
hat, like that worn by the gentlemen of the day, was part of a policeman's uniform.

Mr. Inspector replied, with due generality

very shy characters] 'Shy' here means 'shady', 'disreputable'.

'And I think,' added Mr. Inspector

some lime works anywhere down about Northfleet] Northfleet is on the
Thames estuary. Chalk was quarried, and there were large lime, whiting and
Portland cement factories, sand and ballast yards, and brickworks. Limehouse
itself had long been associated with limeworks: Pepys mentioned the limehouse
'which gives the name to the place'.

Book 1, Chapter 13

TRACKING THE BIRD OF PREY.

As the note in the work-plan indicates, Dickens overwrote the number and was forced to divide this chapter. The chapter title is changed in the MS from 'The Bird of Prey Brought Down'.

The two lime merchants

'a mouthful of fire']   A small amount: in *BL* Mr Snitchey asks for 'a mouthful of ink' (1).

'They burn sherry very well

a piece of local intelligence.]   The change from the MS reading 'a piece of local news' introduces a play on newspaper headings like 'City Intelligence', 'Foreign Intelligence', etc.

'I am not at all obliged to it

Guy Fawkes in the vault and a Sneak in the area]   Great and petty underground crime: Guy Fawkes (1570–1605) was the leader of a group who attempted to blow up the Houses of Parliament by amassing explosives in the vault; area sneaks 'go down into the areas, and open the safes where provisions are kept . . . and carry off the spoil . . . another class . . . try to make their way to the butler's pantry . . . and carry off the basket of plate' (Mayhew 4.291).

'Invisible insects of diabolical activity

the myrmidons of justice]   In Homer, the Myrmidons are the warlike race of men Achilles leads to the siege of Troy.

'I am quite as bad,' said Lightwood

going through some wonderful evolutions, in which his head had been the lowest part of him.]   'Evolutions' in the sense of movements in gymnastics, dance, etc., and possibly in relation to biological theories of evolution.

I felt like Gulliver with the Lilliputians firing upon him.']   In the first chapter of Swift's *Gulliver's Travels* (1726) the sleeping Gulliver is tied down and then fired upon by the tiny Lilliputians: 'an hundred Arrows . . . pricked me like so many Needles'.

'This is my partner,' said Eugene

A fair day's wages for a fair day's work]   A slogan of the Chartists, the working men's movement of the 1840s: in *Past and Present* Carlyle called the slogan 'as just a demand as Governed men ever made of Governing' (1.3).

As the time so passed, this slinking business

him invested with the dignity of Labour!]   A conventional phrase which is a favourite of the pompous Sir Joseph Bowley in *C*: ' "Now, the design of your creation is; not that you should swill, and guzzle . . . but that you should feel the Dignity of Labor" ' (2).

'If I might so far presume

my honourable and gallant friend]   Mock-parliamentary.

Book 1, Chapter 14   Fifth monthly number
                                                    September 1864

THE BIRD OF PREY BROUGHT DOWN.

As the work plan indicates, Dickens brought forward to this number six pages of what was originally chapter 13.

Cold on the shore, in the raw cold

Cold on the shore]   The passage from the opening of the chapter to Eugene's words 'Hold your tongue, you water-rat!' is not in the MS. Dickens made two long additions, and some small changes, as a result of breaking the chapter. This opening recalls his account of a journey with the river police in 'Down With the Tide' (*RP*): 'A very dark night it was, and bitter cold; the east wind blowing bleak, and bringing with it stinging particles from marsh, and moor, and fen . . . O! It was very very dark upon the Thames, and it was bitter bitter cold.'

the vital force]   According to Robert Chambers, the idea of 'a mystic something', a vital force or principle independent of matter which marked the

Settle Bella with the Boffins. Her father? <u>Yes</u>
   also Rokesmith   <u>Yes</u>
   and establish Wegg at the Bower.
                    on a false scent.   <u>Yes</u>
                      The orphan? <u>Yes</u>

The Hexams. <Jennie> Lizzie? <u>No</u> | Hold over for
                and the boy? <u>No</u> | the new 'book'

Wind up the book I as <u>skilfully and completely</u> as I can.

   Mem: for the N^{o}.
   6 pages of the N^{o}. brought forward. 20 to write

Chapter XIV.

The Bird of Prey Brought Down

River description (touched for the new purpose) from overwritten last N.º

Death of Gaffer

> 'Father, was that you calling me?'

Indication of what has become of Eugene

Chapter XV <I>.

Two New Servants

Mr and Mrs Boffin

To them Rokesmith. Engaged.

Over the house, all.

Mrs Boffin and the faces. – Her memory awakened without her knowing how. – By Rokesmith's face

Chapter XVI <I>

Minders and Reminders

Work on

Detach the Secretary from Lightwood

To Brentford. Mrs Betty Higden.

End with Bella. Sloppy.

Chapter XVII <I>

A Dismal Swamp.

all that besets the fortunate man

Charities

Begging letters

Projectors   Indicate Wegg, poking about

The End of the First Book.

border between animate and inanimate, was 'on the decline' (*Vestiges of the Natural History of Creation*, 1844, 113). An *AYR* article agreed: 'Are the forces of organic matter, then, different in kind from those of inorganic? All the philosophy of the present day tends to negative the question' ('Heat and Work', 14.33).

As if with one accord, they all turned

Perhaps fire, like the higher animal and vegetable life it helps to sustain] Fire was anciently believed, by Heraclitus and others, to be 'the seed of the generation of all things, or that from which all things draw their original' (Berkeley, *Siris*, 1733). There are *AYR* articles on the four elements: 'Fire' in 1862; 'Water', 'Air' (two articles) and 'Earth' (two articles) in 1864; and 'Is Heat Motion?' and 'Heat and Work' in 1865. The articles provide accounts of the outmoded theories of the elements and replace them by the findings of modern science. Thus 'Fire is no longer a thing . . . The physical forces now acknowledged are Heat, Light, Electricity, Magnetism, Chemical Affinity, and Motion. Consequently, Fire is only an energetic manifestation of one of these forces' (6.395–6). The author of the article on 'Heat and Work', a report on lectures by Professor Tyndall, was led to ask the questions: 'Has not the human will, power to create strength, energy, and endurance? . . . has not volition . . . a creative power, a faculty of calling up a force out of nothing – that is, out of no material source?' The answer is 'no': 'The strong will . . . can *create* nothing!' (14.32).

'All right. Give way!'

Give way!'] The order to a boat's crew to begin rowing.

They were all shivering

wharves and warehouses . . . like inscriptions over the graves of dead businesses.'] Challenged by the railways, the fortunes of the docks and the Pool were beginning to flag. In *Our Old Home* (1856) Hawthorne saw signs of decrepitude:

> the shore is lined with the shabbiest, blackest, and ugliest buildings that can be imagined, decayed warehouses, with blind windows, and wharves that look ruinous; insomuch that, had I known nothing more of the world's metropolis, I might have fancied that it had already experienced the downfall which I have heard commercial and financial prophets predict for it, within the century. ('Up the Thames')

As they glided slowly on, keeping

as to threaten to crush it.] Compare 'Down With the Tide': 'Uncomfortable rushes of water suggestive of gurgling and drowning, ghostly rattlings of iron chains, dismal clankings of discordant engines, formed the music that accompanied the dip of our oars and their rattling in the rollocks' (*RP*).

the dreadfully facetious Wolf in bed in Grandmamma's cottage]　In 'Little Red Riding-Hood' the wolf eats the grandmother and slips into bed wearing her night-clothes. Red Riding-Hood is astonished: '*Grandmamma, what great eyes you have got!* It is to see thee better my child. *Grandmamma, what great teeth you have got!*'

'I am not going to do either

not even to your Grandmother]　Facetious allusions to grandmothers abounded in colloquial speech: 'So's your grandmother', 'all my eye and my grandmother', 'this beats my grandmother' and so on.

Father, was that you calling me?

Father, was that you calling me?]　This paragraph is not in the MS. The elements sport with Gaffer's body as they do with that of Quilp in *OCS*, chapter 57.

thus baptized unto Death]　Romans 6.3–4: 'Know ye not, that so many of us as were baptized into Jesus Christ were baptized into his death? Therefore we are buried with him by baptism into death: that like as Christ was raised up from the dead by the glory of the Father, even so we also should walk in newness of life.'

'Now see,' said Mr. Inspector, after mature deliberation

towing by the neck and arms.']　The words 'and arms' are not in the MS. This would indeed have been to 'Kill Gaffer retributively' (plan for chapter 13). In *OT* Sykes hangs himself as he tries to escape from the pursuing mob (50).

'Now see,' said Mr. Inspector

The lecturer held up the tightly clenched right hand.]　The dead hand grasping its silver inevitably suggests Judas. It has been suggested (by Patterson, 1970) that there is a pattern of allusions in *OMF* to Izaak Walton's *The Compleat Angler* (1653). The work begins with a debate between a fisherman, Piscator, a hunter, Venator ('a lover of *Hounds*'), and a fowler, Auceps ('a lover of *Hawks*'). Piscator cites Scripture in defence of the angler; anglers pity 'money-getting men' and are 'such simple men as lived in those times when there were fewer lawyers'. Instructing Venator in the art of angling, Piscator's manner resembles that of the Inspector here:

> Well Scholar, you must endure worse luck sometime, or you will never make a good Angler. But what say you now? Here is a *Trout* now, and a good one too,

111

if I can but hold him: Now you see he lies still, and the sleight is to land him: Reach me that Landing Net. So (Sir) now he is mine own.

We could, and we did

outward and visible notice]   The definition of the Sacraments in the Catechism: 'an outward and visible sign of an inward and spiritual grace'.

'My dear fellow,' said Eugene

every crime in the Newgate Calendar.]   Subtitled the 'Malefactors' Bloody Register', the original calendar was published about 1774, and dealt with crimes dating from around 1700. Two later series, *The Newgate Calendar, Comprising Interesting Memoirs of the Most Notorious Characters* and *The New Newgate Calendar*, were issued about 1826.

Book 1, Chapter 15

TWO NEW SERVANTS.

Mr. and Mrs. Boffin sat after breakfast

that busy member had so often interposed]   Like a Member of Parliament.

Mr. Rokesmith again explained

or man of business.]   A number of substantial MS passages are omitted in this and the next chapter, perhaps because Dickens included material in this number from the overwritten previous monthly number. The omitted passages, some of which were already rewritten in the MS, are nearly all concerned with Harmon's relationship with Mrs Boffin. The MS has the following passage after the words 'or man of business':

> 'Sort of foreman in short, eh?' said Mr. Boffin.
> 'Exactly.'
> 'Much as I was here?' said Mr. Boffin.
> 'Just so.'
> 'Mr. Rokesmith, however, cannot be expected to know what you were here, Noddy,' hinted Mrs. Boffin. 'It was in the old man's time; him and the dear lost boy's.'
> 'Who was buried, I have understood,' said Mr. Rokesmith, 'near his father?'
> Mrs. Boffin nodded assent and shook her head.
> There was something so very pleasant in the genial breadth of her, there was

something so generous in her manner, something so truly womanly and tender in the musing look of the moment which she seemed to devote to the slain man once the frightened boy she had pitied and protected, that apparently it quite won Rokesmith over and absorbed his attention.

'Now for instance—'. As Mr. Boffin thus resumed, the candidate for employment became sensible of having completely lost himself.

The passage running from 'There was something so very pleasant' to 'completely lost himself' is on a strip of paper pasted down to the MS leaf (now lifted). Underneath Dickens had written:

Why, the remarkable tendency in that handsome face to become overclouded and downcast, without apparent cause? why, did it droop when Mrs. Boffin's open and genial breadth of face was musingly addressed towards it, as she thought of the slain man once the timid boy she had loved and pitied?

Mr. Boffin embraced his spouse

So did Mrs. Boffin.]   An omitted MS passage follows these words:

It was a decidedly handsome face, that face of Rokesmith's, though darkened by a shadow which it would have been hard for the wisest student of the human face that ever lived to define. Such a student might have said that it meant concealment; but would have found the word insufficient, and yet could have found no other. Under the influence of her momentary touch this shadow could hardly have been said to be upon the face; yet the next instant, looking again, you would have seen it there.

In the MS the words from 'Mr. Boffin embraced his spouse' to 'you would have seen it there' in the omitted passage are on another pasted-down slip. Underneath Dickens had written:

Mr. Boffin embraced his spouse for these words of wisdom, and then, congratulating John Rokesmith on the brilliance of his achievements, cordially gave him his hand in pledge of their new relations. So did Mrs. Boffin [*illegible words*] the midst of his successful smiles, and that smote [*illegible words*] his head down like a blow.

'Ah!' said Mr. Boffin. 'Perhaps.

"This Eminently Aristocratic Mansion to be let or sold."]   G. A. Sala commented on the typical house-agent's advertisements: 'A House to Let may be a mansion, a noble mansion, a family mansion, a residence, a desirable residence, a genteel residence ... Rarely do the advertisements bear reference only to a house' (*Gaslight and Daylight* 210). The terms of this advertisement suggest a major attraction of a West End address. In Hood's 'Miss Kilmansegg and Her

Precious Leg' the heroine's home is referred to as 'a SPLENDID FAMILY MANSION' (1208).

Mrs. Boffin replies

' "The gay, the gay and festive scene]   Wegg's rendering of the opening lines of the song 'The Light Guitar', words by H. S. Van Dyk and music by John Barnett. On a sheet published in 1827 it is described as 'The Celebrated Serenade, Sung by Madame Vestris':

> Oh! leave the gay and festive scene,
> The halls, the halls of dazzling light

Mrs. Boffin complied, by reciting

' "I'll tell thee how the maiden wept]   Wegg's version of the second stanza of 'The Light Guitar':

> I'll tell thee how the maiden wept,
>   When her true love was slain,
> And how her broken spirit slept,
>   Never to wake again.
> I'll tell thee how the steed drew nigh,
>   And left his lord afar,
> But if my tale should make you sigh,
>   I'll strike the light guitar.

'So it is, my dear,' said Mr. Boffin

'when not literary. But when so, not so.]   Dickens had made asides about the literary world in *OT*, chapter 14, and *NN*, chapter 48. His quarrel with Thackeray in 1858 perhaps informs the statement. The two men were not reconciled until shortly before Thackeray's death in 1863.

'I should greatly like it.

I have heard so much of its story.']   Another long MS passage was omitted here:

> Meeting the clear wholesome eyes of Mrs. Boffin as she caught at the proposal, the Secretary smiled, and hoped she would not trouble herself to accompany him.
> 'Lord bless you!' returned Mrs. Boffin, 'I am fond of sights.'
> 'But it's no sight to you,' said the Secretary. '– at least, I suppose, that you have lived here some years?'
> 'Some?' repeated Mrs. Boffin, shaking her honest sides. 'More years than you are old. I meant that I like strangers to see sights. Not that the Bower's

much of a sight (though the Mounds are much noticed in the neighbourhood), but that you seemed to value it as one, Mr. Rokesmith.'

'I do. I mentioned the reason. I have heard so much of its story.'

Mrs. Boffin nodded and sighed again and that former winning look of remembrance – almost of motherly remembrance – passed over her face as she forgot the Secretary and thought of the old days of the house.

The passage from ' "Well!" said Mr. Boffin' (six paragraphs above the paragraph beginning 'I should greatly like it') through to 'the old days of the house' in the omitted passage is on a pasted-down sheet. Underneath:

'Well,' said Mr. Boffin, after considering the point, 'Suppose you keep as you are for the present – we'll decide by and by. You'll take charge at once of all that's going on in the new house, will you?'

'I will begin this very day.'

'Thankee. Being here would you care at all to look round the Bower?'

'I should greatly like it. I have heard so much of its story.'

Surely those were easy words to say. Yet he said them in so indistinct a manner that Mr. Boffin asked him to repeat his answer. And when Mr. Boffin moved to go before and show him the house and Mrs. Boffin moved to follow them, he stood faltering between the two.

'Don't let me trouble *you*,' he said to Mrs. Boffin.

'Bless you!' cried that cheerful creature, touching him on the arm. 'I like it.'

At her touch he shrank again but looked at her. As she looked at him with her wholesome eyes, he lowered his own eyes, but without avoiding her, and set his mouth as to compress his under lip. The wisest student of the human face that ever lived, could not have said then what his face meant, except it meant concealment. Not then whether it was a good or bad face, a naturally strong or weak face. Nothing could have been derived from it but that it was fixed in a determined purpose of concealing something that it knew, and biding its time.

A gloomy house the Bower

Whatever is built by man for man's occupation, must, like natural creations, fulfil the intention of its existence]   The common idea that natural creations had a particular function to fulfil was a consequence of the view that nature evidenced design: for instance, in the second volume of *Modern Painters* (1846), Ruskin defined 'Vital Beauty' as 'consisting in "the appearance of felicitous fulfilment of function in living things" ' (Cook and Wedderburn 4.146).

The bedroom where the clutching old man

a jail-like upper rim of iron and spikes]   This would have supported the bed curtains.

115

the old patch-work counterpane.] Made from waste fabric. Patchwork was one of the cheapest forms of covering: when Oliver Twist's mother is in the workhouse she is covered with a 'patchwork coverlet' (1).

receding atop like a bad and secret forehead] For phrenology, the 'science' of reading the character from the contours of the skull, see page 96.

They had opened the door

that touched the Secretary.] An omitted passage follows these words in the MS:

> 'You must know, Mr. Rokesmith,' said Mr. Boffin as they stood in the yard while that gentle creature stole away, 'that she strove and mourned for those children like a mother.'
> 'Good woman!' said the Secretary.
> 'You'll never speak truer,' said Mr. Boffin, 'if you live to be a hundred and fifty.'

'Well, it ain't that I'm in a mortal hurry

a mortal hurry] 'Mortal' was a colloquial intensive: ' "I was a mortal sight younger then" ' (*BH* 5).

For these reasons Mr. Boffin passed

Bully Sawyers] 'Bully' is colloquially a sort of title or name, as in Shakespeare's Bully Bottom in *A Midsummer Night's Dream*. Belisarius made his name in the wars against the Persians (AD529–32) in the reign of Justinian. His Carthaginian campaign earns him the title of the 'Africanus of new Rome' from Gibbon. Wegg has now reached chapters 41–3.

'Let me get on my considering cap

considering cap] A cliché which probably originates from the caps donned by judges when passing the sentence of death.

'No, Mr. Boffin, not you, sir.

Would Stepney Fields be considered intrusive?] Stepney is beyond Whitechapel on the Mile End Road, over four miles from Boffin's new house.

"Thrown on the wide world] The first four lines of 'The Peasant Boy'(1825) written and composed by John Parry. The singer is instructed to be 'plaintive':

> Thrown on the wide world, doomed to wander and roam,
> Bereft of his parent, bereft of a home,
> A stranger to pleasure, to comfort and joy,
> Behold little Edmund, the poor Peasant boy.

In *BH* Skimpole sings the song on the night he suggests that the sick Jo be sent away from Bleak House (31).

'That, sir,' replied Mr. Wegg, cheering up

Weep for the hour]   A version of the first stanza of one of Thomas Moore's *Irish Melodies* (1807–35), 'Eveleen's Bower':

> Oh! weep for the hour
> When to Eveleen's bow'r
> The Lord of the Valley with false vows came;
> The moon hid her light
> From the heavens that night,
> And wept behind the clouds o'er the maiden's shame.

'I suppose it would, sir. You are right

Then farewell my trim-built wherry]   The first stanza of a song from Charles Dibdin's ballad-opera *The Waterman* (1774). Disappointed in love, Tom joins the Navy.

Book 1, Chapter 16

MINDERS AND REMINDERS.

Mr. Boffin dismissed the matter

this advertisement appeared at the head of all the newspapers] Columns of advertisements covered the whole of the front page of newspapers at this time.

Mr. and Mrs. Milvey had found

five thousand per cent discount ... five thousand per cent premium] Share prices are quoted as above or below a par of one hundred; here the possible fluctuation is comically exaggerated.

The market was 'rigged']   In financial slang to 'rig' is to cause an artificial rise or fall in prices with a view to personal profit: 'To effect this, the most legitimate means are not always resorted to. Rumours violently exaggerated, predictions the most opposed to truth, are but too frequently the machinery employed' (*HW* 8.521).

scrip]   Scrip, or omnium, as it was sometimes called, consisted of unregistered receipts issued to subscribers, upon which one payment or more had been made. In popular language the term 'scrip' was extended to shares in general.

fluctuations of a wild and South-Sea nature]   The South Sea Bubble was a series of financial projections which originated with the incorporation of the South Sea Company in 1711, and ended nine years later in general disaster. Thousands of speculators were ruined.

The Secretary proposed to Mrs. Boffin

the hammer-headed young man behind them.]   A long MS passage following these words is omitted:

John Rokesmith's manner towards Mrs. Boffin was more the manner of a young man towards a mother, than that of a Secretary's towards his employer's wife. It was marked by an absolute affectionate deference that had sprung up on the very day of his engagement. Whatever was odd in her – meaning in her dress and manners – seemed to have no oddity for him. He would sometimes bear a quietly amused face in her company, but it rather seemed as if the pleasure her genial temper and sound nature yielded him, could have been quite as naturally expressed in a tear as in a smile. She for her part was responsive to the young man's manner and felt pleased with it, and interested by it; while it stimulated her curiosity to know more about him.

'It's a shame of me,' said Mrs. Boffin as they jogged along, 'to drag you all this way, Mr. Rokesmith. But Lor, I know you don't mind it, or I wouldn't.'

'I would be dragged a much longer way and in a much more laborious manner to do you a service,' he replied.

'Thank you kindly, I believe you would. Considering where we are going, I hope you like children.'

'I hope Everybody does.'

'They ought, but we don't all of us do what we ought; do us?'

John Rokesmith replied, 'Some among us make up for the deficiencies of the rest. You have loved children well, Mr. Boffin told me.'

'Not a bit better than he has, but that's his way; he puts all the good upon me! You speak rather sad, Mr. Rokesmith.'

'Do I?'

'It sounds so. Were you one of many children?'

He shook his head.

'An only child?'

'No; there was another. Dead long ago.'

'Father or mother alive?'

'Dead.'

118

'And the rest of your relatives?'

'Dead – if I ever had any. I never heard of any.'

'Now don't you mind an old lady's talk. Are you quite sure, Mr. Rokesmith, that you have never had a disappointment in love?' said Mrs. Boffin in her simple, woman's way.

'Quite sure. Why do you ask me?'

'Why, for this reason. Sometimes you have a kind of kept-down manner with you, which is not like your age. You can't be thirty.'

'I am not thirty.'

'And you can't be like yourself either,' said Mrs. Boffin, 'because it never comes quite easy to you. Excuse an old lady's freedom. Are you unhappy?'

He answered with a smiling face, 'Not at all.'

'If you were my son, I should say then, you have been unhappy, I think?' the good soul pursued with an observant glance.

'Ah! That's another thing. I have been. Very unhappy.'

That kept-down manner, which might almost have been brooding, remorseful, or one of half a dozen other moods which it not quite was, passed over him. Then he said wistfully:

'If I thrive in my present endeavour, I am content. You give me wonderful encouragement, Mrs. Boffin, showing your interest in me, knowing little of me. When you know me better, I hope you may think no worse of me!'

'Surely I hope not!' said Mrs. Boffin. She was very quick with the retort, for his tone had rather startled her by sounding like a tone of alarm.

'That I have something of a questionable air about me; that I am not quite like other men; that I would speak plainer but that I dare not; I cannot dispute,' said the Secretary.

'Then after all you have some weight on your mind?' said Mrs. Boffin.

'In vain to deny it. I have.'

'Is it good at your time of life to keep it there, Mr. Rokesmith?'

'I don't say that it is. But it must bide its time now. What is done, is done. What is to come of it, will come of it in its own good or evil hour.'

Mrs. Boffin turned her eyes quickly upon him, as if there were a sound in these closing words, spoken in a lower voice, that jarred upon her. 'Yes,' said he, answering a question she had never asked, 'This is the town. And I thank you with all my heart for having spoken to me in such great confidence and kindness by the way.'

The passage from ' "I hope you like children" ' to ' "I never heard of any" ' appears almost unchanged in the MS and text of book 2, chapter 10. See page 172.

The abode of Mrs. Betty Higden

complicated back settlements of muddy Brentford]   Brentford is on the Thames, six miles from central London. Thorne (1876) quoted the poet Thomson's phrase 'Brentford town, a town of mud' and Gay's reference to its 'dirty streets': 'The town, with its long narrow High-street, back-slums, factories, and rough river-side and labouring population, has always borne an unenviable reputation for dirt and ill odours' (56).

at the sign of the Three Magpies]   Altered in the MS from the real name of the building, the Three Pigeons, perhaps because 'magpie' is the term used to describe black and white half-timbered buildings. The inn is well known in literary history: John Lowin, one of Shakespeare's company, became its landlord; Ben Jonson mentioned it in *The Alchemist*; Tony Lumpkin sings of it in the first act of Goldsmith's *She Stoops to Conquer* (1773).

At first, it was impossible

smiling peace was gradually wooed back]   Shakespeare uses the phrase 'smiling peace' in *King John* (3.1.246).

It was then perceived to be a small home

However propitious ... in the matter of beans, they had not been very favourable in the matter of coins]   In the tale of 'Jack and the Beanstalk', Jack swaps his mother's cow for a handful of beans from which a great beanstalk grows. Jack climbs up into the land of giants from where he steals bags of coins and other valuables.

'For I ain't, you must know,' said Betty

He do the Police in different voices.']   Like Wopsle in *GE* (18), Sloppy gives dramatized readings from the 'Police' column in the newspapers, where the proceedings of the magistrates' courts were reported. From these readings Betty would have learnt of the cruel treatment of the poor.

'Dislike the mention of it?'

'Kill me sooner than take me there.]   It has been suggested (by Nelson, 1965) that Dickens may have known Mayhew's interview with an old woman who was a 'pure' finder ('pure' was dog excrement, valued for its cleansing and purifying properties):

> There's such a dizziness in my head now, I feel as if it didn't belong to me. No, I have earned no money to-day. I have had a piece of dried bread that I steeped in water to eat. I haven't eat anything else to-day; but, pray, sir, don't tell anybody of it. I could never bear the thought of going into the 'great house'; I'm so used to the air, that I'd sooner die in the street, as many I know have done ... I'd sooner die like them than be deprived of my liberty, and be prevented from going about where I liked. (2.145)

Mayhew records many such responses: ' "I'd sooner die on the step of a door, any time, than go there and be what they call kept" ' (1.344); ' "it *does* hurt him every day to think that he must be buried by the parish after all" ' (1.386); ' "all yesterday I only took a farthing. But anything's better than the house" ' (1.394). He concluded 'I have heard it stated that the utter repugnance to a workhouse existence was weaker than it used to be among the poor, but I have not met with anything to uphold such an opinion' (1.459).

The newspapers told the same story. In *Sesame and Lilies* (1864) Ruskin quoted from a report in the *Daily Telegraph*:

> Coroner: 'It seems to me deplorable that you did not go into the workhouse.' Witness: 'We wanted the comforts of our little home.' A juror asked what the comforts were for he only saw a little straw in the corner of the room, the windows of which were broken. The witness began to cry, and said that they had a quilt and other little things. (Cook and Wedderburn 18.92)

set a light to us . . . sooner than move a corpse of us there!']   Dickens had described the callous behaviour of the authorities at a pauper funeral in *OT*, chapter 5.

A surprising spirit in this lonely woman

my Lords and Gentlemen and Honorable Boards!]   Dickens added 'and Honorable Boards' above the line in the MS each time he addresses these bodies in this chapter. The members of the two Houses of Parliament were at this time being asked to consider changes in the existing Poor Law legislation. After the 1834 Act, the Poor Law was administered in each union of parishes by annually elected boards of guardians: 'Our Union comprises five-and-twenty parishes, or places maintaining their own poor, which return altogether twenty-eight elected guardians' (*AYR* 10.160).

What is it that we call it in our grandiose speeches? British independence, rather perverted?]   The MS reads 'you call it in your grandiose speeches'. Dickens made similar changes in the MS of book 3, chapter 8. Both sides in the debate expressed this view (as, indeed, through Betty, Dickens does himself): for instance, *The Times* commented on a death by destitution:

> This aversion . . . of the poor from the workhouse in all its forms of relief is a feeling more deeply seated in a sense of honour and pride than is generally realized; and, except so far as to give way to it . . . is to commit a protracted *felo da se*, it is impossible to wish it otherwise. (11 May 1864, 9)

'Do I never read in the newspapers

'Do I never read in the newspapers]   Dickens repeatedly draws his reader's attention to the newspapers: later in this chapter Betty speaks of ' "those Cruel Jacks we read of" '; in book 2, chapter 9, reference is made to 'the shameful accounts we read every week in the Christian year'; in book 3, chapter 8, Betty is said sometimes to 'hear a newspaper read out'; in the 'Postscript' reference is again made to 'the records in our newspapers'.

how they are put off . . . how they are grudged]   Dickens had described the callous begrudging behaviour of workhouse authorities in *OT* (5) and in *C*. A case that was widely reported in the 1860s was that of Mary Anne Anfield:

> She came [to the workhouse] in a cab with her husband. They got out of the cab and wanted witness to allow Mrs. Anfield to sit down in the lobby. He did not allow her because he was not permitted to do so . . . Deceased stood leaning against the workhouse wall, and others were about her. Mr. Anfield came out, and said he could not get an order.

Mrs Anfield was ultimately admitted to the workhouse infirmary but died shortly afterwards of 'congestion of the lungs' brought on by 'exposure and want of nourishing food and stimulants' (*The Times*, 6 May 1864, 9).

A brilliant success, my Lords

Under submission]   In legal terminology 'submission' is agreement to abide by a decision or to obey an authority.

'He lives more here than anywhere.

a weak ricketty creetur]   Rickets is a disease especially incident to children, consequent on a deficiency of vitamin D (found in eggs and milk). It is characterized by softening of the bones, particularly of the spine; bow legs or in-bent knees; enlargement of the wrists; and distortion of the pelvis.

Of an ungainly make was Sloppy.

the Awkward Squad]   'The awkward squad consists not only of recruits at drill, but of formed soldiers that are ordered to exercise with them, in consequence of some irregularity under arms' (James's *Military Dictionary*, 1802, *OED*).

standing true to the Colours.]   Traditionally soldiers have been expected to fight to the last rather than let their regimental standard fall into the hands of an enemy in battle.

'I say,' repeated Mrs. Wilfer

Lavater]   Johann Kaspar Lavater (1741–1801) was a Swiss poet and an enthusiastic physiognomist. Translations of his *Physiognomische Fragmente zur Befördergun der Menschenkenntnis und Menschenliebe* (1775–8) made him famous in France and England.

Book 1, Chapter 17

A DISMAL SWAMP.

And now, in the blooming summer

all manner of crawling, creeping, fluttering, and buzzing creatures, attracted by the gold dust]　　There is an echo of Genesis 1.20, 24: 'And God said, Let the waters bring forth abundantly the moving creature that hath life, and fowl that may fly above the earth . . . And God said, Let the earth bring forth the living creature after his kind, cattle, and creeping thing, and beast of the earth after his kind: and it was so.' There may also be a recollection of lines from Pope's 'Epistle to Dr Arbuthnot' (1735):

> Yet let me flap this Bug with gilded wings,
> This painted Child of Dirt that stinks and stings.
> 　　　　　　　　(309–10)

Foremost among those leaving cards

One copper-plate Mrs. Veneering]　　A card inscribed with copper-plate writing was more expensive than a printed card because copper plate requires the laborious process of engraving in reverse; contrast the charity appeals 'lithographed by the hundred'. When visiting, a lady would sit outside in her carriage while her footman rang the front-door bell to inquire if the mistress of the house was at home. If the answer was 'No', she would give him three visiting-cards to hand in, one for herself and two for her husband.

Miss Tapkins . . . Miss Malvina Tapkins, and Miss Euphemia Tapkins]　　It was the practice to distinguish the eldest unmarried son or daughter by the omission of the Christian name and the use of 'Mr' or 'Miss'. Malvina is a name of Irish origin. Euphemia was popular because of the heroine of Scott's *The Heart of Midlothian* (1818).

Tradesmen's books hunger

Mr. Boffin or Lady]　　Tradesman's jargon.

The gaping salmon and the golden mullet]　　Salmon is the 'King of Fish' (Izaak Walton) and, according to Mrs Beeton, mullet was 'in high request'. Dickens may have remembered the style of Pope's lines in 'Windsor Forest' (1713):

> The silver Eel, in shining Volumes roll'd
> The yellow Carp, in Scales bedrop'd with Gold.
> 　　　　　　　　(143–4)

But no one knows so well as the Secretary

And then the charities, my Christian brother!]   Dickens had considerable personal experience of appeals from charities. He complained to Edmund Yates:

> For a good many years I have suffered a great deal from charities, but never anything like what I suffer now. The amount of correspondence they inflict upon me is really incredible. But this is nothing. Benevolent men get behind the piers of the gates, lying in wait for my going out; and when I peep shrinkingly from my study-windows, I see their pot-bellied shadows projected on the gravel. Benevolent bullies drive up in hansom cabs (with engraved portraits of their benevolent institutions hanging over the aprons, like banners on their outward walls), and stay long at the door. Benevolent area-sneaks get lost in the kitchens and are found to impede the circulation of the knife-cleaning machine. My man has been heard to say (at The Burton Arms) 'that if it wos a wicious place, well and good – *that* ain't door work; but that wen all the Christian wirtues is always a-shoulderin' and a-helberin' on you in the 'all, a-tryin' to git past you and cut upstairs into Master's room, wy no wages as you couldn't name wouldn't make it up to you.'
>
> Persecuted Ever.
>
> (28 April 1858, Nonesuch 3.19)

Dickens was particularly critical of ostentatious or unnecessary charities, those which 'did a little and made a great deal of noise', as Esther says in *BH*, in contrast to 'the people who did a great deal and made no noise at all' (8).

Large fat private double letter, sealed with a ducal coronet.]   'It was a double letter, and the Major commenced perusing the envelope before he attacked the inner epistle' (Thackeray, *Pendennis*, 1848, 1). Each rank of the nobility is distinguished by a coronet of a particular shape.

the forthcoming Annual Dinner]   Dickens satirized charity dinners in *SB* ('Public Dinners'), and complained about them in letters, but he was in great demand as an after-dinner speaker.

a List of Stewards]   Stewards were the officers forming the executive committee of a charity.

the Duke of Linseed]   Linseed oil is used in painting, so there may be a suggestion of aristocratic family portraits, like the 'Family Varnish' at Snigsworthy Park (2.3). Alternatively, since association with the Duke feeds middle-class snobbery, there may be a suggestion of the linseed cake fed to cattle: in a letter to Douglas Jerrold (3 May 1843), Dickens had described 'your City aristocracy' at a banquet as 'Sleek, slobbering, bow-paunched, over-fed, apoplectic, snorting cattle' (*Letters* 3.482).

These are the corporate beggars.

the individual beggars]   Dickens's account of the begging-letter writers draws on his own experience: as a public figure with a reputation for geniality and kindness, he was an obvious target for fraudulent appeals. The case of Mrs Antonia Matthews, who plagued Dickens and Miss Burdett Coutts for some years, serves as an example. Dickens acted as an unpaid secretary for Miss Burdett Coutts rather as Harmon acts for Boffin. On 19 May 1853, Dickens wrote to Miss Burdett Coutts asking 'will you read the enclosed from Mrs. Matthews (in answer to questions of mine) and tell me what I shall do'. The initial impression seems to have been favourable but, on 18 January 1854, Dickens wrote: 'I send £35 to Mrs Matthews, with an intimation that this closes the correspondence.' It did not, for, on 4 October 1857, Dickens sent Mrs Matthews a further £20. A year later she was still pressing: 'Mrs Matthews is by far the most perplexing female I have ever encountered in that way ... She has certainly become hardened in begging – gradually and surely, since she first began, as I remember, a dozen years ago, or more – in a very remarkable manner. I suppose her statements are correct' (27 October 1858). Two months later Dickens concluded that 'Mrs Matthews's case is clearly hopeless. I have had another letter from her this morning, which I have put in the fire' (13 December 1858, *Letters: Coutts* 225, 257, 349, 364–5). In April 1864, replying to another begging-letter writer, Dickens impersonated his own secretary: 'This is one of hundreds constantly addressed to Mr. Dickens, the briefest replies to which under his own hand would absorb his whole time' (*Nonesuch* 3.385).

Mayhew gave some remarkable facts about the begging-letter writers: 'Most of the "professionals" of this class include a copy of the "Court Guide" among their stock in trade. In this all the persons known to be charitable, have the mark ⊕ set against their names.' The names of both Dickens and Miss Burdett Coutts appeared in the list of 'an old stager' Mayhew interviewed. Mayhew described the reading tastes of this 'pattering fraternity': 'Mr. Dickens *was* a favourite, but he has gone down sadly since his *Household Words* "came it so strong" against the begging letter department' (1.314–15, 250).

The article in question, 'The Begging-Letter Writer' (18 May 1850, *RP*), was by Dickens himself, and based on 'actual experiences'. He particularly attacked the writers for interposing 'between the general desire to do something' for the poor and 'the suffering poor themselves'. The account of the devices of the begging-letter writer in Dickens's article closely parallels that in the novel: 'He is fond of enclosing something – verses, letters, pawnbrokers' duplicates, anything to necessitate an answer'; he 'can quote Latin in his letter (but generally mis-spells some minor English word)'; 'Sometimes he has never written such a letter before. He blushes with shame. That is the first time; that shall be the last'; 'He is very severe on "the pampered minion of fortune," who refused him the half-sovereign referred to in the enclosure number two'; 'Don't answer it, and let it be understood that, then, he will kill himself quietly'; 'He has wanted a greatcoat, to go to India in; a pound, to set him up in life for ever; a pair of boots, to take him to the coast of China; a hat to get him a permanent situation under Government'; 'He has enlisted in the Company's service, and is off directly – but he wants a cheese'.

their gallant fathers waged war in the peninsular]   That is, under the command of the Duke of Wellington in the Peninsular War in Spain and Portugal against the forces of Napoleon (1807–14). The daughter of a sponger described in Mayhew would refer to her father as 'an old Peninsular officer – as would be seen by reference to the Army List'; he 'had received a wound in his leg at Barrossa, under the Duke' (4.408).

a lucifer match]   A type of friction match, similar to the present-day match, which became available in the late 1830s.

the beggars on horseback too, in another sense from the sense of the proverb.]   There are two proverbs: 'If wishes were horses, beggars would ride' and 'Set a beggar on horseback and he'll ride a gallop (to the devil)'.

an electrifying machine]   A hand-operated machine to produce static electricity by friction.

In such a Dismal Swamp

a Dismal Swamp]   Like the 'dismal swamp' at Cairo, site of a projected settlement, which Dickens described in *AN*, and which became the Eden of *MC* (23). The then new science of geology had revealed that England itself had once been such a dismal swamp:

> England was once a steaming morass, covered with the rank tropical vegetation of the tree-fern groves; its awful silence only broken by the hum of the shardy beetle, the rush of the hideous flying-lizards through lofty woods of ferns and reeds. ('England, Long and Long Ago', *AYR* 2.562)

Alligators]   'There were crocodiles' and a huge fish-lizard 'with a head and teeth like a crocodile' in the ancient English swamps: 'Many of these animals were like an enormous crocodile' (*AYR* 2.564–5). Venus has an alligator in his shop (3.14) (see p. 231).

But the old house.

fish of the shark tribe]   The earliest fish were 'like the sharks of our day . . . voracious creatures, armed with powerful means of destruction, and clothed in complete armour' (*AYR* 2.563).

hops up ladders, like some extinct bird]   Probably not the harmless dodo, though it interested Professor Owen in the mid-1860s, but the fearsome pterodactyl, one of 'nature's first attempts at anything in the bird line'. 'Grewsome beasts they seem to be. Even if the pre-Adamite man is ever proved to have been existing at that epoch, we cannot imagine his wife making pets of them, or his children liking to have them hung about the house in cages' (*AYR* 13.62).

BOOK THE SECOND.
BIRDS OF A FEATHER.

The proverb is 'Birds of a feather flock together'.

Book 2, Chapter 1
Sixth monthly number
October 1864

OF AN EDUCATIONAL CHARACTER.

The school

The school at which young Charley Hexam had first learned from a book] Identified in the chapter plan as 'A ragged School'. The ragged school movement was, in the words of Lord Shaftesbury, first president of the Ragged School Union, 'commenced by persons of comparatively humble station in society, who were oppressed by alarm, pain, fear, and shame at the state of things they saw around them, and by the scenes which they witnessed amongst the neglected and impoverished classes' (Montague, 1904, 31). A number of schools, some dating from about 1800, were founded in London and elsewhere, but the ragged school idea achieved effectiveness through the activities of a young lawyer's clerk named S. R. Starey. Starey, who was treasurer of the school at Field Lane, invented the name 'ragged schools', and his efforts led to the establishment of the Ragged School Union (Collins, 1959, 95). The Union's work as a central propagandist and fund-raising body was so successful that by the nineteenth annual meeting (1863) it incorporated 180 Sunday schools with 26,360 scholars, 199 day schools with 17,970 scholars, and 205 weekday schools with 8,320 scholars and 2,850 industrial scholars. There were 2,700 voluntary teachers, 360 paid teachers, and 460 paid monitors (*The Times*, 12 May 1863, 14).

In 1843, Dickens visited the school at Field Lane on behalf of Miss Burdett Coutts. He recommended the school to her, but was critical of some aspects of the teaching. To Starey, he argued that it was

> of vital importance that no persons, however well intentioned, should perplex the minds of these unfortunate creatures with religious Mysteries that young people with the best advantages, can but imperfectly understand. (24 September 1843, *Letters* 3.574)

<u>3 chapters</u>

  Lizzie Hexam. <u>Yes</u>

               and her brother?   <u>Yes</u>

               and Eugene?   <u>Yes</u>

Mr Venus?   <u>No</u>

any new character?   <u>Yes. Schoolmaster</u>

                         and Mistress

                         Miss Pitcher

Podsnappery? only <u>incidentally</u>   and her pupil

Mr and Mrs Alfred Lammle. <u>No</u>   Mary Anne

Miss P<u>ee</u>cher – Not Pitcher.

Book The Second. Birds of a Feather.

Chapter I.

Of an Educational Character

A ragged School

a better sort of school

The Schoolmaster

Smith Square

Amos Headstone

Amos Deadstone

Bradley Deadstone

Bradley Headstone

Miss Pitcher

and hailing pupil

Selfish boy

and Selfish Schoolmaster. Very particular within

Smith Square, Westminster

'The person of the house' – Dolls' Dress Maker

Chapter II

Still Educational

Eugene, and his proposal

Why the Dolls' Dressmaker is 'the person

of the house'

Her drunken father

Her imaginative side, and earthy side

Chapter III.

A Piece of Work

Veneering in Parliament

For Ticklepocket?

Twitchpocket?

'We must work'   Pocket Breaches

Veneering's two neat points

Dickens continued to support the movement, but he became increasingly concerned that the schools would come to be regarded as an adequate substitute for a national system of education. In a *HW* article, 'Boys to Mend', written with Henry Morley, he remarked that

> People are naturally glad to catch at any plea, in mitigation of a great national wickedness. Many good persons will urge, now-a-days, as to this neglected business of boy-mending, 'O! but there are the Ragged Schools!' Admitting the full merit of the ragged schools . . . we still must not disguise the plain fact that they are, at best, a slight and ineffectual palliative of an enormous evil. They want system, power, means, authority, experienced and thoroughly trained teachers. (5.597)

In a *HW* article of 1852, 'A Sleep to Startle Us', Dickens indicated the improvements that had taken place at Field Lane over ten years, and called on government to give support to the ragged schools, but he again criticized the methods of teaching: with 'trained knowledge' and a 'sound system', he believed, 'their usefulness could be increased fifty-fold' (*MP*).

a miserable loft in an unsavoury yard.]   Describing the Field Lane school in 1843, Dickens told Miss Burdett Coutts 'the house they are in, is like an ugly dream' (*Letters* 3.564). In 'A Sleep to Startle Us' he elaborated this description:

> It was held in a low-roofed den, in a sickening atmosphere, in the midst of taint and dirt and pestilence: with all the deadly sins let loose, howling and shrieking at the doors . . . The Dormitory was, in all respects, save as a small beginning, a very discouraging Institution. The air was bad; the dark and ruinous building, with its small close rooms, was quite unsuited to the purpose. (*MP*)

By 1852 the buildings were greatly improved.

The teachers, animated solely by good intentions]   Non-professional teachers were frequently unable to bridge 'the enormous social and cultural distance' between them and their pupils. But voluntarism was thought to be essential to the evangelicalism of the movement. Shaftesbury believed that there must be 'an ungovernable impulse' to go among the ragged classes and 'bring them out of vice and institute them in the ways of truth and holiness; and this cannot be done by the established principle; it must be done by the voluntary principle, and the voluntary principle alone' (Pope, 1978, 194).

It was a school for all ages

partitioned off into square assortments.]   At the Field Lane school each class was partitioned off by screens adjusted 'like the boxes in a coffee-room' ('A Sleep to Startle Us', *MP*).

a grimly ludicrous pretence that every pupil was childish and innocent.]   This was far from being the case. In the early days at Field Lane

the pupils, with an evil sharpness, found them out, got the better of them, derided them, made blasphemous answers to scriptural questions, sang, fought, danced, robbed each other; seemed possessed by legions of devils. The place was stormed and carried, over and over again; the lights were blown out, the books strewn in the gutters, and the female scholars carried off triumphantly to their old wickedness. ('A Sleep to Startle Us', *MP*)

It was ragged school policy to concentrate on particular classes of children, among them the children of convicts, thieves and worthless or drunken parents.

the good child's book, the Adventures of Little Margery]   Stories in the Union's magazines had titles like 'A Boy Happy in his Misery', 'The Dying Child to her Mother', 'The Little Boy that Died', 'The Effects of Bad Company' and 'The Dying Missionary' (Pope, 1978, 190; Collins, 1964, 91).

mudlarks]   Mudlarks were described by Mayhew:

> they are commonly known by the name of 'mud-larks,' from being compelled, in order to obtain the articles they seek, to wade sometimes up to their middle through the mud left on the shore by the retiring tide . . . They may be seen of all ages, from mere childhood to positive decrepitude, crawling among the barges at the various wharfs along the river . . . The mud-larks collect whatever they happen to find, such as coals, bits of old-iron, rope, bones, and copper nails that drop from ships while lying or repairing along shore. (2.155)

Several swaggering sinners had written their own biographies]   In his *HW* article 'Pet Prisoners' (*MP*), Dickens criticized what he described as the 'pattern penitence' and the 'overweening readiness to lecture other people' of the convicts in the model prison at Pentonville. He returned to the subject in chapter 61 of *DC*.

black spirits and grey, red spirits and white, jumbled jumbled jumbled jumbled, jumbled every night.]   An allusion to Hecate's song in the fifth act of Davenant's 1674 version of *Macbeth*:

> *Macbeth:*
> Black Spirits and white,
>   Red Spirits and Gray;
> Mingle, mingle, mingle,
>   You that mingle may . . .
> *Chorus.* Around, a round, about, about,
> All ill come running in, all good keep out. (4.1)

With Locke's music, the song was used in productions throughout the nineteenth century.

the beautiful coming to the sepulchre]   In *The Life of Our Lord*, the version of the gospels he prepared for his children, Dickens wrote 'in a new tomb or sepulchre'. The 'Teacher's Column' in the Union's magazine advised '*Don't Use Dictionary Words*'. One teacher was said to have asked children 'What is the ostensible design of Sabbath Schools?' Another defined the word 'summary' as 'synonymous with synopsis' (Collins, 1959, 108).

Even in this temple of good intentions

an exceptionally sharp boy ... could learn something, and ... could impart it much better than the teachers]   Dickens noticed a 'sharp boy' in a class at the Field Lane school. There, too, 'The best and most spirited teacher was a young man, himself reclaimed through the agency of this School from the lowest depths of misery and debasement, whom the Committee were about to send out to Australia' ('A Sleep to Startle Us', *MP*).

'If you please, Mr. Headstone.'

Mr. Headstone]   In the MS the name is 'Amos Deadstone' the first few times Bradley is named. The names 'Bradley' and 'Amos Headstone' are in the lists in the *Book of Memoranda*.

'Look here, Hexam.'

highly certificated stipendiary schoolmaster]   The term 'stipendiary' is used ironically to suggest a pretension to respectability; in *OT* Bumble asks: ' "Are you aweer, Mrs. Mann, that you are, as I may say, a parochial delegate, and a stipendiary?" ' (2).

Bradley, like M'Choakumchild in *HT*, is a product of a teacher training college. By the late 1830s the pioneer educationalist Kay-Shuttleworth had come to realize that pupil teachers required a further period of education in an institution designed for the training of teachers. In 1840 he opened a private college in Battersea, which he largely financed himself. Numbers of colleges were founded in imitation of this model, and by 1861 there were thirty-five colleges, seventeen for men, fourteen for women, and four for both sexes. After 1846 pupil teachers who had completed their apprenticeship were encouraged to compete for queen's scholarships which provided between £20 and £25 a year. In 1861, of just over two thousand scholars in attendance at colleges 1,676 were queen's scholars. After a two-year training, colleges provided the much-prized certificate, 'the hallmark of professional ability' (Tropp, 1957, 19). The certificated teacher had his salary augmented by a direct grant from the government of between £10 and £30 (women: £6 13s 4d to £20).

Dickens was not alone in criticizing the mechanical acquisition of facts in the training of teachers. A principal of a training college testified to the Newcastle Commission (1858): 'Vast demands are made on the memory, little is done for the improvement of the judgement or reasoning powers ... To use a very significant and very intelligible expression, the great feature of the course of study pursued in training colleges is *cram*.' A government inspector complained of pupil teachers: 'They become overlaid with facts. Playing upon the surface of many objects, and mastering none, their memory is unwholesomely stimulated, their judgement stunted and baffled' (Collins, 1964, 151, 152). Examining pupil teachers, Matthew Arnold was 'much struck ... with the utter disproportion between the great amount of positive information and the low degree of mental culture which they exhibit' (19).

Pupil and certificated teachers were both frequently criticized for their conceit and ambition:

> The certificated teacher was said to have been over-educated for his position ... His discontent with his position was said to lead him to move constantly from school to school and finally to desert the profession and compete with the children of the middle classes in the new white-collar occupations. (Tropp, 1957, 60)

'Conceit ... was particularly galling' to school managers who 'were not always the most tactful of people, and who often saw in the school teacher a fit object of condescension' (Rich, 1933, 173). The teachers resented, and were uncomfortable in, their position. A controversial article in the *Educational Expositor* (1853) put their case:

> The qualifications now required of schoolmasters are such as would grace any rank of society, or fit their possessor for almost any sphere of usefulness ... If we ask what position in society the schoolmaster ought to occupy, it will be evident at once to all disinterested and unprejudiced persons that he should rank on a level with the other learned professions, with the clergyman, the doctor and the lawyer. (Tropp, 1957, 36)

Charley tells Lizzie that Bradley has come to her ' "out of the sphere to which he is an ornament" ' (3.15); in confrontation with the barrister Eugene he is said to be 'unused to the larger ways of men' (2.6).

Claims like that in the *Educational Expositor* served to infuriate a proportion of the middle-class public and their representatives. In the critical examination of the education system in the late 1850s and early 1860s a marked animus against the teachers and their social pretensions is evident. The judgement of the *Edinburgh Review* is typical:

> The whole course of instruction is regulated by examinations which cannot fail to stimulate personal feelings in a very high degree; and these feelings are certainly inconsistent with the homely duties, the quiet position, and the simple habits of a teacher's after life. They render him, on the contrary, conceited, assuming, and discontented. (114, 1861, 15)

Criticism found its occasion when the Newcastle Commission revealed that the basics of education – the three Rs, writing, reading and arithmetic – were being neglected. As *The Economist* put it, '*we were over-teaching our masters and under-teaching our children*' (1861, 1037); or, in the words of the *Quarterly Review*, 'the Privy Council have been long manufacturing razors for the purpose of cutting blocks, and in future the instrument must be better adapted for the purpose' (110, 561). The *Edinburgh Review* commented:

> It is impossible to carry bathos further. This vast expenditure, this huge machinery, this office of State, this army of examiners and inspectors, and this elaborate Report of a Royal Commission, end with the admission that

everything is most perfect, *except* that the majority of children do not learn, or learn imperfectly, the rudiments of human knowledge which we profess to teach them. (114, 1861, 17)

Dickens had remarked of M'Choakumchild: 'If he had only learnt a little less, how infinitely better he might have taught them more!' (1.2).

In August 1861 the Revised Code was published. It abolished all direct payments to teachers and pupil teachers without exceptions. All the existing classes of annual grants were merged into one payment of so much per child to the *managers*. The engagement of pupil teachers was to be contracted not with the teachers but with the managers. The number and value of queen's scholarships was reduced. The training college course was to be ruthlessly cut down (Tropp, 1957, 81). The system was one of payment by results: in the epigram of the day, 'If it is not cheap it shall be efficient, if it is not efficient it shall be cheap'. The teachers' position was severely affected. 'To Sir James Kay-Shuttleworth the Revised Code meant the undoing of his work' (Smith, 1923, 274). An inspector said: 'Teaching, in its highest sense ... is almost extinct, and teachers seem inclined to think that the responsibility is now limited to training children to "pass" the examinations prescribed in the New Code' (Morley, 1873, 24). Kay-Shuttleworth believed that the higher aims of education had been sacrificed to 'attaining the mechanical standard of the revised code' (1861, 56).

The parliamentary attack on the certificated schoolmaster continued after 1861. It was led by J. Walter, MP for Berkshire and proprietor of *The Times*. On 5 May 1863, Walter denounced the ambitions of the schoolteachers:

These gentlemen wish to place themselves on the same footing as the lawyers, doctors, and other learned bodies. One great objection to this ought to strike every one – that it is not at all necessary to increase the self-importance of the scholastic profession. (Hear, hear.)

Walter (in words like Eugene's) feared that England would become 'a schoolmaster-ridden country'. On the other hand, an *AYR* article, 'In and Out of School', was opposed to the Revised Code: 'it would be, in short, to put the clock back four or five hours because it was as many minutes slow' (6.80).

'You see, Hexam, you will be one of us

pass a creditable examination]   Pupil teachers took an exam at the end of five years' apprenticeship. They had to show proficiency in the composition of an essay on some subject connected with teaching; in the rudiments of algebra, or the practice of land surveying and levelling; in syntax, etymology and prosody; in the use of the globes, or in the geography of the British Empire and Europe; more completely in the Holy Scriptures, Liturgy and Catechism in Church of England schools; and in their ability to give a gallery lesson, and to conduct the instruction of the first class in any subject selected by the inspector (Rich, 1933, 121).

'Bradley Headstone, in his decent black coat

decent pantaloons of pepper and salt]   The respectable pepper-and-salt cloth seems to have been worn by all classes: in *C* Mr Filer 'kept his hands continually in the pocket of his scanty pepper-and-salt trousers' (1); and in *OCS* as a servant Kit wears 'a coat of pepper-and-salt' (22).

recalling some mechanics in their holiday clothes. He had acquired mechanically]   In the MS: 'recalling a mechanic in his holiday clothes. He so far belonged to that order as that he had acquired mechanically'.

the habit of questioning and being questioned]   A witness before the Select Committee on Education (1834) described how he proceeded with his pupils: 'By requiring the meaning of every word they read, and of every word they write, and of every thing they do. We never allow them to do any thing without asking them how to do it, and why they do it. We avail ourselves very fully of the principle of interrogation' (quoted by Altick, 1957, 151). The practice of question-and-answer is well illustrated by the widely used question-and-answer books of the period (Shatto, 1974).

Suppression of so much

he would not have been the last man in a ship's crew.]   These words suggest the Short Time system of education which Dickens advocated in a chapter of *UCT*, 'The Short-Timers', which first appeared in *AYR* in June 1863. The system, which was supported by the reformer Edwin Chadwick, had been established by the Stepney Union. It had proved that (for working-class children) 'eighteen hours a week of book-learning are more profitable than thirty-six'. It was cheaper than other systems and had the advantage of taking up less of the pupils' time, 'a most important consideration, as poor parents are always impatient to profit by their children's labour'. Army and navy drill were part of the system: watching the boys at drill Dickens thought he saw 'a perfect uniformity, and yet an individual spirit and emulation' among them. Three other *AYR* articles supported the Short Time system: 'Stomach for Study' (4.42–5), 'Children of all Work' (5.254–8) and 'In and Out of School' (6.77–80).

The schools – for they were twofold

that district of the flat country tending to the Thames, where Kent and Surrey meet]   Stanford's *Library Map* of 1862 shows a national school on Spa Road, Bermondsey, a point where market-gardens and built-up areas met and were crossed by the South Eastern railway line.

The schools were newly built, and there were so many like them all over the country]   So many that the weekly magazine *The Builder* began a column entitled 'School Building News' in 1860. The subject was surveyed by Edward Robert Robson, *School Architecture* (1874). By 1856 the efforts of government departments had been 'so directed to the economy of school planning that an

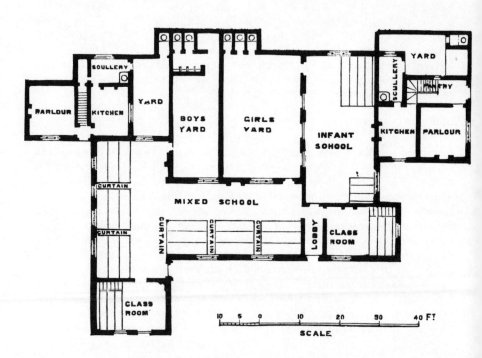

3 Elevation and ground plan of a school, as suggested by the Education Department. From Edward Robert Robson, *School Architecture*, 1874

excellent foundation has been laid for the labour of School Boards and their architects . . . The accompanying plan, taken from the well-known "Rules," is a sufficient reminder of the kind of school alluded to' (15). See Plate 3.

But even among school-buildings

Miss Peecher]   Dickens wrote 'Pitcher' for 'Peecher' throughout the MS for this chapter.

Miss Peecher's favourite pupil

double wallflowers]   'Wallflower' was used as early as 1820 to describe women to whom men do not pay attention (*OED*).

Miss Peecher inverting

a Jack's beanstalk before morning]   In the nursery tale 'Jack and the Beanstalk' Jack exchanges his mother's cow for a hatful of beans. His angry mother throws them out of the window, but by the morning a beanstalk has grown up into the sky.

'Oh, Mary Anne, Mary Anne!'

Part of Speech They?']   Miss Peecher adapts to her purposes the exercises in Lindley Murray's *An English Grammar* (1795; many editions), a work which would have been familiar from childhood to many of Dickens's readers.

Bradley Headstone and Charley

a very hideous church with four towers at the four corners]   The church of St John the Evangelist, Smith Square, Westminster, completed in 1728 after the designs of Archer, a pupil of Vanbrugh. It began to settle, and a tower and lantern turret were added at each corner to strengthen the main building; they were intended to complement a central tower and spire which were never built. Dickens's criticism had precedents: Lord Chesterfield was reminded of an elephant thrown on its back, with its four feet erect in the air; Charles Mathews compared it to a dining-table upside down, with castors on the legs.

a rusty portion of a boiler and a great iron wheel . . . lying half-buried in the dealer's forecourt]   Similar details appear in the description of a 'narrow water-side street by Millbank' in *DC*, chapter 47. There also are 'Handbills offering rewards for drowned men'.

Like the Miller of questionable jollity]   The song 'The Miller of Dee' became well known after it was sung by John Beard in Bickerstaffe's *Love in a Village*, performed at Covent Garden in 1762:

> There was a jolly miller once,
>   Lived on the river Dee;
> He worked and sang from morn till night,
>   No lark more blithe than he.
> And this the burden of his song
>   Forever used to be,
> I care for nobody, no! not I,
>   If nobody cares for me.

The boy knocked at a door

a child – a dwarf – a girl – a something]   Dickens described his idea of Jenny Wren in a letter to Marcus Stone discussing the cover design: 'The doll's dressmaker is immensely better than she was. I think she should now come extremely well. A weird sharpness not without beauty is the thing I want' (23 February 1864, *Nonesuch* 3.380).

'You can't tell me

the name of my trade]   Jenny is a dolls' dressmaker (her father is a tailor). A *HW* article, 'Dolls', which describes the manufacture of dolls, mentions the 'doll's milliner and dressmaker ... earnestly preparing the attire for the young lady' (7.353). Dolls were often expensively and lavishly dressed. An article in the *Strand Magazine* for 1891 described the life of the girls who assisted their mothers at home 'in tailoring and dolls' clothes-making':

> The united work of mother and child yields only a wretched pittance and carried on as it is in a room where sleeping, eating and living go on, is of all forms of labour the saddest and most unhealthy. Meals consist of bread and tea, and work is prolonged till midnight by the light of one candle with the consequence that the children are prematurely aged and diseased. (1.510)

'You make pincushions

pincushions]   In the nineteenth century the pin-cushion occupied a far more important place on a woman's dressing-table than today.

'Penwipers,' said Bradley Headstone.

'Penwipers]   Made of one or more pieces of cloth folded or fastened together in various forms, such as a 'brush penwiper', 'tassel penwiper'.

'A schoolmaster, and says dinner-mats!

I love my love with a B]   This is the game called Forfeits: the players worked through the whole alphabet, the letters Q, X and Z presenting the greatest difficulties. The Blue Boar, an ancient inn on the south side of High Holborn, was pulled down in 1864. Jenny suggests the life of a fallen woman (compare Miss Mowcher in *DC* 22).

'Busier, I'm slack just now

Doll I work for lost a canary-bird.']　A fashionable lady mourning for her pet bird has been a poetic subject since the Roman poet Catullus's two poems (*Carmen* 2–3) on the death of his mistress's pet sparrow (*passer*, frequently translated as 'canary').

'When are you going to settle

some Christian sort of place]　Colloquially 'Christian' meant decent, respectable, presentable.

The boy looked doggedly

They were at Millbank, and the river rolled on their left.]　The old Millbank riverside (described in *DC* 47) had been transformed by the building of the Thames Embankment, which was begun in 1854 and completed shortly afterwards. Dickens described it as 'a splendid broad esplanade' in a letter to W. F. de Cerjat (*Nonesuch* 3.209–10).

The master and the pupil

a gentleman came coolly sauntering]　Eugene walks with the 'Pall-Mall saunter' that distinguishes him from those with a purpose or with business to do.

Their walk was almost

not much encouraged in the unscholastic art of needlework by Government.]　One of the complaints made of the schoolteachers was that the mistresses were ignorant of needlework. Dickens himself did not believe that educationalists were aware of 'the immense uses . . . of needlework':

> I think Shuttleworth and the like, would have gone on to the crack of doom, melting down all the thimbles in Great Britain and Ireland, and making medals of them to be given for a knowledge of Watersheds and Pre Adamite vegetation (both immensely comfortable to a labouring man with a large family and a small income) (*Letters: Coutts* 321)

Miss Burdett Coutts offered prizes at a number of institutions for essays on 'Common Things', subjects like cookery, needlework and household management. *The Times* supported the idea and it was recommended in articles in *HW*, for instance 'Not Very Common Things' (14.39–41).

Book 2, Chapter 2

STILL EDUCATIONAL.

'This is what your loving Jenny Wren

Jenny Wren] Jenny Wren is the nursery name for the wren. In nursery lore Jenny Wren is the wife, bride or sweetheart of Robin Redbreast or Cock Robin. One of the nursery rhymes about Jenny Wren (first published about 1800) suggests an aspect of Jenny's idea of herself:

> Jenny Wren fell sick
>   Upon a merry time,
> In came Robin Redbreast
>   And brought her sops and wine...
>
> Jenny Wren got well,
>   And stood upon her feet;
> And told Robin plainly,
>   She loved him not a bit.

'You're more to be relied upon than silver and gold.'

'Who comes here?] The first stanza of a rhyme recorded in 1725–6. It was probably originally a catch sung in Stuart alehouses after the formation of the grenadier units:

> Who comes here?
>   A grenadier.
> What do you want?
>   A pot of beer.
> Where's your money?
>   I forgot.
> Get you gone,
>   You drunken lot.

'It won't break my heart,' laughed Eugene

Sir Eugene Bountiful] Lady Bountiful is a character in Farquhar's *The Beaux' Stratagem* (1707). She is 'one of the best of women. Her last husband, Sir Charles Bountiful, left her worth a thousand pound a year; and, I believe, she lays out one-half on't in charitable uses for the good of her neighbours' (1.1).

'No, no, no,' said Eugene; shocked

If we all set out to work as soon as we could use our hands, it would be all

over with the doll's dressmakers.'] A version of the commonplace rational-
ization of the economic inequalities of the day; for instance, in his article 'On
Strike' Dickens wrote: 'It is a melancholy thing that it should not occur to the
Committee to consider what would become of themselves, their friends, and
fellow operatives, if those calicoes, silks, and satins, were *not* worn in very large
quantities' (*MP*).

'I dare say my birds sing better than other birds

my birds] Jenny's account of her sufferings and fancies is similar to that of a
crippled bird-seller whom Mayhew interviewed:

> I couldn't walk at all until I was six years old, and I was between nine and ten
> before I could get up and down stairs by myself . . . When I could get about and
> went among other boys, I was in great distress, I was teased so. Life was a
> burthen to me, as I've read something about. They used to taunt me by offering
> to jump me' (invite him to a jumping match), 'and to say, I'll run you a race on
> one leg. They were bad to me then, and they are now. I've sometimes sat down
> and cried, but not often . . . When I was thirteen my father put me into the bird
> trade . . . I liked the birds and do still. I used to think at first that they was like
> me; they was prisoners, and I was a cripple . . .
>
> 'I dream sometimes, sir,' the cripple resumed in answer to my question, 'but
> not often . . . I've never seemed to myself to be a cripple in dreams. Well, I can't
> explain how, but I feel as if my limbs was all free like – so beautiful. (2.67–8)

**All in white dresses, and with something shining on the borders, and on
their heads . . . They used to come down in long bright slanting rows**]
Other sick children in Dickens are granted visions of angels and heaven, for
instance the child who sees the angels 'come out from the long rows in which they
stood' and draw people down 'avenues of light' in 'A Child's Dream of a Star'
(*RP*). The 'slanting rows' recall Bible illustrations of Jacob's dream of angels
ascending and descending the ladder to heaven and of the ranks of bright angels
and cherubim above the (sometimes appreciative) infant Jesus in some nativity
scenes.

'Don't go away, Miss Hexam

It ain't – ain't catching.'] Jenny's grandfather was also a drunkard. Dickens
could argue that drunkenness 'is quite as often the consequence as the cause of
the condition in which the poor and wretched are found' ('Demoralization and
Total Abstinence', *Examiner*, 27 October 1849; reprinted *Dickens Studies Annual*
9.4–14). He was also critical of the temperance societies because of their failure
to understand that 'exactly in the ratio' that people had to work 'long and
monotonously' they would crave drink (*HT* 1.5) and that 'Gin-drinking is a great
vice in England, but wretchedness and dirt are a greater' ('Gin-Shops', *SB*).
Nevertheless, he was severe on the infirmities of the individual working-class
alcoholics who appear in his novels, such as Stephen Blackpool's wife in *HT*.

141

'I wish you had been taken up

poked into cells]   Jenny adds a colouring of childish horrors and a suggestion of the horrors of delirium tremens to the threat to have her father imprisoned for drunkenness. The standard fine for drunkenness was five shillings.

'Here's but seven and eightpence

'Oh, you prodigal old son!]   The parable of the Prodigal Son, who 'wasted his substance with riotous living' in Luke 15.11–32. Jenny refers to the parable again in book 3, chapter 10.

'If you were treated as you ought

the skewers of cats' meat]   Horsemeat, boiled down in knackers' yards, was sold for cat food at the rate of 2½d a pound. It was sold in small pieces impaled on wooden skewers, which cost a farthing, halfpenny or penny each (Mayhew 1.182).

As they went on with their supper

of the world, worldly; of the earth, earthy.]   1 Corinthians 15.47–9:

> The first man is of the earth, earthy: the second man is the Lord from heaven. As is the earth, such are they also that are earthy: and as is the heavenly, such are they also that are heavenly. And as we have borne the image of the earthy, we shall also bear the image of the heavenly.

Book 2, Chapter 3

A PIECE OF WORK.

Perhaps with a suggestion of Hamlet's words: 'What a piece of work is a man! How noble in reason! how infinite in faculties!' (2.2.299–300).

Britannia, sitting meditating

Britannia]   The seated figure of Britannia, with helmet, spear and shield, appeared on the copper coinage from the time of Charles II. Dickens elsewhere used the figure of Britannia for comic effect: for instance, in *DC* David imagines 'Britannia, that unfortunate female ... like a trussed fowl: skewered through and through with office-pens, and bound hand and foot with red tape' (43).

a 'representative man']   See page 94.

a legal gentleman of her acquaintance]   A solicitor acting for the person who controls the borough. Professional election agents were usually solicitors.

'put down' five thousand pounds]   In 1864 *The Economist* reported a speech by John Stuart Mill which claimed that bribery at elections was increasing in England: it made for a Parliament of rich men (479). An *AYR* article of 1864, 'Election Time', claimed that 'we may all learn, if we will, from what we see in a general election time, that except in very special cases, it is money not merit that makes the member of parliament' (13.606). The article recommended parliamentary reform to lessen the power of rich men in general, and of the railway interest in particular (see notes to 3.17 below).

The legal gentleman

rally round him.']   A political cliché: 'the Lord Mayor made a note of the neat expression, rallying round, as available for various public occasions' ('Reflections of a Lord Mayor', *MP*).

Veneering then says to Mrs. Veneering

a Hansom cab]   A speedy low-hung two-wheeled cab, holding two persons inside, the driver mounted on a dickey or elevated seat behind, the reins going over the roof.

a distracted and devoted manner, compounded of Ophelia and any self-immolating female of antiquity]   Dido, Queen of Carthage, committed herself to the flames out of grief over the departure of Aeneas. In book 4, chapter 5, Bella is described as 'putting back her hair with both hands, as if she were making the most business-like arrangements for going dramatically distracted'.

Veneering having instructed

like the Life-Guards at Waterloo]   The Allied armies under the command of the Duke of Wellington inflicted a final defeat on Napoleon at the battle of Waterloo (1815). The Life Guards are a cavalry regiment.

the Monument on Fish Street Hill]   The monument commemorating the Great Fire of London (1666) is from a design by Wren; the 202-foot pillar is surmounted by a vase of flames. In *MC* Dickens described it 'with every hair erect upon its head, as if the doings of the city frightened him' (9).

King Priam on a certain incendiary occasion not wholly unknown as a neat point from the classics.]   It has been pointed out that the detail from the account of the burning of Troy in the second book of the *Aeneid* shows that Dickens must have read Dryden's translation: 'Dryden makes Aeneas say, after seeing Priam murdered, "My hair with horror stood," without any such detail in the Latin text. So Dickens may have associated the upright hair with the scene of Priam's murder, though he gave it to the wrong person' ('V. R.', *Notes and Queries* 187.232–3).

'I think,' rejoins Twemlow, feelingly

it is the best club in London.']

> 'House of Commons, sir! House of Commons is the best club in London,' said a new member, repeating an old boast.
> 'Yes,' was the reply – 'The best club in London – in the worst part of it.'
> 'That's too bad,' was the retort – 'for we pay the deuce of an entrance fee.' (Doré and Jerrold, 1872, 99)

Veneering again blesses him

directs the driver to be up and at the British public]   The command attributed to the Duke of Wellington at the crisis of the battle of Waterloo: 'Up Guards and at 'em.'

Meanwhile Twemlow

Pocket-Breaches]   Dickens created a number of telling names for constituencies, such as Eatanswill (*PP*) and Groginhole, Gammonrife and Drowsyshire ('A Few Conventionalities', *MP*). Pocket-Breaches is a pocket borough, one in which the parliamentary representation is under the control of one person or family. The Reform Act of 1832 had not removed all such abuses. After 1832 about forty peers could still nominate Members, and in the five general elections between 1832 and 1847 the average number of contested seats was just over 50 per cent.

a Parliamentary agent]   Lady Tippins describes herself as an 'electioneering agent'. The election agent organized the team which canvassed for a candidate.

From Twemlow's, Veneering

Italy is not England.]   Conservative opinion was unsympathetic to Italian unification and Italy was an election issue between Conservatives and Liberals in 1859. Italy allied with the France of Napoleon III in the war with Austria of 1859, and French aggrandizement was much mistrusted. Garibaldi's visit to England in 1864 was the occasion of working-class celebration.

Veneering immediately mentions

at a hand-gallop]   An easy gallop, in which the horse is kept well in hand.

Mrs. Veneering, during the same

the Belgravian Borders]   Belgravia was 'the collective appellation of that "City of Palaces" which lies to the southwest of Hyde Park Corner, stretching away towards Pimlico and Chelsea . . . icy cold, from its stiff and unbending habit of fashion, form and ceremony' (Thornbury and Walford 5.4).

'My love,' says Lady Tippins

they have a house out of the Tales of the Genii, and give dinners out of the Arabian Nights.] *The Arabian Nights' Entertainments*, or *The Thousand and One Nights*, is a collection of linked stories written in Arabic which was translated into French and then into English in the early eighteenth century. *The Tales of the Genii* (1764), by James Ridley ('Sir Charles Morell'), is a collection of eastern tales on the model of *The Arabian Nights*. As a child, Dickens read and reread both collections: they deeply influenced his imagination, and he refers to them repeatedly in his writings.

plumpers] Votes given solely to one candidate at an election when the voter has the right to vote for two or more.

Now, the point of view

promote a railway, or jockey a railway] To 'jockey', as opposed to promote or to carry, a railway was to prevent a motion in Parliament proposing its establishment. Railways could not be laid without Acts of Parliament.

Probably because this reason

baiting-place] A point where food and water were provided for horses.

'I'll keep about the lobby

the lobby] In the House of Commons the lobby is a large entrance-hall chiefly used for interviews between MPs and the public (see 'A Parliamentary Sketch' in *SB*).

When the time comes

a feeble little town hall on crutches] An example of the pillared halls of Elizabethan date, which persisted in type throughout the seventeenth and eighteenth centuries, often containing the town hall or guildhall in the rooms above the pillared space where traders had their stalls.

Veneering speaks to the listening earth.] The phrase 'the listening earth' is from Addison's hymn 'The Spacious Firmament on High' ('An Ode', *Spectator* 465):

> Soon as the evening shades prevail,
> The Moon takes up the wonderous tale;
> And nightly, to the listening Earth,
> Repeats the story of her birth. (9–12)

145

Point the first is this.

an original comparison between the country and a ship] The comparison, in fact, goes back to Roman times: the platform for public speeches in the Roman forum (the *rostrum*) was ornamented with the prows of captured galleys (*rostra*). Dickens probably had in mind George Canning's well-known poem in praise of William Pitt, 'The Pilot That Weathered the Storm' (1802).

Then, dinner is had

nomination, and declaration.] Nomination normally preceded the candidates' speeches. There would then be a vote by a show of hands. Normally this would be contested, and the election would be decided by a poll of registered voters. Once votes were counted the returning officer declared the successful candidate or candidates elected.

Book 2, Chapter 4

Seventh monthly number
November 1864

CUPID PROMPTED.

To use the cold language

the warm language of Mrs. Lammle] In his *Book of Memoranda* Dickens made the note: 'The lady who lives on her enthusiasm – and hasn't a jot' (7). Some of Dickens's most calculating and unfeeling ladies affect attitudes and emotions derived from the cult of sensibility which flourished at the end of the eighteenth century and the beginning of the nineteenth. In *DS* Mrs Skewton, who was a fashionable beauty at the turn of the century, claims that her ' "whole Soul and Being" ' is ' "inspired by the sight of Nature" '; her family suffers from being too enthusiastic, but ' "Our own emotions are our recompense" ' (21, 27). To Mrs Merdle, in *LD*, a ' "more primitive state of society would be delicious" ' (1.20). Compare the opening chapters of Mrs Radcliffe's *The Mysteries of Udolpho* (1794).

Whenever Georgiana could escape

elderly osteologists] Osteology is the science which deals with bones: the allusion is to Professor Owen (see p. 27).

grasp at the hem of his mantle] When Jesus walked through a crowd a sick woman 'touched the hem of his garment' and was healed (Matthew 9.20).

the pale reflected light of the watery young moon his daughter] An allusion to Oberon's words in *A Midsummer Night's Dream*:

> But I might see young Cupid's fiery shaft
> Quench'd in the chaste beams of the wat'ry moon;
> And the imperial vot'ress passed on,
> In maiden meditation, fancy-free. (2.1.161–4)

There is perhaps also a suggestion of Milton's 'dim religious light' ('Il Penseroso' 160).

setting his obstinate head in his cravat and shirt-collar, much as if he were performing on the Pandean pipes, in his own honor, the triumphal march, See the conquering Podsnap comes, Sound the trumpets, beat the drums!] Pandean pipes, or Pan-pipes were played by the musicians who accompanied the popular Punch and Judy shows. In order for the musician to play the pipes whilst beating the drums or playing some other percussion instrument with the hands, the pipes were fastened around the neck, and the player sunk his chin into his stock to keep them in place. Podsnap pipes the famous march from Handel's *Judas Maccabaeus* (words by T. Morell; first performed in London, 1747). The Victorians venerated Handel, and his works were widely performed, particularly in 1859, the centenary of his death. Morell's words, 'See the conqu'ring Hero comes./Sound the Trumpet, beat the Drums', derive from Dryden, 'Alexander's Feast; Or the Power of Musique': 'The jolly God in Triumph comes;/Sound the Trumpets; beat the Drums' (49–50).

It was a trait in Mr. Podsnap's character

I have licensed this person.] In his *Book of Memoranda* Dickens made the note:

> I stand by my friends and acquaintance; – not for their sakes, but because they are *my* friends and acquaintance. *I* know them, *I* have licensed them, they have taken out *my* certificate. Ergo, I champion them as myself. (19)

In book 3, chapter 17, the Veneerings are said to have taken out Podsnap's 'permit'.

The handsome fittings

the skeleton up-stairs . . . 'Here I am in the closet!'] According to *OED*, the phrase 'skeleton in the closet' was brought into literary use by Thackeray, though it is known to have been current at an earlier time. Dickens had used the phrase in a letter of 1856: 'I find that the skeleton in my domestic closet is becoming a pretty big one' (*Nonesuch* 2.765).

The orphan and Sloppy?   No. – Next N.º

Lizzie? Very slightly. carry through

Mr & Mrs Lammle and Miss Podsnap?   Yes

        –and a new man?   Yes

                                  Young Fledgeby

                                  Conversation Fledgeby

Rumty   Fascination Fledgeby

Mortimer Lightwood and Eugene together?   No

                          Yes   Elaborately

Chapter IV

Cupid <Prompting> Prompted

Mr and Mrs Lammle following up their plot
    Consequently: – Georgina Podsnap
    and – Conversation Fledgeby
        Fascination

Dinner. Opera. Lammles make all the love
all done by deputy   But they won't come together, no!
Mrs Lammle pats her head as   Alfred would like to knock 'em
if it was Fledgeby patting it   together by their heads
Soda-water touch   'Money in her own right?'
                       'Aye Sophronia.'

Chapter V

Mercury Prompting

Quarrel scene between the two; one dastard just getting
the start of the other.
        'Give me your nose Sir, give me your nose!'
To St Mary Axe?   The gentle Jew
   Crutched Friars?   – Oden?
   Minories?   – Reheiah?
   Goodman's Fields   – Riah?
The Christian employing the Jew. 'But they won't believe me.'
   House-top.   Lizzie – Jenny Wren.

Chapter VI

A Riddle without an answer

Mortimer and Eugene living together

[The domestic virtues]   To Them, Young Hexam and Bradley

So work to 'What is the end of it? What are you
  doing <What> Where are you going?
        'I am an embodied conundrum. Riddle-me, riddle-me
        ree, perhaps you can't tell me what this may be? No, upon my life and
        soul I can't!'

'You do, my darling

young Fledgeby's name.]   Fledgeby suggests 'fledgling'. In *The Book of Snobs* Thackeray has 'Fledglings from the army, Goslings from the public schools' (41).

In perturbation of mind

preceded six feet one of discontented footman]   Well-to-do young ladies walking out were sometimes escorted by a footman who carried their library books and protected them from any undesirable encounter with the opposite sex. Footmen were selected for height and good physique; their supposed vanity, laziness and discontent with their positions were established subjects for humour: there are many cartoons about footmen in *Punch*, for instance.

Georgiana had by this time

a certain handsome room with a billiard table]   The billiard room was the centre of the male domain in large Victorian homes. There the men could smoke and relax free from the constraints of female company. Lammle may derive some of his income from betting on his game. In *Vanity Fair* the disreputable Rawdon Crawley is 'a consummate master of billiards' and makes part of his living by that means (36).

men of pleasure]   'Man of pleasure' was a phrase for one devoted to the pursuit of sensual pleasure; a licentious person; a profligate.

the Bourse]   The Parisian stock exchange, characterized in *HW* as a 'great screaming, tumbling, Temple of Mammon' with 'its hot, reeking atmosphere, the snow storm of torn scraps of paper on its pavements; the great inner and outer rings where the bulls and bears offer, refuse, scream, and gesticulate at each other like mad men' (10.441). Dickens described the volatile atmosphere in a letter:

> Concierges and people like that perpetually blow out their brains, or fly into the Seine, *'à cause des pertes sur la Bourse.'* On the other hand, thoroughbred horses without end, and red velvet carriages with white kid harness on jet black horses, go by here all day long, and the pedestrians who turn to look at them, laugh, and say, *'C'est la Bourse!'* (*Letters: Coutts* 313 n).

Greek and Spanish and India and Mexican]   After excited speculation in the 1820s, Greek, Spanish and Mexican stocks had long languished in the 'rubbish' market. By 1863 their recovery, stimulated by political events in the respective countries, had excited a 'foreign Stock Mania': 'a speculative *furore*' about Greek securities; an 'advance on Spanish'; an 'improvement of nearly twenty percent' in Mexican. They soon reached the 'middle, or highest parts of the market' and for a time dominated trading, but 'It was not to be supposed they could be sustained at this dizzy pinnacle, and therefore the first slight sand crack in the foundation has brought the whole fabric tumbling' (Evans, 1864, 179).

Their fall brought about a Stock Exchange panic in 1864. India was in a different category ('India' is added above the line in the MS both times these stocks are listed): the restructuring of the finances of the country after the Mutiny (1857) and the establishment of free trade (1858) created many opportunities for projects, notably railway companies.

asthmatic and thick-lipped . . . with gold pencil-cases which they could hardly hold because of the big rings on their forefingers]   Jews were conventionally represented as 'bloated and bejewelled' in *Punch* cartoons: 'Leech, in a representative cartoon, drew a picture of the House of Commons populated by a grossly caricatured array of pudgy thick-lipped, dusky-chinned Jews' (Stone, 1958–9, 227). Dickens's Jews are often asthmatic: ' "Bister Sikes!" exclaimed Barney, with real or counterfeit joy; "cub id, sir; cub id" ' (*OT* 22).

Young Fledgeby was none of these

a peachy cheek, or a cheek compounded of the peach and the red red red wall on which it grows]   Dickens plays on the line in many songs 'The red red red rose'.

'By Jupiter]   In Roman mythology Jupiter was the bearded father of the gods.

leaning on a chimneypiece, like as on an urn.]   The phrase 'like as' is a characteristic Miltonic introduction to the epic simile. In funerary sculpture and in paintings of the eighteenth century a figure of a youth or, more commonly, of a young woman is often represented leaning on a funerary urn.

Not so was Fledgeby

Arrayed in superb raiment]   Fledgeby is wearing a dress suit and an opera cloak. Opera cloaks were dark on the outside with richly coloured linings.

A handsome little dinner

his servant behind his chair]   It was the practice for the butler to stand behind and to the left of his master's chair during dinner.

'Georgiana,' said Mr. Lammle

sparkling all over, like a harlequin]   Harlequin was the young lover of Columbine in the English harlequinade and pantomime. He wore a visor and was conventionally dressed in particoloured tights decorated with sequins.

Still, it wouldn't do

mightn't, couldn't, shouldn't, wouldn't]   Dickens plays on the conjugations of the verb 'to be', familiar to readers of Lindley Murray's *An English Grammar* (Hill).

151

More prompting was necessary

Cupid must be brought up to the mark.]   In boxing, from whence the phrase 'up to the mark' derives, the mark was the line at which the opponents faced each other.

'Why, then,' said Mrs. Lammle

the discovery which flowed from the premises]   The usual description of a syllogism is that a conclusion 'follows' from the premiss.

Content perforce with this

green tea]   Tea roasted almost immediately after gathering, often also artificially coloured. It was often associated with puerile femininity: Fitzjames Stephen referred to Dickens and his set as 'bacchanals, drunk with green tea, and not protected by petticoats' ('The License of Modern Novelists' 152).

Book 2, Chapter 5

MERCURY PROMPTING.

Mercury was the Roman god of merchants; the name is linked with the root *merx* ('merchandise') and *mercari* ('to deal, trade'). In Roman art Mercury is represented with a purse in his hand.

Fledgeby deserved

instinct (a word we all clearly understand)]   In *HT*:

> 'Thquire, you don't need to be told that dogth ith wonderful animalth.'
> 'Their instinct,' said Mr. Gradgrind, 'is surprising.'
> 'Whatever you call it – and I'm bletht if I *know* what to call it' – said Sleary, 'it ith athtonithing.' (3.8)

Darwin discussed the confusing nineteenth-century debate about the relations of instincts to the higher faculties in the first part of *The Descent of Man* (1871).

The father of this

the Registrar-General]   See page 34.

Fledgeby's mother

clean outside the cousinly pale]   The phrase 'beyond the pale' derives from the English occupation of Ireland; the pale was that part of Ireland occupied by the English (usually taken as the district around Dublin).

Among her pre-matrimonial transactions

a certain reversionary interest.]   In law a reversion is the return of an estate to a donor or granter, or his heirs, after the expiry of a grant, or its transfer to another party, especially upon the death of the original grantee.

subjective differences of opinion, not to say objective interchanges] The modern meanings of the terms 'subjective' and 'objective' derive from the philosophy of Kant (1724–1804). Ruskin was impatient of their popularization: 'German dulness and English affectation have of late much multiplied among us the use of two of the most objectionable words that were ever coined by the troublesomeness of metaphysicians, – namely, "Objective," and "Subjective" ' (*Modern Painters*, Vol. 3, 1856: Cook and Wedderburn 5.201).

backgammon boards]   Backgammon was a favourite Victorian pastime.

He lived in chambers

the Albany]   Situated on the north side of Piccadilly, the Albany, which was established in 1804, was let by the proprietors to single gentlemen who did not carry on a trade or profession in the chambers. The Albany had been a fashionable place of residence, associated with the names of 'Monk' Lewis, Byron, Bulwer Lytton and Canning.

'Never mind. It seemed so

I saw a man examined as a witness in Westminster Hall.]   The Hall of the Palace of Westminster, erected in the fourteenth century. The chief courts of English law sat in the hall from medieval times until 1825, when the new Law Courts, designed by Sir John Soane, were erected nearby. Consequently the name Westminster Hall was often used for the law itself (Wheatley and Cunningham 3.483).

'Why, of course it is

our little compact of advantage]   MS: 'our little compact of mutual advantage'.

Whether this young gentleman

He was sensible of the value of appearances]   A *HW* article by John Hollingshead, 'New Puppets for Old Ones', contrasts the traditional miser of literature with his real modern equivalent:

All this time the real miser has been walking about the great world, unnoticed and undepicted. Sometimes he takes the form of a small fundholder, living in an inaccessible lodging, upon a very small portion of his annual dividends. His face is not dirty; nor are his clothes ragged; for he finds it profitable to be decent, like his fellow-men. (19.210–11)

Your concentrated Fox . . . your concentrated Ass] Suggestive of the animal fables of Aesop and of the French verse tales of La Fontaine (1621–95), though no particular original seems intended.

Fascination Fledgeby feigned

a touch of the outlaw, as to their rovings in the merry greenwood of Jobbery Forest, lying on the outskirts of the Share Market and the Stock Exchange.] The legendary outlaw of the Middle Ages, Robin Hood, is supposed to have inhabited Sherwood Forest in Nottinghamshire. The 'greenwood' is the traditional scene of outlaw life, as in Scott's *The Lady of the Lake* (1810): 'Merry it is in the good greenwood' (4.12). Norman Russell explains that 'To belong to the Stock Exchange after 1800 was to advertise yourself as a man of integrity: less reputable jobbers and brokers were not admitted to "the House", but plied their trade in 'Change Alley, Sweeting's Alley, and the adjoining streets. These often "shady" figures were known in the early nineteenth century as "little go men" or "alley men".' 'Shady' meant disreputable; a 'jobber' is strictly someone in possession of stocks and shares; Dr Johnson's definition of a stockjobber in the *Dictionary* (1755) as 'a low wretch who gets money by buying and selling shares in the funds' defines the traditional literary point of view (Russell, 1979, 17).

The other smiled

tapped one tap upon his nose.] A gesture that intimates that one is sly enough; 'up to' something; 'awake'.

'My late governor

Geor – is the right name Georgina or Georgiana?'] Fledgeby's confusion may have been a private joke between Dickens and his sister-in-law, Georgina Hogarth.

'Why, you coarse and vulgar

'if your servant was here to give me sixpence of your money to get my boots cleaned . . . I'd kick you.'] To offer to kick someone for sixpence or to pull someone's nose were conventional pieces of bravado (see *NN* 29 and *MC* 4).

Little recked Mr. Podsnap

she, Georgiana, should take him, Fitz-Podsnap, who with all his worldly goods should her endow.] 'Fitz' was the Anglo-French word for 'son', used in later times to create surnames for the illegitimate children of royal princes (in *BH* Miss Flite refers to the illegitimate Esther as 'Fitz-Jarndyce').

It was a public holiday

the precincts of St. Mary Axe]   St Mary Axe, running from Leadenhall Street to Houndsditch, was at the heart of one of the Jewish quarters of mid-nineteenth-century London.

Pubsey and Co.]   Dickens noted the names 'Pudsey – Pedsey' in his *Book of Memoranda* (22).

He addressed an old Jewish man

an old Jewish man]   The presence of Riah in *OMF* is in part a consequence of Dickens's growing awareness that he had not hitherto fairly represented the Jews in his writings. This fact was impressed upon him by Mrs Eliza Davis, the wife of J. P. Davis, the 'Jew Money-Lender' as Dickens then called him (*Nonesuch* 3.171), who had purchased Tavistock House from him in 1860. Contrary to his expectations, Dickens had been favourably impressed by Davis: 'I cannot call to mind any occasion when I have had money-dealings with any one that have been so satisfactory, considerate, and trusting' (*Nonesuch* 3.176).

On 22 June 1863, Mrs Davis opened a correspondence with Dickens (published by Cumberland Clarke, *Charles Dickens and His Jewish Characters*, 1918, and in the *Dickensian* as 'Fagin and Riah', 1921, 144–52) on the subject of the representation of the Jews in his work. 'It has been said', she wrote,

> that Charles Dickens, the large hearted, whose works plead so eloquently and so nobly for the oppressed of his country, and who may justly claim credit, as the fruits of his labour, the many changes for the amelioration of the condition [of the] poor now at work, has encouraged a vile prejudice against the despised Hebrew. (145–6)

'Fagin', she went on, '... admits only of one interpretation', and she invited Dickens to 'atone for a great wrong'. Dickens defended himself, arguing that 'that class of criminal almost invariably *was* a Jew' and claiming that Fagin was 'called "The Jew," not because of his religion, but because of his race' (10 July 1863, 146). But, as Mrs Davis pointed out, 'the Jewish *race* and *religion* are inseparable', and in *OT* there are '*good Christians*' whereas 'this poor, wretched Fagin stands alone – "The Jew" '. She added:

> I hazard the opinion that it would well repay an author to examine more closely into the manners and character of the British Jews and to represent them as they really are to 'Nothing extenuate nor aught set down in Malice.' (14 July 1863, 147)

Though Riah is not the product of such an approach, Mrs Davis was pleased: 'your introduction of the Jew, Riah, in the 7th No. of "Our Mutual Friend," impels me to thank you very earnestly for what I am so presumptuous as to think a great compliment paid to myself and to my people' (13 November 1864, 148). Though she made some criticisms of detail, she seems to have approved of the way Dickens developed the character, for three years later she made him a gift of a richly bound copy of the new Benisch edition of the Bible, which she inscribed 'in grateful and admiring recognition of his having exercised the noblest quality man can possess; that of atoning for an injury as soon as conscious of having inflicted it'.

an ancient coat, long of skirt, and wide of pocket. A venerable man]   In her letter of 13 November 1864, Mrs Davis wrote: 'I am acquainted with an aged Hebrew living not far from the house in St. Mary Axe whose physique and courteous deportment it very well describes; the costume, however, differs; ordinarily these people dress as their neighbours do, and before the present fashion of beards prevailed, did not wear theirs unless, indeed, they are Polish Jews' (149). A *HW* article, 'Old Clothes!', observed that 'Old Jewry – old, bearded, gaberdined, bent-backed Jewry is nearly extinct . . . Very rarely now is the gaberdine – that long, loose, shapeless garment, the same on which Antonio spat – to be seen in the London streets' (5.94). The allusion is to Shylock's speech in *The Merchant of Venice*: 'You call me misbeliever, cut-throat dog,/And spit upon my Jewish gaberdine' (1.3.106–7). Later in the chapter Dickens describes Riah's 'long black skirt' as 'a very gaberdine'. In his reply to Mrs Davis, Dickens wrote: 'The peculiarities of dress and manners are fixed together for the sake of picturesqueness' (16 November 1864, 149).

a graceful Eastern action of homage]   Riah's salaam is broadly oriental.

'Generous Christian

'Generous Christian master]   Mrs Davis wrote that 'The phrase "generous Christian Master" is not characteristic'. Otherwise she seems to have found Riah's speech convincing: 'I conclude from his language that Riah is an English Jew' (13 November 1864, 149).

With his former action

Foreign toys, all.]   Meason's character Grass began business as 'a toyshop-keeper in a very humble way in Whitechapel' (14.370). Albert Gottheimer began as a partner in a foreign 'fancy' goods business in Newgate Street. See p. 23.

'The Jews,' said the old man

'They hear of poor Jews often, and are very good to them.']   Mrs Davis's first letter to Dickens invited him to contribute to the Lady Montefiore Memorial, which was to take the form of a convalescent home for the Jewish poor. Lady Montefiore was the wife of Moses Montefiore (1784–1885), who, retiring a wealthy man from the Stock Exchange in 1821, was made Lord Mayor of London in 1855, and a baronet in 1864. Montefiore's philanthropy was on a large scale: he aided Jewish refugees in Syria, Russia and Morocco, and Christian refugees in the Lebanon. After 1859 the Jews in London had their own highly efficient Board of Guardians, and their Free School was the largest public school in England.

'Don't go on posturing

a Deaf and Dumb School] Dickens had taken an interest in deaf and dumb schools in Boston on his first American tour and in Switzerland in 1846. A number of *HW* articles discuss the need for such institutions.

He made a little gesture

as though he kissed the hem of an imaginary garment] Later he does 'put the hem of his coat to his lips'. Mrs Davis objected: 'I conclude from his language that Riah is an English Jew, but the action of kissing the hem of a garment is strictly Polish. A Turkish Jew might use it; but we have few of them in England. I have never myself seen it practised but by a Polish Jewess' (13 November 1864, 149). The first Jews to settle in London in large numbers were well-to-do Spanish and Portuguese Jews from Amsterdam who came at the end of the seventeenth century. German and Polish Jews emigrated to England in the eighteenth century. Nineteenth-century immigrants were usually Polish or Russian Jews. Dickens may have been following Scott, *Ivanhoe* (1819), in which the Jewess Rebecca 'after the Oriental fashion in addressing superiors' kisses the hem of Rowena's garment (19).

'You won't say any more

extracting a double-tooth or two] Dickens had described the persecution of a wealthy Jew of Bristol by King John in *CHE*:

> Until such times as that Jew should produce a certain large sum of money, the King sentenced him to be imprisoned, and, every day, to have one tooth violently wrenched from his head – beginning with the double teeth. For seven days the oppressed man bore the daily pain and lost the daily tooth; but, on the eighth, he paid the money. (14)

It is recorded that, having noticed the big house the great financier Rothschild was building, Carlyle 'delighted Dickens' by declaring that

> I do not mean that I want King John back again, but if you ask me which mode of treating those people I hold to have been nearest to the will of the Almighty about them – to build them palaces like that, or to take the pincers for them, I declare for the pincers.

Carlyle then acted 'in the very style of Dickens' the part of an 'up-to-date King John' forcing Rothschild to part with 'some of those millions' for the state (Wilson, 1929, 430).

'Sir, I tell them no more

curse me in Jehovah's name.]   Mrs Davis objected that 'no Jew ever utters this appellation of the "Creator," even in his prayers' (13 November 1864, 148). Dickens admitted his mistake: 'The error you point out to me had occurred to me – as most errors do to most people – when it was too late to correct it. But it will do no harm' (19 November 1864, 149).

'And at other times

"Can it never be done without these tricks]   The money-lending business was traditionally in the hands of the Jews, a practice dating from the times when usury was forbidden to Christians. In *NN* Ralph alludes to the conventional fiction that the person arranging the loan was not himself the principal: 'Will you take the money – down, mind: no delay, no going into the City and pretending to negotiate with some other party who has no existence and never had' (34). Meason has three *AYR* articles about money-lenders: 'Wanted to Borrow, One Hundred Pounds' (13.164–8), which describes the experiences of a man driven into bankruptcy after backing a bill for a friend; 'Accommodation' (13.260–4), the confession of a military man who acts as a tout for money-lenders; and 'How I Discounted My Bill' (13.557–61), an account of the practices of a City money-lender. Meason's money-lenders are usually Jews with rather repulsive manners.

Mr. Riah]   The name Riah is not a Jewish one, nor does it appear in the Bible. Dickens invented a name which would sound exotic and biblical (compare Uriah, Jedidiah, Hezekiah, Jeremiah, Nehemiah, Obadiah, Neariah, etc.) (Stone, 1958–9, 241 n).

'Look here, Riah,' said Fledgeby

buying up queer bills]   Fledgeby deals in ' "waste paper" ' (3.1), bills which seem difficult to collect and which are therefore sold by the creditor at a fraction of their paper value. Fledgeby buys the bills, becomes the creditor, and then brings pressure to bear (through Riah) on the debtor, forcing him to pay higher rates of interest, or suffer the confiscation of his goods or other legal action.

Riah drew some folding

folding tablets]   Hinged sheets or leaves for writing memoranda on, made of ivory or of cardboard or the like, and carried in the pocket.

Lizzie Hexam and Jenny Wren.

Lizzie Hexam and Jenny Wren.]   In depicting Riah's kindness to Lizzie and

Jenny, Dickens challenges the prejudice mentioned by Scott in *Ivanhoe* that Jews are as 'reluctant and churlish' in their charities to non–Jews as they are 'liberal' to their own people (10). Mrs Davis had reminded Dickens that 'the acts of benevolence of Sir Moses and Lady Montefiore were never limited by distinctions of creed' (146). She thought Riah's 'kindness to the two girls' was 'very truthful': 'I believe we do perform the enjoinder to "show kindness unto the stranger because ye know the heart of the stranger for ye were strangers in the land of Egypt" – and, to a certain extent, we are yet strangers here' (13 November 1864, 149). Dickens may have been following Thomas Dibdin's farce *The Jew and the Doctor* (1800) or Richard Cumberland's play *The Jew* (1816), in both of which a Jew, respectively an apparent miser and a money-lender, is charitable to a Christian girl. In Smollett's novel *Ferdinand Count Fathom* (1753) the 'benevolent Jew' (47), the merchant of London, Joshuah Manasseh, comes to the aid of the Christian hero and heroine (Stone, 1958).

'At all events,' observed Fledgeby

put any chap up to the fastenings]   Instruct an accomplice how to break in: what the Bow Street officers in *OT* call a 'put-up robbery' (31).

Book 2, Chapter 6

A RIDDLE WITHOUT AN ANSWER.

'Do me the favour,' said Eugene

his chum]   'Chum' was schoolboy, particularly public schoolboy, usage: an *AYR* article has the phrase 'my chum at Eton' (3.346).

'You must take your friend

The old nursery form runs, "Riddle-me-riddle-me-ree, p'raps you can't tell me what this may be?"]   The *Oxford Dictionary of Nursery Rhymes* gives two rhymes with this opening, one of which, first recorded in 1844, suggests the bird of prey Eugene is becoming:

> Riddle me, riddle me ree,
> A hawk sat up in a tree;
> And he says to himself, says he,
> Lord! what a fine bird I be!

'Two belated wanderers

On the hat of wanderer number two, the shorter one, I drop this

pellet.]   When Dickens was a boy working in the offices of Ellis & Blackmore in Raymond Buildings 'clerks had a second-floor office overlooking Holborn from which the boy amused himself by dropping cherry stones on the hats of passers-by' (Johnson 1.52).

He said it so tauntingly

could have wound it round his throat and strangled him]   At the time of publication the reader might have been reminded of the attacks on London pedestrians by garrotters in 1862 and 1863 which had caused great public alarm.

The boyish weakness of this speech

Bradley Headstone, used to the little audience of a school]   In his essay 'The Old and New Schoolmaster' in *The Essays of Elia* (1820–3) Charles Lamb asked:

> Why are we never quite at our ease in the presence of a schoolmaster? – because we are conscious that he is not quite at his ease in ours. He is awkward and out of place in the society of his equals. He comes like Gulliver from among his little people, and he cannot fit the stature of his understanding to yours. He cannot meet you in the square. He wants a point given him, like an indifferent whist player.

'I assure you, Schoolmaster

'I don't think about you.']   This exchange recalls the confrontation between Steerforth and Mr Mell in *DC*, chapter 7. In 1851, Dickens played the part of the dandy, Wilmot, in an amateur production of Bulwer Lytton's play *Not So Bad as We Seem*. Wilmot, like Eugene, is shadowed by a friend and imitator (Softhead). His foil is the 'self-made man', Hardman. Their confrontation over the girl they both love (5.2) resembles that between Wrayburn and Headstone (see Purton, 1978).

'Mr. Wrayburn, at least I know

half-a-dozen branches of knowledge]   Educationalists' jargon: in *HT* Mr M'Choakumchild 'had taken the bloom off the higher branches of mathematics and physical sciences, French, German, Latin, and Greek' (1.2).

'My dear fellow,' said Eugene, as he lighted

If as a set-off (excuse the legal phrase)]   In legal parlance a 'set-off' is a counter-claim, or a counterbalancing debt, pleaded by the defendant in an action to recover money due.

'My dear Mortimer, not that tone

"**Away with melancholy**]   The song is an adaptation of 'Das klingst so herrlich' from Mozart's *The Magic Flute* (*Die Zauberflöte*, 1791):

> Away with melancholy
> Nor doleful changes ring,
> On life and human folly
> But merrily merrily sing fal la!

'I concede both admissions

'**I concede both admissions**]   Legal language.

'My dear Mortimer, one would think

you only saw them as in a glass darkly]   1 Corinthians 13.12: 'For now we see through a glass, darkly; but then face to face: now I know in part; but then shall I know even as also I am known.'

Book 2, Chapter 7   Eighth monthly part
                                              December 1864

IN WHICH A FRIENDLY MOVE
IS ORIGINATED.

The arrangement between Mr. Boffin

those enervated and corrupted masters of the world]   Dickens parodies such thematic phrases in Gibbon as 'the conquerors were enervated by luxury, which is always fatal', and 'enervated by luxury, despotism, and superstition' (42).

Even those born governors . . . who have been the most imbecile in high places]   This comment recalls Dickens's satire on the monopoly of government by aristocratic factions in *BH* and *LD*.

'Bring me round

old Jamaikey warm]   Jamaica rum, taken with hot water.

161

Mr Wegg?   Yes. And Venus

The Boffins?

      and the Secretary?

      and Bella?   Yes

Pursue the orphan and Sloppy

Work on the story

          With the Secretary and Bella

Rumty? Reserve him to be Bella's friend and confidant

Mem: Two more interviews between Bradley Headstone and

Lizzie before the close of Book The Second. One in N? IX?

                and one in N? X?

Note. Boffin was left one mound, before the whole property

reverted to him through the death of the son.

Chapter VII
In which a friendly move is originated

Wegg and Venus

To search together, and divide together.
Master George, Aunt Jane, and Uncle Parker, those great
creatures – all superseded and gone.

Chapter VIII
In which an innocent elopement occurs

Pave the way to Rumty's being Bella's friend and confidant

They have a day out together.

She spends her money in buying him clothes
and treating him.

says she is mercenary and why. But indicate better qualities.

Interest the reader in her

Chapter IX
In which the Orphan makes his will

Carry through Betty Higden

So to the children's Hospital

'Him! – Those'

and 'a kiss for the boofer lady'

<Chapter X>

<Not room for 4 chapters. N.° in 3 >

Chapter X.
A Successor.

Sloppy appointed

'No, Mr. Wegg,' replies Venus.

'I am not above a parcel.']   Venus does not object to appearing to be a messenger paid to carry parcels.

'You can't buy human flesh

'You can't buy human flesh and blood in this country, sir; not alive, you can't]   From 1772, when a slave set foot on English soil he became free.

Having said which, Mr. Wegg

Charity; as if he had caught that cardinal virtue by the skirts]   The four cardinal, or fundamental, virtues in scholastic philosophy were Justice, Prudence, Temperance and Fortitude. Later writers added the three 'Theological' virtues, Faith, Hope and Charity, making seven cardinal virtues. Charity is traditionally personified as a woman in long robes.

' – Him that shall be nameless

tackled the Romans, both civil and military]   The distinction between civil and military history was a common one.

'It is true, sir,' replies Venus

Since that, all is fled, save gall.']   Like 'the world may deem it harsh' below, a melodrama phrase.

'As one that was ever

'Helm-a-weather, now lay her close]   Perhaps with a memory of lines from Charles Dibdin's song, 'The Tar for All Weathers':

> Helm-a-weather the hoarse boatswain cries;
> Brace the foresail athwart; see she quivers,
> As through the rough tempest she flies.

true British Oak]   Of which British ships were said to be made, and hence figuratively used of the men who sailed them.

See into what wonderful

featherless ostriches plunge their heads]   The belief was that the ostrich, when hunted, ran a certain distance and then plunged its head into the sand, supposing that if it could not see it could not be seen.

'No, sir! Remembrances of Our House

all laid waste!] 'Laid waste' is a biblical phrase: for instance, Isaiah, 64.11: 'Our holy and our beautiful house, where our fathers praised thee, is burned up with fire: and all our pleasant things are laid waste.'

the minion of fortune and the worm of the hour!] Henry IV says that Hotspur is 'sweet Fortune's minion and her pride' (*1 Henry IV* 1.1.83). 'The man of the hour' was a newspaper phrase.

Book 2, Chapter 8

IN WHICH AN INNOCENT ELOPEMENT OCCURS.

The minion of fortune

Legacy Duty] A duty charged by the state upon personal property devolving upon the legatees or next of kin of a dead person, first imposed in 1780.

The front garden-gate clanked

'we have at present no stipendiary girl] In book 1, chapter 4, the Wilfers had a 'servant girl'. 'The middle class was defined essentially as the servant-keeping class. Even the humblest householders in the lower middle classes expected to be able to have a servant of some kind, though she might be only a young girl of 12 or 14 who made the fires and helped with the cleaning and washing' (J. F. C. Harrison, 1979, 136).

'We have been quarrelling

like a female Lieutenant of the Tower] Dickens was probably thinking of scenes from Shakespeare's history plays, such as Act 1, scene 1 of *Richard III*, in which Clarence is led to the Tower by the Lieutenant.

As she was uninformed

'a slap-up girl in a bang-up chariot.'] Slang terms meaning 'first rate', 'grand'.

Rumty himself, with his pen

What a lovely woman you are!] Perhaps with a recollection of Goldsmith's

165

song from *The Vicar of Wakefield* (1766), 'When lovely woman stoops to folly'; or, more probably, of lines from Byron's 'I would I were a careless child': 'And woman, lovely woman! thou,/My hope, my comforter, my all!' In *BH* Mr Turveydrop says: 'But Wooman, lovely Wooman . . . what a sex you are!' (14).

'Why, my dear, I have already

Saveloy]   Saveloys are highly seasoned cooked and dried sausages. When Dickens was a child working in the blacking factory, his dinner was ' "commonly a saveloy and a penny loaf" ' (Forster 1.33).

'Truly, it ain't as much

Small Germans]   Another kind of sausage, the stuffing of which is spiced and partly cooked.

It demanded cogitation

'**Near the garden up by the Trinity House on Tower Hill.**']   The garden is in Trinity Square on the north side of Tower Hill. Trinity House is a large public building in the Ionic style, from where the nation's lighthouses and buoys were administered and apprentices to the sea bound and enrolled. The area around Tower Hill has traditionally been noted for its salubrity.

'Greenwich!' said Bella, valiantly.

'**Greenwich!**']   Greenwich is about three miles by river from Tower Bridge. Thackeray described the particular appeal of an outing to Greenwich in his essay 'Greenwich – Whitebait':

> You . . . leave the cares of London behind you – the row and struggle, the foggy darkness, the slippery pavement where every man jostles you, striding on his way, preoccupied with care written on his brow. Look out of the window, the sky is tinted with a thousand glorious hues – the ships pass silent over the blue glittering waters – there is no object within sight that is not calm, and happy, and beautiful.

Dickens and his friends frequently made the excursion.

'We-ell, ye-es,' he returned

the Dead March in Saul]   The Dead March from the oratorio *Saul* by Handel. The *AYR* reporter at the Handel Festival at the Crystal Palace, Sydenham, wrote: 'There is in the Dead March an element of discord imparted by the peculiar note of the drum which is almost horrible in its harsh grandeur' (1.278). In *BH* Trooper George tersely remarks ' "That's the Dead March in Saul. They bury soldiers to it" ' (21).

dancing a hornpipe]   In the musical melodrama, the jolly British tar frequently broke into a hornpipe.

The little expedition

the little room overlooking the river]   'In the days when Greenwich was famous for its whitebait dinners, the town was noted for its hotels overlooking the waterside. The chief of these was the Ship, whilst another notable one was the Trafalgar' (Matz, 1922, 209).

And then, as they sat looking

And then, as they sat looking at the ships]   This long paragraph is not in the MS or the proofs. The added material celebrates the great world of Victorian commerce of which the Thames was the heart: there, according to a *HW* writer, were 'the glories of the British inscribed' (4.254).

to China . . . to bring home opium]   The bulk of the British opium trade was export from India to China, not import from China to Britain.

just the article]   A commercial phrase.

a band playing on deck]   Bella may be thinking of the Royal Navy, or of the popular river steamboat excursions: ' "Then, we shall hire a steamer expressly for our party, and a band, and have the deck chalked, and we shall be able to dance quadrilles all day" ' ('The Steam Excursion', *SB*).

held her state aboard . . . like a modern Cleopatra]   Cleopatra refused Antony's invitation to dine and instead received him splendidly on her barge. The effect she created is described by Enobarbus in Act 2, scene 2, of *Antony and Cleopatra* in the famous speech beginning 'The barge she sat in, like a burnish'd throne/Burn'd on the water' (194–5).

that troop-ship when she got to Gravesend]   Gravesend is a town in Kent, some twenty-seven miles down-river from London. Like Tilbury opposite, it has been of strategic importance historically because it commands the mouth of the river.

red coats and blue jackets]   The popular terms for soldiers and sailors.

a cargo of sweet-smelling woods]   In *MED* Mr Sapsea speaks of ' "bamboo and sandal-wood from the East Indies" ' (4). In the 1860s sandalwood came mainly from the Pacific islands, such as the Sandwich Islands.

an Indian Prince, who was a Something-or-Other, and who wore Cashmere shawls all over himself, and diamonds and emeralds blazing in his turban]   Bella and Pa cannot remember Indian titles such as 'maharaja' or 'nawab'. Fine and costly cashmere shawls, brought back from India by English residents and travellers, had long been fashionable. Bella is thinking of Golconda diamonds, rather a literary convention than an actuality: Golconda, near

Hyderabad, had formerly been a centre of gem-cutting rather than a source of gems. 'Oriental emerald', specimens of which were sent from India to England in the eighteenth century, is green corundum.

as willing to put his head into the Sultan's tub of water as the beggar-boys below were to put *their* **heads in the mud]**   In the *Spectator* (94, 18 June 1711) Addison tells of a sultan who, dipping his head in a bucket of water, seemed to undergo the experiences of a lifetime. Blanchard Jerrold commented on the practice of the beggar-boys (mentioned again in 4.4): 'The Greenwich boys were busy in the mud below, learning to be vagabond men, by the help of the thoughtless diners flushed with wine, who were throwing pence to them' (Doré and Jerrold, 1872, iv).

Book 2, Chapter 9

IN WHICH THE ORPHAN MAKES HIS WILL.

John Rokesmith hoped the child

the doctor's shop]   An apothecary's shop, like that in which Mr Dolls dies in book 4, chapter 9. According to Dickens's and Henry Morley's *HW* article, 'Drooping Buds', because of inadequate specialization, most medical men, when confronted with children's illnesses, could do no more than 'sympathize with the distress of the parents, look at a sick child's tongue, feel its pulse, send powders, and shake their heads with vain regret over the little corpse, around which women weep so bitterly' (5.46). Morley made the point again in a subsequent *HW* article: 'No medical man is altogether competent to treat a sick child, if he has not made of the diseases of children a distinct matter of study' (18.380).

something as wos wery long for spots.']   Johnny has the symptoms of smallpox, but he is not, apparently, infectious.

Sloppy knew his ground

the Christian year]   The phrase is used of the events in the Church of England calendar. Dickens may have intended an allusion to John Keble's widely read collection of poems *The Christian Year* (1827). Keble had been one of the leaders of the Oxford Movement, and Dickens was critical of clergymen who involved themselves in 'Pusey controversies, and Newman controversies' rather than attending to the condition of the poor: he advised them to 'be simply Apostolic thus low down' ('A Sleep to Startle Us', *MP*).

God save the Queen and Con-found their politics]   An allusion to lines from the version of the national anthem, 'God Save the King', by Henry Carey (1693?–1743): 'Confound their politics/Frustrate their knavish tricks.'

Punctual to the time

the rumble]   The hind part of the carriage, provided as sitting accommodation for servants or attendants, or to carry luggage.

But, on the way down

a Noah's ark]   Dickens mentioned these popular toys, which Caleb makes in *CH* (2), when describing the Hospital for Sick Children in Great Ormond Street in his speech of 9 February 1858: 'each poor sufferer is supplied its tray of toys; and, looking around, you may see how the little tired, flushed cheek has toppled over half the brute creation on its way into the ark' (*Speeches* 251).

a yellow bird with an artificial voice]   Simple mechanical singing birds were popular toys.

'He's bad! He's bad!'

the Power and the Glory]   The phrase is used at the conclusion of the Lord's Prayer.

'I don't know why else

as if he had hold of a finger that I can't see]   Suggestive of the biblical phrase 'the finger of God', which signifies divine power and operation.

The terror, the shame

it 'crops up' – as our slang goes]   'Crops up' was originally a collier's term used of areas of coal appearing on the surface: as, for instance, in Disraeli, *Sybil*: 'the great veins of coal and ironstone cropped up, as they phrase it' (1845, 3.4). The earliest figurative use in *OED* is Disraeli, *Coningsby*: ' "We shall have new men cropping up every session" ' (1844, 2.6).

'Now see, Betty,' pursued the sweet

a place set up on purpose for sick children]   Of the 50,000 people who died annually in London in the 1850s, 21,000 were children under the age of 10. In 1852 the Hospital for Sick Children had been started in a house in Great Ormond Street. A *HW* article by Dickens and Henry Morley, 'Drooping Buds', stressed the need for doctors who had specialized in children's ailments and praised the admirable arrangements at the hospital (5.45–8). Six years later, in 1858, the hospital still had only thirty-one beds. In that year, Dickens gave a speech on behalf of the hospital at the Freemason's Hall. He described a sick child he had

4   A ward in the Great Ormond Street Hospital for Sick Children, by Gustave Doré. From
     London, 1874

seen in the slums of Edinburgh: 'there lay, in an old egg-box which the mother had begged from a shop, a little feeble, wasted, wan, sick child'. Since then, whenever he had come across 'a poor child, sick and neglected', he had thought of his 'poor little drooping friend in his egg-box' who seemed to be asking 'why, in the name of gracious God, such things should be' (*Speeches* 250–1). The speech was a great success and Dickens was later made an honorary governor. On 15 April he gave a reading of *CC* on behalf of the hospital. A follow-up article in *AYR* in 1862, 'Between the Cradle and the Grave', mentioned that the number of beds had risen to fifty; there was an infant nursery; and similar institutions had been established in Edinburgh, Birmingham, Liverpool and other places (6.454–6).

However, they were all carried up

another Johnny seated on the knee of some Angel surely who loved little children.] 'Suffer little children, and forbid them not, to come unto me' (Matthew 19.14). Dickens described the hospital wards in his speech: 'On the walls of these rooms are graceful, pleasant, bright, childish pictures. At the bed's heads, are pictures of the figure which is the universal embodiment of all mercy and compassion, the figure of Him who was once a child himself, and a poor one' (*Speeches* 251).

Moorish tumblers] 'There were little tumblers in red breeches, incessantly swarming up high obstacles of red-tape, and coming down, head first, upon the other side' (*CH* 2).

Book 2, Chapter 10

A SUCCESSOR.

Some of the Reverend Frank Milvey's brethren

they were required to bury the dead too hopefully.] Some Anglican clergymen had come to believe that reading the burial service amounted to a pronouncement of the actual salvation of every person over whom it was read: as a result, some argued that the words of the service should be changed, others that church discipline should be strengthened so that the service need never be read over someone whose life had been, in some interpretation, unchristian. The majority of clergymen, however, interpreted the words in the burial service about salvation as the expression of hope, rather than the pronouncement of a certainty (*The Times*, 26 December 1863, 9).

one or two other things (say out of nine-and-thirty) calculated to trouble their consciences] The Thirty-Nine Articles of the Church of England, the confession of faith for ministers promulgated by the Church in 1571. Many Victorian clergymen had difficulty subscribing to the articles.

Indeed, the Reverend Frank Milvey

many sad warps and blights in the vineyard wherein he worked] The vineyard is a frequent setting in biblical parables, signifying the place of human endeavour, the sphere of one's efforts.

savagely wise.] The oxymoron suggests Honeythunder in *MED*. The first half of the 1860s was a time of much dissension within the Church of England and between denominations. Dickens expressed his impatience in a letter to W. F. de Cerjat:

> As to the Church, my friend, I am sick of it. The spectacle presented by the indecent squabbles of priests of most denominations, and the exemplary unfairness and rancour with which they conduct their differences, utterly repels me. (25 October 1864, *Nonesuch* 3.402)

John Rokesmith's manner

John Rokesmith's manner] The long passage from the beginning of this paragraph to Harmon's words 'I am not yet thirty' is largely taken from a long passage in the MS and proof of book 1, chapter 16, which was omitted from the published chapter. See page 119. Here Dickens added a sentence appropriate to the context of little Johnny's death ('The completeness of his sympathy . . .') and brought in Bella to overhear the conversation.

The consideration of Mrs. Boffin

a perfect Argus in the way of buttons] In Greek mythology Argus was a monster with a hundred eyes, set by the goddess Hera to watch over her rival Io, whom Zeus had turned into a cow. Hermes lulled Argus to sleep with his lyre and killed him. Hera then put his eyes into the tail of the peacock.

a hatband of wholesale capacity] In the 1830s English crape production grew and men's hats got taller and taller. Hence the typical Victorian mourner's and mute's chimneypot topper with massive 'weepers' hanging behind nearly to the waist.

Book 2, Chapter 11

Ninth monthly number
January 1865

SOME AFFAIRS OF THE HEART.

Little Miss Peacher

her faithful slate had the latent qualities of sympathetic paper]
'Sympathetic ink' becomes visible when the paper is held in direct sunlight
or near a flame; to balance 'faithful slate' Dickens attributes the sympathetic
quality to the paper.

Was Geography in question?]   The particular facts alluded to are all to be
found in the widely used question-and-answer books of the period. Thus in
Chambers, *Miscellaneous Questions*, in the chapter 'Geology-Mineralogy': '*How is
the central heat of the globe manifested on the surface?* – By volcanoes and hot
mineral springs ... *Which are the more remarkable in Europe?* – Etna in Sicily,
Vesuvius in Italy, and Hecla in Iceland ... *What are geysers?* – Boiling springs in
Iceland, in which the water is ejected in a column to a great height' (19–20); and in
the 'Geography' chapter: '*Name a large river in India.* – The Ganges ... *What river
flows through Egypt?* – The Nile' (25–6).

four-score and four neck-ties]   Sums were often given the form of tradesmen's bills: Mr Murdstone gives David Copperfield a sum beginning 'If I go into a
cheesemonger's shop, and buy five thousand double-Gloucester cheeses at
fourpence-halfpenny each ...' (4).

'Who gave her that name?

**theological impatience to strike in with her godfathers and her god-
mothers**]   The second question in the Catechism of the Church of England
is 'Who gave you this Name?', to which the catachumen must answer: 'My
Godfathers and Godmothers in my Baptism; wherein I was made a member of
Christ, the child of God, and an inheritor of the kingdom of heaven.'

'Right, Mary Anne.

any Lizzies in the early Christian Church]   Some people distinguished
between 'truly Christian names' and names of pagan derivation, but Miss
Peecher's objection is really to the use of the familiar 'Lizzie' for Elizabeth.

She was right touching

the wisdom of his ancestors]   Among the false book-backs with which
Dickens decorated his study at Gad's Hill was a set called 'The Wisdom of Our

<u>Lizzie Hexam.</u>   <u>Yes</u>

        and Bradley.   <u>Yes</u>

        Miss Peecher?   <u>Yes</u>

        Jenny Wren   <u>Yes</u>

        Riah   <u>No</u>

Veneerings, Twemlow, Tippins, Boots and Brewer.   <u>No</u>

<u>The Fellowship Porters</u>

           Miss Potterson

             and her brother (from page 23)   <u>No</u>

Riderhood?

      and his Daughter?

            <u>Yes</u>

Work up to scene in next N^{o} between Lizzie, Her brother,
and Bradley Headstone.

Chapter XI
Some affairs of the Heart.

The State of Miss Peecher's heart
       of Bradley's
       of Lizzie's (extracted by Miss Wren)
Lead on to another scene between Bradley and Lizzie.

Chapter XII
More Birds of Prey.

Riderhood's abode
    Miss Pleasant Riderhood: A leaving shop.
    Secretary disguised. Work on to possessing the reader with
    the fact that he is John Harmon

Chapter XIII.
A Solo and a Duett

John Harmon as he goes, recalls the whole story
       all but proposes then – opportunity is fitting when
       he gets back – to Bella
              Bella impatient and resentful
Bury John Harmon under mounds and mounds! Crush
him! Cover him! Keep him down!

Ancestors – I. Ignorance. II. Superstition. III. The Block. IV. The Stake. V. The Rack. VI. Dirt. VII. Disease.' House (1941) observes that Bentham had described phrases like 'the Wisdom of our Ancestors', 'the Wisdom of the Ages' and 'the Wisdom of Old Times' as mischievous and absurd fallacies (35).

some form of tribute to Somebody for something that was never done, or ... that was done by Somebody Else]   In *BH* the philanthropists who trouble Mr Jarndyce 'were going to give a testimonial to Mrs. Jellyby; they were going to have their Secretary's portrait painted, and presented to his mother-in-law' (8). In his *Latter-Day Pamphlets* (1850) Carlyle wrote: 'Poor English Public, they really are exceedingly bewildered with Statues at present. They would fain do honour to somebody, if they did but know whom or how ... They have raised a set of the ugliest Statues, and to the most extraordinary persons, ever seen under the sun before' ('Hudson's Statue'). Recently, the Shakespeare Committee for the Tercentenary celebrations (1864) had been widely accused of paying greater tribute to its own leading spirits than to Shakespeare.

Book 2, Chapter 12

MORE BIRDS OF PREY.

Rogue Riderhood dwelt deep

waterside characters, some no better than himself, some very much better, and none much worse]   The reports of Mr Jones, the rector of St Anne's, Limehouse, between 1851 and 1870, provide a comment on the character of the population of the district:

1857. – The greater part of the parishioners are very poor – dependent upon casual employment at the docks. There is a sad amount of ignorance and vice. The pulling down of many houses in Shadwell for the enlargement of the docks has materially contributed to the deterioration of the moral character of the inhabitants of this parish during the past year by causing the immigration of a large number of degraded women and the establishment of many new lodging houses for seamen.

1863. – The greater part of the parishioners are very poor, obtaining precarious employment at the Docks and elsewhere. Some are a very low and vicious class, frequenting sailors' lodging houses, etc., but many are decent and respectable.

1869. – The parishioners are for the most part poor, comprising a large number of persons, employed at the Docks, and in engineering and shipbuilding yards. There is an increase of low lodging houses for sailors and a corresponding increase in immorality, and the removal of the greater part of the more respectable families to other localities has also contributed to deteriorate the character of the population. (Birch, 1930, 123–4)

Had it not been for the daughter

a Leaving Shop]   An unlicensed pawnbroker.

Why christened Pleasant

Pleasant]   The name is among those Dickens listed in his *Book of Memoranda*.

As some dogs have it

to worry certain creatures to a certain point]   The allusion is to the bulldog, which will seize a bull by the nose and cling to it until the bull stands still; this is called 'pinning' the bull.

a Wedding in the street]   A walking wedding; if too poor to hire a carriage or a cab, a wedding party proceeded to the church or chapel on foot, in a more or less formal procession. Dickens had described a walking wedding in Limehouse in *DS*, chapter 60.

a Funeral . . . a black masquerade, conferring a temporary gentility on the performers]   Pleasant's view was Dickens's own: see Jenny Wren's comments on elaborate funerals in book 4, chapter 9.

among groves of bread-fruit, waiting for ships to be wafted from the hollow ports of civilization.]   Ironically attributing to Pleasant a view of 'Society' such as Mrs Merdle affects in *LD*: ' "We know it is hollow and conventional and worldly and very shocking, but unless we are savages in the Tropical seas (I should have been charmed to be one myself – most delightful life and perfect climate, I am told), we must consult it" ' (1.20). In the *UT* essay 'Bound for the Great Salt Lake', Dickens observed: 'Down by the Docks is the road to the Pacific Ocean, with its lovely islands, where the savage girls plait flowers, and the savage boys carve cocoa-nut shells, and the grim blind idols muse in their shady groves to exactly the same purpose as the priests and chiefs.' He added the remark: 'the noble savage is a wearisome impostor wherever he is' (22). Compare the essay 'The Noble Savage' (*RP*).

It was a wretched little shop

SEAMAN'S BOARDING-HOUSE]   There were 'successive gradations' of seamen's lodging-houses in the waterside districts, 'from decent lodging houses to the lowest dens of infamy where, – if stories told, be true, – even a man's life is not safe'. A 'decent specimen of the class' in the 1850s had a small common room, a kitchen where food and alcohol were available, and small crowded dormitory rooms, fitted out with bunks (Beames, 1852, 100–1).

The conversation had arrived

a short jagged knotted club with a loaded head]   Clubs with heads loaded with lead, intended for self-defence, were called 'life-preservers'.

bristling oakum-coloured head and whiskers]   Oakum is the loose fibre obtained from unpicking old rope. Picking oakum was a common employment of convicts and workhouse inmates. The loose fibre was put to various nautical uses, and it was also used to dress wounds.

'To wile away the time

is there much robbing and murdering of seamen about the water-side now?']   'What villainous cruelty, complicated with lamentable sin, sailors just turned adrift from their ships, with their pay in hand, are exposed to – is almost beyond belief. A class of men exists – forming a distinct body – and organized as such by the name of "Crimps" . . . who look out for sailors as their destined and natural prey' (*HW* 2.164).

'You're right. Their money may be soon

Their money may be soon got out of them]   'Sailors are proverbially ignorant of the world; they live for years together at sea; and having few opportunities on shore, they never go far inland; whilst they are at sea, their wages accumulate, and they come home with full pockets, more imprudent than children.' They are 'like boys let loose from school' (Beames, 1852, 100, 105).

With his Fortunatus's goblet

Fortunatus's goblet]   The phrase is 'Fortunatus's purse'. In Thomas Dekker's comedy, *Old Fortunatus* (1599), based on a German story, Fortunatus receives a purse from which he can at any time draw ten pieces of gold.

'That there article of clothing

dull Old Bailey evasion.]   The central criminal courts were at the Old Bailey.

Book 2, Chapter 13

A SOLO AND A DUETT.

Dickens employs the alternative spelling of 'duet' (from the Italian, *duetto*).

He tried a new direction

narratives of escape from prison . . . where the little track of the fugitives in the night always seems to take the shape of the great round world] Dickens may have been thinking of tales told of North American backwoodsmen. See Hardy, *The Mayor of Casterbridge* (1886): 'his wandering, like that of the Canadian woodsman, became part of a circle of which Casterbridge formed the centre' (44).

'I have no clue to the scene

Limehouse Church]   The church of St Anne's, Limehouse, is about half a mile from Limehouse Hole. It stands in a large churchyard at the corner of the Commercial Road and Church Row (now Newell Street). The church is by Hawksmoor, and was built between 1712 and 1724. The interior was completely burnt out in 1850 but restored by 1857. The tower has four angular turrets and a more lofty turret in the centre: 'a most magnificent pile, exhibiting the most solemn, reverend aspect when viewed in front, and when at an angle the most gay and airy'. It is conspicuous from the river, and sailors were said to steer by it. In the burial registers at St Anne's are entries like 'Found drowned, man unknown'; 'a drowned woman'; 'a young man unknown drowned'; 'a drowned man unknown'. The oldest inscription in the church crypt, dated 1733, reads:

> Man but dives to Death
> Dives from the sun in fairer day to rise,
> The grave his subterranean road to bliss.
>   (Birch, 1930, 61, 99)

'It is a sensation not experienced

A spirit that was once a man . . . going unrecognized among mankind]   This suggests the ghosts in *CC* and *HM*. In his *Book of Memoranda* Dickens made the note 'The Invisible One' (18).

'When I came back to England

shrinking from my father's money]   Harmon's story may owe something to a humorous *HW* article, 'My Two Partners' (19.275–80), by John Hollingshead.

179

5 St Anne's, Limehouse, by Nicholas Hawksmoor

The narrator wakes one morning to find he has inherited 'a bone-boiling factory, a skin-drying settlement, and a patent manure depot'. He is appalled by the sources of his wealth: 'I had bartered my soul for worldly goods . . . The name of bone-boiler was always hissing in my ears. The horrid effluvium, which had always prevented me from exploring my own premises, seemed to cling to my clothes, and exude from the roots of my hair' (276). But his fears that his fiancée and her father will reject him because of the nature of his business are misplaced: both are attracted by the profits.

However, a sociable word

So the plot was made out]   This part of Harmon's story recalls the *Memoirs* of the clown Joseph Grimaldi (1779–1837), which Dickens edited in 1837 (1838; reprinted, ed. Findlater, 1968). In 1803 two men called on Grimaldi in the green room. They seemed to him to be strangers, but one of them greeted him warmly: 'He looked about Grimaldi's own age, and had evidently been accustomed to a much warmer climate than that of England' (132–3). The man revealed himself to be Grimaldi's long-lost brother, John, who had run away to sea fourteen years previously. The brother had in his pocket 'a coarse canvas bag, stuffed full of various coins'. Grimaldi arranged to meet him after he had changed out of his clown's costume, but when he returned his brother had disappeared: 'Grimaldi could scarcely persuade himself but that the events . . . were a delusion of his brain.' As he puzzled over the disappearance, he became aware that his brother's companion had been dressed exactly as his brother, 'in precisely the same attire as John, even down to the white waistcoat'. Grimaldi and his friends could only conclude that John must have been 'lured into some infamous den . . . and afterwards either murdered in cold blood or slain in some desperate struggle to recover his gold' (134, 138, 140).

'His advantage in all this

Mr. Jacob Kibble]   Dickens listed the name 'Kibble' in his *Book of Memoranda*.

'He had carried under his arm

I was to buy slops.]   In *DS* Dickens mentioned the waterside slop-sellers' shops, 'with Guernsey shirts, sou'wester hats, and canvass pantaloons, at once the tightest and the loosest of their order, hanging up outside' (9).

'I had drank some coffee

I saw a figure like myself lying dressed in my clothes on a bed.]   MS and proof read: 'I saw myself lying dressed in my clothes on a bed.'

'What would I have? Dead, I have found

I have found them, when they might have slighted my name and passed greedily over my grave . . . lingering by the way, like single-hearted children] In Wordsworth's poem 'We Are Seven', which Dickens admired, a little girl will not believe that her brother and sister, who are buried in the churchyard where she is sitting, are dead:

> 'But they are dead; those two are dead!
> Their spirits are in heaven!'
> 'Twas throwing words away; for still
> The little Maid would have her will,
> And said, 'Nay, we are seven!' (65–9)

She was on a low ottoman

a little shining jewel of a table] In *BH* Lady Dedlock has 'a golden talisman of a table' at her elbow (2). There were several styles of small circular pedestal table in the nineteenth century which were intended for ornament rather than use on account of their highly decorated surfaces. The surfaces might be of boulle (a form of marquetry produced with thin tortoiseshell), inlaid mother-of-pearl, papier mâché, or perhaps mosaic. In *LD* the guests at Merdle's are described 'marrying golden liqueur glasses to Buhl tables' (2.12).

Book 2, Chapter 14   Tenth monthly number
                                          February 1865

STRONG OF PURPOSE.

'I don't know whether

books of African Travel] In 1848, Dickens had reviewed the *Narrative of the Expedition Sent by Her Majesty's Government to the River Niger in 1841, under the Command of Captain H. D. Trotter, RN*, by Captain William Allen and T. R. H. Thomson, MD, 2 volumes (1848) ('The Niger Expedition', *MP*). His criticisms of the expedition underlie the satire on the Borrioboola-Gha project in *BH*. Dickens mentioned a number of African kings in the article, all of whom failed to keep their treaties with the expedition. King Obi, 'one of the falsest rascals in Africa', is described dressed in 'a sergeant-major's coat . . . and a loose pair of scarlet trousers . . . and a black velvet hat'. In his *Book of Memoranda* Dickens made the note

<By> Buying poor shabby – FATHER? – a new hat. So incongruous, that it makes him like African King Boy, or King George; ∧ who is ∧ usually full dressed in a cocked hat or *a* waistcoat – and nothing else. (1)

'I was going to say

a London hat only, or a Manchester pair of braces]   A 'London hat' was probably one of the styles of the popular top hat. 'Manchester' braces were of ordinary cotton, rather than, say, embroidered silk or indiarubber. 'Manchester' was used in the names of various cotton goods produced there.

'Not in this case, Mr. Rokesmith.

league and covenant]   A common legal phrase, best remembered from the Solemn League and Covenant for the suppression of Popery adopted by the Scottish Parliament in 1638.

'Now lookee here, my dear

the poor old people that they brick up in them Unions . . . crawling quite scared about the streets.]   In *LD* old Nandy is described 'creeping along with a scared air' after coming out of the workhouse (1.31). In the *Daily Telegraph* report Ruskin introduced into *Sesame and Lilies* (1865), a witness explained why she and her husband would not go into the workhouse for winter: ' "When we come out in the summer we should be like people dropped from the sky" ' (Cook and Wedderburn 18.93).

I'm a good fair knitter, and can make many little things to sell.]   Mayhew recorded many cases of old people who were street sellers, 'some of the old people being lame or suffering from some infirmity, which, however, does not prevent their walking about with their commodities' (1.145). Women street sellers sold lace and millinery, stockings they had knitted themselves, bootlaces and other small articles.

get my own bread by my own labour.]   Genesis 3.19: 'In the sweat of thy face shalt thou eat bread, till thou return unto the ground.'

'Yes, my deary, but not through letter-writing

letter-writing – indeed, writing of most sorts – hadn't much come up for such as me when I was young.]   The literacy rate in the early part of the century was probably about two-thirds for men, half for women. A parliamentary committee in 1816 estimated that 120,000 London children were entirely without education facilities. Such schools as there were – charity schools and dame schools (see *GE*) – often provided only the rudiments of an education (Lawson and Silver, 1973, 236–7).

Mrs Higden goes into the country – <u>Yes</u>

Declaration scene between Bradley ⎤
and Lizzie ⎦ <u>Yes</u>

Mrs Lammle and Twemlow. <u>Yes</u>. To conclude
the <u>book</u> <u>II</u>

Veneering, Tippins, Boots and Brewer.

Chapter XIV.
Strong of purpose

Gather up Boffin Threads.

    Mrs Higden in her independence goes away

    Patrons and Vice Patrons

Chapter XV.
The Whole Case so far

<City church at>

City churchyard at dusk.

    Bradley Headstone's love

> His hand upon the coping wrenching at it while he speaks

'You could draw me to fire –   Declared

           water   Rejected

           Gallows   Brother renounces Sister

        what not!'

Riah on the scene and glimpses of Eugene:

  Leading on to disappearance.

Chapter XVI.
An Anniversary Occasion.

The Lammles' Wedding Day – First anniversary

    Back to the man from somewhere. Lightwood

                 Lizzie's Disappearance

                 Book of Portraits

Mrs Lammles to Twemlow   Shut the book

The End of The Second Book

The Secretary took that opportunity

a wonderful cabinet-maker]   A small group of six or seven hundred of London's cabinet-makers produced high-quality work while the majority of four or five thousand supplied the mass market. The skilled minority earned perhaps thirty to forty shillings a week, with fair regularity of employment and decent conditions of work (J. F. C. Harrison, 1979, 47).

a foreign monkey's musical instrument.]   Organ-grinding was the livelihood of innumerable Continental immigrants who had begun to arrive in London following Waterloo. There were a few Savoyard and Tyrolean grinders, but the great majority were Italian. Grinders frequently kept a monkey on top of their portable organ. Alternatively, the grinder would play the tabor or a tin whistle while the monkey ground the organ.

'No, no, no,' said Mr. Boffin; 'no patronizing!

no patronizing!]   It appears from the *OED* that the modern senses of 'patronize' and 'patronizing' (condescend and condescending) emerged in the period 1820–40, and are thus a sign of a developing middle-class sentiment. Compare, for example, Hazlitt, *Lectures on Dramatic Literature* (1820): 'Feeling much the same awkward condescending disposition to patronise these first crude attempts'; Scott, *The Fair Maid of Perth* (1828): 'The knight . . . received them with a mixture of courtesy and patronising condescension'; Disraeli, *Sybil* (1845): 'Spruce . . . had a weakness for the aristocracy, who . . . patronized him with condescending dexterity.' In Hazlitt and Disraeli the idea of the patron, respectively of the arts and of a business (Spruce is a bookmaker), is still present. Dickens draws 'patronize' and 'patronizing' into the context of charity patrons, so that the pronunciation must be uncertain (does Boffin say 'I don't want to be Pātronized'?). The most recent use of the verb 'to patron' (pātron) in the *OED* before *OMF* is from 1643 ('Wiser Princes Patron the Arts').

Dickens did not share Tennyson's idealized view of the 'great broad-shouldered genial Englishman,/ . . . A patron of some thirty charities' (*The Princess*, 'Conclusion', 85, 88). Rather, Dickens's view was of the middle classes patronizing the working classes whilst themselves being patronized by their temporary elevation to the role of patrons alongside the names of the aristocracy (see the use of the name of the Duke of Linseed in book 1, chapter 17). The subject repeatedly calls forth an angry response from Dickens in his letters, speeches and journalism. For instance, in 1858 he wrote in response to the request to become a patron:

> I must beg to be excused from complying with the request you do me the honour to prefer, simply because I have a great objection to patronize anything, and hold the opinion that there is a great deal too much patronage in England. (*Nonesuch* 3.52)

In the late 1850s and 1860s, Dickens's particular concern was the independence of working men's clubs.

'I don't. And if they do, my dear

Mr. Tom Noakes . . . Mrs. Jack Styles]   Noakes and Styles are fictitious names used to fill blanks in legal documents.

'Warm!' cried Mr. Boffin. 'It's enough to make a man

Pills, or Hair-Washes, or Invigorating Nervous Essences, to be puffed]   The most famous of the advertised pills was Morrison's Pill, which Carlyle used as an image of the easy remedy in *Past and Present* (see pp. 240–1). Morrison, who called himself the 'Hygeist', and his shop the 'British College of Health', frequently advertised his 'vegetable universal medicine' in the monthly parts of Dickens's novels as did other manufacturers of quack medicines.

'As to the letter, Rokesmith

'you're right as a trivet]   'Thoroughly or perfectly right', referring to a trivet's always standing firm on its three feet.

Book 2, Chapter 15

THE WHOLE CASE SO FAR.

A grey dusty withered evening in London city

a sun-dial on a church-wall]   There is a sundial on the wall of the church of St Katherine Cree, on the north side of Leadenhall Street.

melancholy waifs and strays]

Among the finders there is perhaps the greatest poverty existing, they being the very lowest class of all the street-people. Many of the very old live on the hard dry crusts they pick up out of the roads in the course of their rounds, washing them and steeping them in water before they eat them. (Mayhew 2.138)

dismal Newgate seems quite as fit a stronghold for the mighty Lord Mayor as his own state-dwelling.]   Newgate Prison, 'a grim stone building' (*GE* 20) with 'rough heavy walls and low massive doors' ('Criminal Courts', *SB*), stood at the corner of the Old Bailey and Newgate Street. The official residence of the Lord Mayor is Mansion House, a substantial building with a grand portico and a massive rough-hewn basement. In *CC* Dickens referred to 'The Lord Mayor, in the stronghold of the mighty Mansion House' (1).

'Yes. We are going to walk with you.

Here's a large paved court by this church] The church of St Peter's, Cornhill.

She had not released his hand

a churchyard . . . conveniently and healthfully elevated above the level of the living] Dickens frequently criticized the unwholesome and overcrowded city graveyards, such as that in *NN* where the dead lie 'cheek by jowl with life: no deeper down than the feet of the throng that passed there, everyday, and piled high as their throats' (62), and such as that where Nemo is buried in *BH* (11).

'Not yet. It shall and must be

Here is a man lighting the lamps.] Gas lighting was introduced on to the streets of London in the first decades of the nineteenth century. The lamplighter was still employed.

'Pardon me, young woman

I cannot pass upon my way] Riah's words recall the parable of the Good Samaritan in Luke 10.30–7; the priest and the Levite 'passed by on the other side'.

'He is a thankless dog

Shake the dust from thy feet] Matthew 10.14: 'And whosoever shall not receive you, nor hear your words, when ye depart out of that house or city, shake off the dust of your feet.'

'But, Lizzie, I came expressly

lingering about . . . like a bailiff] Waiting to take possession of a person or property in a case of debt; Jews were often employed in this capacity.

an old clothesman.] German and Polish Jews who came to England in the eighteenth century to escape persecution continued the activities forced upon them by Continental restrictions on their participation in trade and manufacture: dealing in old clothes and peddling. The second-hand clothing business played an important part in London's economy before the development of cheap clothing in the nineteenth century, and the Jewish old-clothes man was a picturesque and familiar figure. Carlyle used the figure of the old-clothes man to comment on the spiritual condition of nations in his *Latter-Day Pamphlets*:

> Did you never hear, with the mind's ear as well, that fateful Hebrew Prophecy, I think the fatefullest of all, which sounds daily through the streets, 'Ou'clo'!

Ou'clo'!' – A certain People, once upon a time, clamorously voted by an over-whelming majority, 'Not *he*; Barabbas, not he! . . .' Well, they got Barabbas; and . . . at this hour, after eighteen centuries of sad fortune, they prophetically sing 'Ou'clo'!' in all the cities of the world. Might the world, at this late hour, but take note of them, and understand their song a little! ('The Present Time')

'Mysteries of Udolpho!'

'Mysteries of Udolpho!']   The famous Gothic novel by Mrs Radcliffe, published in 1794.

'If Mr. Aaron,' said Eugene

Mr. Aaron]   Aaron was the brother of Moses and the first high priest. The name was commonly applied to Jews: ' "Vy don't you talk to your partner, or Saint Giles, if you vant conversation, Aaron?" ' (Ainsworth, *Jack Shepherd*, 1839, 2.12); 'Jew Money-Lenders are numerous as the hairs in Aaron's beard' (Douglas Jerrold, 'The Money-Lender', in *Heads of the People*, 1841, 24).

Book 2, Chapter 16

AN ANNIVERSARY OCCASION.

The estimable Twemlow

the noble animals at livery.]   A horse is 'at livery' when it is kept for the owner, and fed and groomed at a fixed charge; Twemlow requires a servant *in* livery to attend him.

come up and come over]   An ostler's expression used to an animal when it is required to move.

How the fascinating Tippins gets on

arraying herself for the bewilderment of the senses of men]   Perhaps a recollection of Pope, *The Rape of the Lock*: 'This Nymph, to the Destruction of Mankind,/Nourish'd two Locks, which graceful hung behind' (2.19–20). In the poem, Belinda's cosmetic preparations are assisted by 'busy *Sylphs*' as well as by her maid, so that 'Betty's prais'd for Labours not her own' (1.145, 148).

a diurnal species of lobster]   Lobsters shed their shells about every six months, the exact rate depending on water temperature and other factors.

It is the first anniversary

that magnificent Tartar issued the ukase]   'Ukase' derives from the Russian for 'a decree or edict having the force of law'.

Ah! my Twemlow! Say, little feeble grey personage

to stand in the wintry slush giving the hack horses to drink out of the shallow tub]   Like a waterman who attends the horses at a hackney-coach stand. The water was carried in shallow tubs with rope-and-leather handles.

And dear Mrs. Lammle and dear Mr. Lammle

Guy, Earl of Warwick, you know – what is it? – Dun Cow – to claim the flitch of bacon?]   Guy, Earl of Warwick was a hero of romance supposed to have lived in Saxon times. One of his adventures was to overcome the famous Dun Cow, greater in size than an elephant. The Dunmow flitch of bacon, awarded to 'whatever married couple . . . will swear they have not quarrelled nor repented of their marriage within a year and a day after its celebration', was instituted in 1244. The first flitch was awarded in 1445 (Hill).

that stifling place night after night]   There were galleries for visitors and for reporters over the north end of the House of Commons, but the Commons was 'too small for the proper accommodation of the whole body of members, to say nothing of "strangers" ' (Wheatley and Cunningham 2.242).

Veneering, why don't *you* prose]   Dickens began his 'Parliamentary Sketch' in *SB* by assuring his readers that he had not 'the slightest intention of being more prosy than usual'. Veneering has yet to make his maiden speech, traditionally understood to be a test of character.

'It's like,' impatiently interrupts Eugene

I'll tell you a story/Of Jack a Manory]   A nursery rhyme of which the first recorded version is dated 1760. The name varies from version to version.

Eugene says this with a sound of vexation

her dear Bear . . . she . . . is Beauty, and he Beast.]   The fairy-tale of 'Beauty and the Beast', the best-known version of which appeared in the French *Contes* of Mme. de Villeneuve (1744). The Beast is sometimes represented as bear-like, and a 'bear' is someone who is bad-tempered, rough.

Tippins, with a bewitching little scream

we shall every one of us be murdered in our beds.]   'The Metropolitan

Protectives', a *HW* article by Dickens and W. H. Wills, begins with an account of the silly fears of people at the time of the Great Exhibition:

> It would appear that no words can express our fearful condition, so well, as Mr. Croaker's in 'The Good Natured Man.' 'I am so frightened,' says he, 'that I scarce know whether I sit, stand, or go . . . Murder! We shall all be burnt in our beds!' (3.97)

The quotation is from the fourth act of Goldsmith's *The Good-Natured Man* (1768).

However, the great subject

the Parliamentary sing-song]   In 'A Few Conventionalities' (*MP*) Dickens asked:

> why, why, above all, in either house of parliament must the English language be set to music – bad and conventional beyond any parallel on earth – and delivered, in a manner barely expressible to the eye as follows:

⌒
night
_____

to
_____

Sir when I came do   this house
_____

o
_____

o
_____

wn to
⌣   *ters*
Minis
_____

ty's
_____

I found Her   jes
_____

_____

_____

Ma
⌣

while memory holds her seat.]   *Hamlet* 1.5.95–7:

> Remember thee!
> Ay, thou poor ghost, whiles memory holds a seat
> In this distracted globe.

191

Seeing no better way out of it

pulls up his oratorical Pegasus]   Pegasus, the winged horse of Greek mythology, traditionally represents poetic inspiration.

Intensely astonished, Twemlow puts his hand

if the Genie of the cheek would only answer to his rubbing.]   In the story of 'Aladdin and the Wonderful Lamp' in the *Arabian Nights*, Aladdin is able to make a genie appear to carry out his commands by rubbing a magic lamp.

In the drawing-room, groups form as usual

a book of portraits]   The richly bound photograph-albums of the day contained portraits not only of family and friends but also of contemporary celebrities. *Punch* thought portrait-albums 'among the prettiest of the many pretty playthings for grown-up people in these latter days' (47.167).

Then good-bye and good-bye

charming occasion worthy of the Golden Age]   The legendary age in history when life was ideal.

nearly run down by a flushed letter-cart]   As though it, too, has been celebrating; the flush is the red colour of the Royal Mail (Hill).

BOOK THE THIRD.
A LONG LANE.

The proverb is 'It is a long lane that has no turning'. The title of book 4 is 'A Turning'.

Book 3, Chapter 1
Eleventh monthly number
March 1865

LODGERS IN QUEER STREET.

'Queer Street' is an imaginary street where people in financial difficulties are supposed to reside.

It was a foggy day in London

with a haggard and unblest air, as knowing themselves to be night-creatures that had no business abroad under the sun]   In *Hamlet* the ghost disappears when the cock's crow announces daylight (1.1.152–5).

the sun itself . . . showed as if it had gone out and were collapsing flat and cold]   The 'nebular hypothesis' of Laplace (1749–1827) and the work of Kelvin (1824–1907) and others on the dissipation of energy had established the idea that the sun was cooling and that the solar system would in time be reduced to dead matter whirling in space. Tennyson referred to the prospect in the third section of *In Memoriam*: 'From out waste places comes a cry, / And murmurs from the dying sun' (7–8).

the whole metropolis was a heap of vapour]   A suggestion of Hamlet's words: 'this most excellent canopy the air . . . appeareth no other thing to me than a foul and pestilent congregation of vapours' (2.2.300–5).

With another comfortable plunge

Turkish slippers, rose-coloured Turkish trousers . . . and a gown and cap to correspond. . . . further fitted out with a bottomless chair, a lantern, and a bunch of matches.]   In *NN* the fashionable gallant Mantalini wears such a

Position of affairs at the end of the Second Book ($-$ N$^{\underline{o}}$ X).

Lizzie has disappeared, by the aid of the good Jew: leaving as to that part of the story:

> Eugene
>
> The Dolls' Dress Maker
>
> Mr bad child
>
> Bradley Headstone (and Charley?)
>
> Miss Peecher

John Harmon is known to the reader, and involves on to that part of the story:

> Bella
>
> Mr and Mrs Boffin

With the Bower are concerned:

> The Dustmounds
>
> The friendly move between Silas Wegg and Venus
>
> Check-mate on the part of Harmon and Sloppy

With the chorus, rest:

> Humbug, Social and Parliamentary
>
> Twemlow's promise as to Georgiana
>
> Mrs Lammle's development
>
>> Fledgeby's use of power.

There remain, besides, for implements and otherwise:

>> The Wilfers (notably Rumty)
>>
>> George Sampson
>>
>> Riah
>>
>>> Betty Higden
>>>
>>> Lightwood
>>>
>>> Riderhood and his daughter
>>>
>>> The Six Jolly fellowships. $-$ Miss Abbey Potterson
>>>> $-$ Job Potterson
>>>> $-$ Jacob Kibble

Book The Third: A Long Lane

Chapter I.

Lodgers in Queer Street.

Fledgeby's chambers. Fog.

  Riah Lammle

Work up < on > and on

Lizzie Hexam's disappearance

Chapter II.

An < old > respected friend in a new aspect

Dolls' Dress Maker and Riah

  The Great Ladies 'trying on' the dolls' dresses

  To the Fellowship Porters

The litter bumping at the door

  Riderhood brought in, drowned

Chapter III.

The same ∧respected∧ friend in more aspects than one

Process of recovery

  while it is a struggling spark of life, it is not Riderhood

  when it animates Riderhood, it is Riderhood

As if he had had a Fight!   Goes out of the Ring

Chapter IV.

A happy return of the Day.

Mr and Mrs Wilfer's Wedding Day

      Mr George Sampson

Work up to Bella's account of the change in Mr Boffin – broken

to the reader through her –   Mercenary Bella, Money, money, money

Lay the ground very carefully all through

négligé outfit: 'He was dressed in a gorgeous morning gown, with a waistcoat and Turkish trousers of the same pattern, a pink silk neckerchief, and bright green slippers' (10). The fashion for such clothing owed something to the cult of eastern romance associated with the poetry of Byron and Thomas Moore. Two residents of the Albany, Byron and Bulwer, cultivated eastern dress; Bulwer, an admirer of the poet, took what had been Byron's rooms; another literary figure with a taste for eastern dress, Disraeli, negotiated for the same rooms after Bulwer quitted them. The bottomless chair, lantern and bunch of matches would suit Fledgeby because he looks a 'guy': a grotesquely dressed person, a fright. Effigies of Guy Fawkes, which appeared in the streets around 5 November, were equipped with these appurtenances.

'I suppose,' he said, taking one up

what sweating a pound means]   Fledgeby refers to the process of lightening a gold coin by wearing away its substance by friction or attrition.

Mr. Fledgeby was thus amiably engaged

you Pump of Israel]   A 'pump' is colloquially a solemn, foolish, tearful person. In the Bible the Jews are 'the children of Israel'.

'Mr. Riah is bound to observe

made and provided]   A legal phrase.

Mr. Fledgeby took it, saying

Regular flayers and grinders]   In commercial parlance a 'flayer' is someone who strips someone of money or assets by extortion or exaction, a 'grinder' one who makes others work for him at low wages. Fledgeby's language here and below suggests the fates of certain Christian martyrs: St Bartholomew, for instance, is supposed to have been flayed alive.

'Now, old 'un,' proceeded Fledgeby

old 'un]   One of the nicknames of the devil is 'the old one'.

you'd be peppered and salted and grilled on a gridiron]   St Lawrence is supposed to have been slowly roasted to death on a gridiron. Dickens saw 'the gridiron of Saint Lawrence, and the stone below it, marked with the frying of his fat and blood' in Rome ('Rome', *PI*).

'You can't be a gallivanting dodger

you're a regular "pity the sorrows," you know]   Fledgeby alludes to the opening lines of 'The Beggar's Petition', by the Reverend Thomas Moss:

> Pity the Sorrows of a poor old Man!
>   Whose trembling Limbs have borne him to your Door,
> Whose Days are dwindled to the shortest Span,
>   Oh! give Relief – and Heav'n will bless your Store.
> (*Poems on Several Occasions*, 1769)

'The Beggar's Petition' was printed on the moral pocket handkerchiefs to which the elder Mr Weller objects in *PP* (27).

'Cut away,' said Fledgeby

'Start with your motive.']   In *DC* it is Mr Wickfield's failing to be always ' "fishing for motives" ' (15). Dickens was doubtless aware of the frequent use of the word in the writings of utilitarians, particularly in those of Bentham.

With this apostrophe Mr. Fledgeby

anointing of himself with the last infallible preparation for the production of luxuriant and glossy hair]   Quack preparations abounded: for instance, Edward's 'Harlene' was advertised as the 'world-renowned hair producer and restorer. Produces Luxuriant Hair, Whiskers, and Moustaches'; and Latreille & Son offered 'Valuable Hints specially worth reading by Every Person Desirous of Producing Whiskers and Moustachios' (de Vries, 1968, 54, 57).

Book 3, Chapter 2

A RESPECTED FRIEND IN A NEW ASPECT.

Miss Wren expected him

she came to the door . . . aiding her steps with a little crutch-stick.]   The MS continues: 'like that of the little halting old woman who came out of the chest by night, to terrify the merchant Abudah into going in search of the Talisman of Oromanes'. This was an allusion to 'The Talisman of Oromanes; or, The History of the Merchant Abudah' in James Ridley's *The Tales of the Genii*. In the *UT* essay 'Nurses' Stories' Dickens described the fascination this story continued to have for him: 'I was never (thank Heaven) in company with the little old woman who hobbled out of the chest and told the merchant Abudah to go in search of the

Talisman of Oromanes, yet I make it my business to know that she is well preserved and as intolerable as ever.'

'Good evening, godmother!'

'Good evening, godmother!'] The story of Cinderella is from Perrault. Cinderella is ill-treated by her stepmother and stepsisters. Her fairy godmother provides her with beautiful clothes, a coach made from a pumpkin, and six horses, which are transformed mice. Thus equipped, she goes to the ball and meets the prince.

'Well!' exclaimed Miss Wren, delighted.

If we gave prizes at this establishment (but we only keep blanks), you should have the first silver medal] Medals were given as rewards for intellectual and moral achievement by schools, by other educational institutions, and by various associations and societies (including temperance societies). Jenny may also be thinking of lotteries: 'They tell you enough about the great prizes, which very few can gain, but you hear nothing about the numerous blanks' (Copley, 1825, 57).

'Yes, it was truly sharp of you

the bright little books!] Dickens had a life-long affection for fairy-tales and frequently referred to them in his writings. Amongst his earliest reading had been the chapbooks hawked by pedlars which included the old fairy-tales about Jack the Giant-Killer, Bluebeard, Beauty and the Beast, Cinderella, Dick Whittington, the Wandering Jew, and many others. In his *HW* article 'Frauds on the Fairies' he argued that 'in an utilitarian age, of all other times, it is a matter of grave importance that Fairy tales should be respected . . . the little books, nurseries of fancy as they are, should be preserved' (*MP*).

'Dangerous, godmother? My bad child

setting the house on fire] Jenny's fears are appropriate to her father's condition, but they are also like those of a parent: Lizzie recalls the times 'when father was away at work and locked us out, for fear we should set ourselves afire' (1.3).

mind your Commandments and honor your parent] The Fifth Commandment: 'Honour thy father and thy mother' (Exodus 20.12).

'Yes, and then — you know, godmother.

Is it better to have had a good thing and lost it, or never to have had it?'] Probably an allusion to the well-known lines from Tennyson's *In Memoriam* (1850), a poem which Dickens admired:

I hold it true, whate'er befall;
  I feel it, when I sorrow most;
  'Tis better to have loved and lost
Than never to have loved at all. (27.13–16)

'What a mooney godmother you are

There's a Drawing Room, or a grand day in the Park, or a Show, or a Fête]   The London Season coincided with the parliamentary session from Easter to August. Country gentlemen came to town, and ladies had an opportunity to show themselves and their daughters off. Events of the Season included balls, banquets, fêtes, the opera and, above all, the four drawing-rooms held by the queen for the presentation of débutantes 'coming out' in Society for the first time. These were afternoons at which everyone wore full evening dress, and the queues of aristocratic carriages in the Mall on drawing-room day were a popular spectacle. It was the practice to leave the blinds of the carriages up, so the young débutantes remained exposed to the public gaze.

a wax one, with her toes turned in.']   Only the most expensive dolls were made of wax; cheaper dolls were made of leather or coarse linen stuff.

'But first of all,' said Miss Abbey

shrub]   Made with the juice of orange or lemon (or other acid fruit), sugar, and rum (or other spirit) mixed with water.

'You shall try. And, if you find it good

enough to make wigs for all the dolls in the world.]   In the *HW* article 'Dolls': 'the dolls' peruquier is not idle; he is at work on the beautiful ringlets, and perhaps eye-brows and eye-lashes; he employs real human hair, and is not unworthy of the rank of a wig-maker' (7.353).

'Tell 'em to put on all the kettles!'

Heat some stone bottles.]   Stoneware bottles used as hot-water bottles, sometimes with one side concave to fit the body.

Boats were putting off

the unpopular steamer]   Steamboats were introduced on to the Thames in 1814. By the 1860s there was a great volume of traffic. The steamboats were unpopular with the waterside community at the best of times because their introduction had greatly diminished the number of watermen and because their speed and swell made life on the river more dangerous. A waterman told Mayhew: 'many of us watermen saved money then, but now we're starving . . . steamers came in, and we were wrecked' (3.327).

the Murderer, bound for Gallows Bay . . . the Manslaughterer, bound for Penal Settlement]   The steamboat is identified with one of its possible cargoes, convicted prisoners being transported to the penal settlements in Australia and elsewhere (though transportation virtually ended in 1852). Murderers were normally executed in England. 'Gallows Bay', on the model of Botany Bay, is formed by the association of two forms of punishment: hanging and transportation. No place of that name existed.

burning blue-lights. These made a luminous patch about her]   Flares were made by firing a tar-barrel, powder or other combustible material.

'That's the stretcher, or the shutter

the shutter]   A litter or stretcher improvised from a window shutter.

Book 3, Chapter 3

THE SAME RESPECTED FRIEND IN MORE ASPECTS THAN ONE.

The doctor-seeking messenger

The doctor-seeking messenger]   Mock-Homeric.

the spark of life within him is curiously separable from himself now]   The idea that there was a principle of life, a vital spark or fire, which distinguished the animate from the inanimate, was common in poetry of earlier centuries. Though increasingly discredited among nineteenth-century scientists (see p. 107), it still had some scientific advocates.

Captain Joey, the bottle-nosed

the body should be hung up by the heels . . . and should then . . . be rolled upon casks.]   In her remarks on first aid, Esther Copley thought it necessary to warn against the ideas of the old school about treatment in cases of drowning: 'All violent and rough usage is to be avoided, such as shaking the body, rolling it over a cask, holding it up by the heels, also rubbing it with salt or spirits, or injecting the smoke of tobacco' (1825, 152).

Mr. Riderhood next demands

exactly as if he had just had a Fight.]   In *UT* Dickens described a visit to the Paris Morgue:

This time, I was forced into the same dread place, to see a large dark man whose disfigurement by water was in a frightful manner comic, and whose expression was that of a prize-fighter who had closed his eyelids under a heavy blow, but was immediately going to open them, shake his head, and 'come up smiling.' Oh what this large dark man cost me in that bright city! (7).

Also in *UT*, Dickens mentioned an 'offensive' young man he encountered on the way to Wapping Workhouse:

with a puffed sallow face, and a figure all dirty and shiny and slimy, who may have been the youngest son of a filthy old father, Thames, or the drowned man about whom there was a placard on the granite post like a large thimble, that stood between us. (3)

Book 3, Chapter 4

A HAPPY RETURN OF THE DAY.

Mr. and Mrs. Wilfer had seen

kept morally, rather as a Fast than a Feast]   An allusion to the designation of the days in the Church of England calendar: a section of the Book of Common Prayer is entitled 'Tables and Rules for the Feasts and Fasts through the whole Year'.

The revolving year now bringing

The revolving year]   The phrase occurs in Shelley's *Adonais* (155 and 472); Moore's translation of Anacreon's Ode 25 begins: 'Once in each revolving year,/ Gentle bird! we find thee here.' In *MED* Miss Twinkleton says: ' "Ladies, another revolving year has brought us round to that festive period" ' (13).

a plum-pudding carriage dog with as uncomfortable a collar on as if he had been George the Fourth]   Both the spotted Great Dane and the Dalmatian were known as plum-pudding or carriage dogs. They were trained to trot with the entourage of horse and carriage. Carriage dogs were especially fashionable in the early part of the century: Dickens compares the dog's collar to the high collar, worn with a cravat, which was part of the dress of the Regency dandy.

Yet she had sufficient curiosity

stands of books, English, French, and Italian]   Harmon was educated in Brussels (1.2). The knowledge of modern languages distinguishes him from a public-school boy, like Richard Carstone in *BH*, who can 'make Latin verses of several sorts', but is ill-equipped for the world: modern languages were regarded as important qualifications for commerce.

'But what,' said Bella, as she watched

what . . . makes them pink inside]   Making the point that 'Great would be the advantage to the community, if cookery were made a branch of female education', a *HW* article about 'Common Things' (see p. 139) complained of 'poultry rendered . . . tempting to the eye, till dissection reveals red and uncooked joints' (1.140).

So, the gridiron was put in requisition

often as un-cherubically employed . . . as if he had been in the employ-ment of some of the Old Masters. . . . staring about him (a branch of the public service to which the pictorial cherub is much addicted) . . . performing on enormous wind instruments and double-basses . . . fore-shortening himself in the air]   There is a witty allusion to the 'HOW NOT TO DO IT' (*LD*, 1.10) tendencies of government departments. Dickens would have remembered the famous frescoes by Correggio in the Duomo in Parma which he had dismissed as 'a labyrinth of arms and legs' in *PI* ('To Parma, Modena, and Bologna'); among the flying figures are many strikingly foreshortened youthful angels and cherubs, some playing flutes, horns, cymbals and tambourines; one cherub appears to be playing a stringed instrument like a double bass.

'Would you take a merry-thought

a merry-thought]   The merrythought is the portion of the chicken which contains the wishbone.

'Your grandpapa,' retorted Mrs. Wilfer

a tall member of society . . . the weakness . . . of King Frederick of Prussia.']   Carlyle had described 'that unique giant regiment, of which the world has heard so much in a vague half-mythical way. The giant-regiment was not a myth, however, but a big-boned expensive Fact.' The Potsdam Giant Regiment, which was in fact formed by Frederick's father, Friederich Wilhelm, contained some 2,400 men: 'the shortest man of them rises . . . towards seven feet, some are nearly nine feet high' (*History of Frederick the Great*, 1858–65, 5.5).

Book 3, Chapter 5 Twelfth monthly number
April 1865

THE GOLDEN DUSTMAN FALLS INTO BAD COMPANY.

Dickens derived this part of the plot of *OMF* from another play by Knowles, *The Hunchback*, first performed at Covent Garden in 1832. Fanny Kemble, in her first triumph in comedy, played the part of Julia, a girl from the country, who is taken to London. She rapidly becomes vain and mercenary, and quarrels with her intended husband, Clifford, who has been disappointed of the riches he expected to inherit. To win her back to good-heartedness, the hunchback, Master Walter, who is her guardian, pretends to encourage her designs to make a mercenary marriage. Here he recommends a rich suitor:

> Is this a lover? Look! Three thousand pounds
> Per annum for your private charges! Ha!
> There's pin-money! Is this a lover? Mark
> What acres, forests, tenements, are tax'd
> For your revenue; and so set apart
> That finger cannot touch them, save thine own.
> Is this a lover? (3.2)

Clifford appears before Julia as the secretary of the rich man she had intended to marry. They are reconciled. By this time Julia's estimate of wealth has changed ('Wealth – a feather!'), but at the conclusion of the play Clifford is shown to be rich again. Master Walter turns out to be her father. Dickens had a copy of the 1832 edition of *The Hunchback* in his library at Gad's Hill; autographed 'Charles Dickens, July 1832', it was a well-read copy with a few manuscript notes apparently by Dickens himself.

'Don't be above calling it wages

'Don't be above calling it wages] The word 'salary', as opposed to 'wages', was normally used of the remittance for non-manual or non-mechanical work; even overseers or clerks in a factory were said to draw a salary.

'I don't say, you know,' Mr. Boffin stipulated

the duties of property] A much-used phrase, originally from Thomas Drummond's *Letter to the Landlords of Tipperary* (22 May 1838): 'Property has its duties as well as its rights.' In the view Boffin is assuming, the duty is ' "to other men of property" '.

Mr Boffin

    Wegg?   **Yes**

    Venus?

Work the Lammles into the Boffins' house?   **Yes**

Mr Wegg's unspeakable affection for Mr Venus.

Chapter V.

The Golden Dustman falls into bad company

Mr Boffin and Rokesmith and Mrs Boffin, having, unknown to the reader,
arranged their plan, now strike in with it

    She always touched and < sore? > hurt by even the pretended

    change in her husband. Can't bear Bella to see him so.

Work in The < Misers > Misers – to bring out his pretended love of money

Lay the ground for Mrs Lammle

Bella at war with herself.

> Keep Bella watching and
> never suspecting

Chapter VI.

The Golden Dustman falls into still worse company

The Bower, and Wegg and Venus

               Wegg trying to jockey Venus.

More books – and the misers – and about hidden wiles

    relieve by making Wegg as comic as possible

Mr Boffin and the Mounds, and the Bottle he digs up

The Mounds begin to go.

Chapter VII

The friendly move takes up a strong position.

Mr Wegg's discovery   (reserved from Venus until forced out)

        Scene between them how it shall be used against

        Mr Boffin: – 'Wait till the Mounds are gone.'

Venus's love is Pleasant
      Riderhood

> all the property left to the Crown. This
> the last-dated will.

'In bygone days, when I was in service

in service] The phrase was normally used of domestic servants. In this vein Boffin talks of being able to ring a bell for Harmon, and lodges him in a room at the top of the house, the location of the servants' quarters.

'I have let that chap, that young man of mine

that young man of mine] The phrase 'young man' was normally used of youths employed by tradesmen, as in *SB*: 'Mr. Todd's young man over the way, is . . . taking down his master's shutters' ('The Streets – Morning').

'Says too!' cried Mr. Boffin. 'Whatever he says!

There's a golden ball at your feet.] A symbol of the highest rank, as in Tennyson's *In Memoriam*: 'To him who grasps a golden ball,/By blood a king' (111.3–4).

Bella, thus directed, would examine

the Annual Register . . . Mr. Boffin at once bought a whole set] The *Annual Register* was founded in 1758 by Edmund Burke and Robert Dodsley (1703–64) and has continued ever since. Dickens had the volumes from 1758 to 1860 in his library.

It very soon became unnecessary

the ardour of Don Quixote for his books of chivalry] The hero of Cervantes's novel (published in two parts in 1605 and 1615) is addicted to romances of chivalry and, as a result, loses his wits and attempts to become a knight errant himself.

Mrs. Lammle took the friendliest interest

a compound of fine girl, thorough-bred horse, well-built drag, and remarkable pipe.] As *Punch* cartoons suggest, the habit of pipe-smoking gained ground in the 1860s. A 'drag' was a private vehicle resembling a stage-coach, usually drawn by four horses, with seats inside and on the top.

'Hold your tongue!' said Mr. Boffin

the Life of Mr. Elwes?'] John Elwes was the son of a Southwark brewer and grandson of a Member of Parliament. His mother was a miser and, left a widow with a hundred thousand pounds, starved herself to death. His uncle Sir Harvey Elwes was a miser. When he visited him, John would dress in a suit of rags to please the old man. In this he succeeded, for he was left a quarter of a million pounds, though by then he had already amassed that much himself. He was not a complete miser like Dancer: he involved himself in the financial speculation of the day; built much of the district around Portland Place and Portman Square; gambled for high stakes; and was an excellent horseman and kept a stable and hounds. Though there are instances of his generosity, it was said that he never had his shoes cleaned for fear this would wear them out; that he collected stray chips and bones; and that he ate rank meat, including, on one occasion, a complete dead sheep. He died in 1789 and left a property of over eight hundred thousand pounds. Lives of Elwes and Dancer are to be found in Merryweather and Kirby; Caulfield contains a life of Elwes (for the books of misers, see next chapter). An account of Elwes and the other misers is given by G. F. Young (1947).

'He never owned to being rich

Daniel Dancer]   Wegg reads from Merryweather's account of Dancer in the next chapter. Dancer was born in 1716 and died in 1794; by the time of his death his fortune was three thousand pounds a year. He and his sister, whom Merryweather describes as a 'walking dunghill', made their clothing from rags 'collected from the streets, or raked out from the dust heaps' (111).

Book 3, Chapter 6

THE GOLDEN DUSTMAN FALLS INTO WORSE COMPANY.

The Roman Empire having worked out

Rollin's Ancient History . . . the whole of the army of Alexander the Macedonian . . . burst into tears simultaneously, on his being taken with a shivering fit after bathing.]   The French historian Charles Rollin published his *Histoire ancienne des Égyptiens, des Carthaginois, des Assyriens, des Babyloniens, des Mèdes, et des Perses, des Macédoniens, des Grecs* in thirteen volumes between 1730 and 1738. It was translated into English as Rollin's *Ancient History* between 1738 and 1740. Dickens had a copy in his library at Gad's Hill. Wegg's reading stops at the account of an incident when Alexander the Great bathed in the River Cydnus: 'the instant he plunged into it, he was seized with so violent a fit of shivering, that all the standers-by fancied he was dying . . . The news of this sad disaster threw the whole army into the utmost consternation. They all burst into tears' (15.4).

The Wars of the Jews]   'The History of the Jewish War' by Flavius Josephus, whose *Works* were first translated into English by Thomas Lodge in 1602.

Plutarch]   Plutarch's 'Parallel Lives', lives of twenty-three Greeks and twenty-three Romans arranged in pairs, were first translated into English in 1579 by Sir Thomas North as *The Lives of the Noble Grecians and Romanes*. Plutarch was usually read in the translation of J. and W. Langhorne, 6 volumes (1770) at this time; Dickens owned a copy.

One evening, when Silas Wegg

some profane historian]   It was usual to distinguish between 'sacred' and 'profane' history. Dickens may have been remembering Rollin's preface, 'The Usefulness of Profane History, especially with regard to Religion'.

'Walk in, brother,' said Silas

"No malice to dread, sir]   Wegg misquotes a stanza of Mrs Elizabeth Hamilton's 'My Ain Fireside', music by George Frederick Kemp:

> Nae falsehood to dread, nae malice to fear,
> But truth to delight me, and kindness to cheer;
> Nae force now upon me to seem wae or glad,
> I may laugh when I'm merry, and sigh when I'm sad
> Of a' roads to pleasure that ever were tried,
> There's nane half so sure as my ain fireside.
>
> My ain fireside, my ain fireside
> The bonny blithe blink o' my ain fireside.

'We'll devote the evening, brother

crushing a flowing wine-cup]   'I pray come and crush a cup of wine' (*Romeo and Juliet*, 1.2.81).

"And you needn't Mr. Venus be your black bottle]   Wegg's version of the last stanza of Robert Burns's 'Auld Lang Syne':

> And surely ye'll be your pint-stowp,
>   And surely I'll be mine;
> And we'll tak a cup o' kindness yet
>   For auld lang syne.

'Rome, brother,' returned Wegg

a city which . . . originated in twins and a wolf, and ended in Imperial marble]   In legend, Romulus and Remus were twin brothers abandoned as babies but suckled by a she-wolf; they survived to found Rome. It was the boast of the Emperor Augustus Caesar that he found Rome brick and left it marble. Wegg makes 'Imperial marble' sound like a trade name.

'No, sir!' remonstrated Wegg, enthusiastically.

"Charge, Chester, charge]   Wegg adapts the famous lines from Sir Walter Scott's *Marmion*: ' "Charge, Chester, charge! On, Stanley, on!"/Were the last words of Marmion' (6.32).

'But think how little time

the whole framework of society]   A cliché: 'Without mayors and many of them, it cannot be disputed that the whole framework of society – Mr. Sapsea is confident that he invented that forcible figure – would fall to pieces' (*MED* 12). The earliest example in *OED* is dated 1816.

'And here's Kirby's

Kirby's Wonderful Museum . . . and Caulfield's Characters, and Wilson's.]   In his library at Gad's Hill, Dickens had copies of R. S. Kirby, *The Wonderful and Scientific Museum: or, Magazine of Remarkable Characters; Including all the Curiosities of Nature and Art, from the Remotest Period to the Present Time, Drawn from Every Authentic Source*, 6 volumes (1803–20); James Caulfield, *Portraits, Memoirs, and Characters, of Remarkable Persons, from the Revolution of 1688 to the End of the Reign of George II*, 4 volumes (1819); and Henry Wilson, *Wonderful Characters; Comprising Memoirs and Anecdotes of the Most Remarkable Persons of Every Age and Nation*, 3 volumes (1821–2). Dickens makes use of a passage from Kirby in this chapter, but of nothing from Caulfield or Wilson.

'Call him out,' cried Mr. Boffin

Jemmy Taylor of Southwark]   Taylor was a weaver who became a stock-broker, accumulating a fortune of two hundred thousand pounds. He dressed in rags and slept in rags and straw on the bare floor. Kirby describes an occasion when two banker's clerks discovered him boiling a single chop in a large amount of water to make broth for himself and his friend Dancer. He generally ate rank meat, observing that 'meat was nothing unless it smelt as well as tasted'. He died in 1792 and was buried in the church of St Saviour. Kirby and Merryweather give accounts of Taylor.

Jemmy Wood of Gloucester]   Merryweather mentions 'The ever famous Jemmy Wood of Gloucester, who died with nearly two millions of money' (25).

'There!' said Mr. Boffin, gloating

the four-and-twenty fiddlers – all of a row.]   The number four-and-twenty is frequently employed in ballads and popular rhymes, of knights, ladies, boys, etc. Dickens may have had in mind the 'Four-and-twenty blackbirds' who were baked in a pie and the 'fiddlers three' who played to Old King Cole.

209

'This, sir,' replied Silas, adjusting his spectacles

Merryweather's Lives and Anecdotes of Misers]   Dickens owned a copy of F. Somner Merryweather, *Lives and Anecdotes of Misers; or, The Passion of Avarice Displayed* (1850), a small red book. It is from Merryweather that Wegg reads about Dancer and from the table of contents that the list of misers is taken.

'Well, sir,' replied Silas, turning

John Overs]   Overs was a Thames ferryman who became very rich. He had a beautiful daughter who fell in love with a young man but was not permitted to see him. Overs would go out in the night to scrape upon the dunghill; he ate rank meat; and would refuse the lighting of a candle from his because that way some light was taken from him. To save a day's provision he feigned sickness and laid himself out for dead. His servants began to celebrate, and seeing this expensive levity he came to life – only to be struck dead by a frightened servant who thought him the devil. Riding to claim his bride, the daughter's lover fell from his horse and was killed. The daughter founded the church of St Mary Overs, afterwards called St Saviour, in Southwark, where an emaciated figure on an old sepulchre is said to represent her father. An account of Overs is given by both Merryweather and Kirby.

John Little]   Called the Miser of Kentish Town, Little died in 1789 at the age of 84. He was not only a miser, but also a collector of useless rubbish (Merryweather, ch. 5).

Dick Jarrel]   In the MS 'Jarret', which is how Merryweather spells the name. He was called the Miser of Rye, and died in 1806, worth ten thousand pounds. After his death 'three hundred guineas were found under a brick in the floor, and notes were discovered in unsuspected crevices' (86).

the Reverend Mr. Jones of Blewbury]   Dickens added the name above the line in the MS, perhaps because of the potential for Bella's 'Blackberry' mistake (3.15). Jones died in 1827 worth many thousands of pounds. He lived on half a crown a week; ate only bread, bacon and tea; and never lit a fire except on Sunday, when he cooked his meat for the week (Merryweather, ch. 5).

Vulture Hopkins]   Pope mentions Hopkins in one of his *Moral Essays* (1731–5): 'When Hopkins dies, a thousand lights attend/The wretch, who living saved a candle's end' (3.291–2). He is mentioned in Merryweather's chapter 6.

Mr. Wegg pursued the biography

warming his dinner by sitting on it]   This detail is in Kirby, but not in Merryweather.

While speaking, he thrust his hand

a much-dilapidated dark lantern!]   A lantern with a slide which could be closed, thereby concealing the light without extinguishing the candle.

'He's warm,' said Silas in the same tone.

'He's warm]   As in the children's game, which Dickens calls 'hot boiled beans and very good butter' in *MED*, chapter 18.

Book 3, Chapter 7

THE FRIENDLY MOVE TAKES UP A STRONG POSITION.

The friendly movers sat upright

(he looked like a German wooden toy)]   The German wooden toy industry centred on Nuremberg. Carved and painted wooden dolls, soldiers and other figures were popular throughout the century.

'N-no,' returned Wegg, shaking his head

All's Well arranged as a duett]   This was a popular duet by Thomas Dibdin, music by John Braham, from *The English Fleet in 1342: An Historical Comic Opera* (1805). Wegg mangles lines from the first stanza:

> Deserted by the waning moon,
> When skies proclaim night's cheerless noon,
> On tower, or fort, or tented ground,
> The sentry walks his lonely round,
> And should a footstep haply stray,
> Where caution marks the guarded way,
> 'Who goes there? stranger – quickly tell;'
> 'A friend,' – the word – 'Good night – *All's Well.*'

'– Hear me out!' cried Wegg. 'I said so. I paid

I paid a shilling]   The fee for inspection of a will at the Prerogative Office (see p. 76).

my labour of love]   A common phrase derived from 1 Thessalonians 1.3 and Hebrews 6.10.

On this head, Silas Wegg had much to say.

the sharp sword impending over his head]   An allusion to the sword of Damocles. Damocles was one of the companions and flatterers of Dionysus the elder, tyrant of Syracuse (405–367 BC). Damocles called Dionysus the happiest of men because of his wealth and power. To indicate the quality of happiness for monarchs, Dionysus placed Damocles at a banquet with a sword suspended by a single hair hanging over his head.

Mr. Venus, having wafted his attention

a hand which never yet]   A phrase from melodrama: 'A hand which never yet was sullied or did unworthy action, etc.' (Hill).

'And there you sit, sir

assimilating the flagrant article!]   In his poem *The Task* (1785), Cowper described tobacco as 'the fragrant weed' (4.764).

called upon for Home, Sweet Home, and was obleeging the company!]   The song is from *Clari; or, The Maid of Milan* (1823), an opera in two acts by John Howard Payne (1791–1852), also credited to J. R. Planché, music by Henry R. Bishop. Dickens produced the play in private theatricals in 1833. Wegg adapts the second stanza:

> An exile from home, splendour dazzles in vain!
> Oh! give me my lovely thatch'd cottage again!
> The birds singing gaily that come at my call,
> Give me *them*, with the *peace of mind* DEARER than all!
>> Home! sweet home!
>> There's no place like home! (1.1)

Wegg refers to the practice at the song and supper rooms of the day by which those present might be called on for a song by the chairman. 'Obleege' was the standard pronunciation of 'oblige' in the eighteenth century and survived, among the older generation, into the next century.

'I was down at the water-side,' said Venus

'looking for parrots']   'Most of these birds come from South America and the coast of Africa. Jack generally brings home one or two as his own private venture, selling it in London for a sum varying from thirty to forty shillings . . . A parrot which is accomplished enough to rap out half-a-dozen round oaths in a breath, will fetch you fifty shillings, perhaps' (*HW* 4.257).

Book 3, Chapter 8   Thirteenth monthly number
                                        May 1865

THE END OF A LONG JOURNEY.

The train of carts and horses

My lords and gentlemen and honorable boards, when you in the course of your dust-shovelling]   When Gradgrind becomes a Member of Parliament in *HT* he is 'usually sifting and sifting at his parliamentary cinder-heap in London (without being observed to turn up many precious articles among the rubbish), and ... still hard at it in the national dust-yard' (2.9). Such passages recall Carlyle's *Latter-Day Pamphlets* (1850):

> it is felt that 'reform' in that Downing-Street department of affairs is precisely the reform which were worth all others . . . to clean-out the dead pedantaries, unveracities, indolent somnolent impotences, and accumulated dung-mountains there . . . such mountains of pedant exuviae and obscene owl-droppings have accumulated in those regions, long the habitation of doleful creatures. ('Downing Street')

all the queen's horses and all the queen's men]   From the nursery rhyme 'Humpty Dumpty':

> Humpty Dumpty sat on a wall,
> Humpty Dumpty had a great fall.
>   All the king's horses
>   And all the king's men
> Couldn't put Humpty together again.

bury us alive.]   Altered from 'bury you alive' in the MS. So also 'This boastful handiwork of ours' below is in the MS and proof 'This boastful handiwork of yours', and 'it will mar every one of us' is in the MS and proof 'mar you and everyone of us'.

Yes, verily, my lords and gentlemen

adapting your Catechism to the occasion, and by God's help so you must]   In the Catechism the catechumen is asked, with reference to the promises made at baptism by the godparents, 'Dost thou not think that thou art bound to believe, and to do, as they have promised for thee?' and replies, 'Yes verily: and by God's help so I will'.

in the Returns of the Board of Trade]   From 1832 the Board of Trade was required to collect and publish statistical information about the national economy.

213

Betty Higden's Flight and Death
    Lizzie finds her
    Lizzie and Bella come together
                    And Mr Boffin?
                    And Rokesmith?   <u>Yes</u>

Lizzie to work an influence on Bella's character, at its wavering point.

Wrayburn for the last chapter?
                    <u>Yes</u>

Chapter VIII

The End of a Long Journey

Betty Higden's Flight as she finds herself failing

Fear

and Death

Riderhood
Deputy
Lock Keeper

Found by Lizzie – Dies at the Paper Mill

The foot of the Cross

'Now lift me, my dear.'

Chapter IX.

Somebody becomes the subject of a prediction

'This Our Sister'

Mr and Mrs Milvey – Bella – Secretary and Sloppy

Interview with the Secretary, and then with Lizzie

Bella perceived to contrast

Stations shutting their green
eyes and opening their red ones
as they let the Boofer lady go by

herself with Lizzie

Chapter X.

Scouts out

The wretched 'old boy' turns traitor

Scene with Eugene

The Schoolmaster on the watch

'The pleasures of the chase.'

the sturdy breaker of windows and the rampant tearer of clothes]
Paupers broke windows so that they could not be discharged from a workhouse.
Clothes were torn for the same purpose or to get a new suit of clothes. For
instance, *The Times* reported the case of Mary Anne Baker, remanded on the
charge of 'wilfully destroying her clothing in the Rotherhithe-workhouse'; just
before 'being discharged in the morning she tore her clothes up' (27 July 1863,
11). Another pauper 'having torn up his clothes . . . was presented with a canvas
suit. When he got outside the doors of the workhouse he took off his clothes and
threw them over the walls of the workhouse, and then ran naked about the streets.'
He claimed that ' "he had been promised work if he had proper clothes" ' but that
the clothes the workhouse authorities gave paupers were such that they
' "prevented them from getting work" ' (27 January 1863, 9).

Faithful soul! When she had spoken

**That the shadow should be deep as it came on, like the shadow of an actual
presence, was in accordance with the laws of the physical world, for all the
Light that shone on Betty Higden lay beyond Death.]**   A shadow is made
up of a dark centre, the umbra, and a lighter surround, the penumbra. The law of
the physical world which this fact illustrates is that light travels in straight lines.
Christ said 'I am the light of the world' (John 9.5); he told his disciples 'Ye are the
light of the world' (Matthew 5.14): in a world where the Good Samaritan is a
pursuing fury, the Christian light does not shine.

The poor old creature had taken

the track in which her last home lay]   Betty's home was at Brentford, on the
Thames, six miles from London. Chertsey, Walton, Kingston and Staines, all
small market-towns at this time, are further up the Thames valley.

In those pleasant little towns

the pauper-nurse's; death . . . among the pauper-wards.]   Dickens had
described a pauper nurse and death in a workhouse in the first chapter of *OT*.
Among the cases of pauper neglect *The Times* reported in 1864 was that of
Timothy Daly, who had died in a workhouse hospital and was found to have been
suffering from bedsores 'denuding the hipbones of flesh for three inches'. *The
Times* urged that there must be some reform of workhouse conditions: 'Unless this
is done, or at least attempted, even in the Infirmaries of Workhouses, there will be
those who prefer to lie down and die in solitude to the cruel tender mercies of Poor
Law officials' (29 December 1864, 7). On 10 April 1865, *The Times* reported
another case of pauper neglect, 'infinitely more horrifying' even than that of Daly.
Richard Gibson had died of neglect *while in a workhouse infirmary*. *The Times*
described conditions in the ward:

> His bed . . . unmade for five days and nights . . . The doctor orders that his leg
> should be dressed with water dressing every day; the dressing is left to be done

or undone by the pauper nurses; and the paid nurse never sees the order carried out. Lastly, she actually sees vermin on the man's body while he is dying.

The Times insisted that 'Every one, from the highest to the lowest, is guilty' (8–9). In the *Lancet* investigations, to which Dickens refers in the 'Postscript', the workhouse-hospital system was described as 'a disgrace to our civilization' (15 April 1865, 410). Conditions in some wards were horrifying: 'In St. Pancras we found that the majority of the bedsteads were only five feet eight long ... bedridden patients habitually washed their hands and faces *in their chamber utensils* ... we were told that they preferred it' (1 July 1865, 18). On the subject of the pauper nurses, the *Lancet* had this to say:

> We have no wish to make 'sensation' statements against the pauper nurses. But, in the first place, it is notorious that the majority of them are aged and feeble and past work, or have strong tendencies to drink ... Secondly, their inefficiency is borne out by the character of their ward work as to the details of cleanliness.

In addition, 'in the great majority of cases, pauper nurses can only manage their patients by inspiring fear ... their conduct is consequently often brutal' (1 July 1865, 19).

But, the old abhorrence grew

a great blank barren Union House, as far from old home as the County Jail ... and in its dietary, and in its lodging ... a much more penal establishment.]   Workhouses were widely known as 'Poor Law Bastilles'. Their monotonous routine and prison-like discipline repelled the poor. As *The Times* said: 'The nation punishes poverty ... the simple fact of numbers dying because they would rather die ... than go into a workhouse, is enough to prove that the nation holds poverty to be a crime, and treats it accordingly' (17 March 1864, 11). In his *Latter-Day Pamphlets* (1850), Carlyle had attacked philanthropists who concerned themselves with 'Model Prisons' rather than with the condition of the non-criminal poor. Taking up the charge in his *HW* article 'Pet Prisoners', Dickens compared the 'physical condition of the convict in prison, and that of the hard-working man outside, or the pauper outside' and found that the convict was better treated (*MP*). A dietary recommended by the Poor Law Commissioners made this provision for able-bodied men and women: twelve ounces of bread a day (women, ten); one and a half pints of gruel a day; five ounces of cooked meat three times a week; half a pound of potatoes three times a week; one and a half pints of soup three times a week; rice pudding or suet on Fridays (Rose, 1972, 165).

she would hear a newspaper read out ... how the Registrar General cast up the units that had within the last week died ... that Recording Angel seemed to have a regular fixed place in his sum, as if they were its halfpence.]   *The Times* printed a weekly column 'The Public Health', or 'The Health of the Metropolis', subtitled 'The Registrar-General's Weekly Return', which,

217

along with statistics relating to the incidence of disease, general mortality and even the weather, gave reports like 'the daughter of a shoemaker, aged 5 years, was found dead in bed on the 11th of March from "starvation" ' (1 April 1863, 6). The concept of the 'human unit' was the subject of some debate. William Farr (1804–83), compiler of abstracts in the office of the Registrar-General, wrote glowingly of its usefulness: 'the people of England ... appear divested of all colour, form, character, passion, and the infinite individualities of life; by abstraction they are reduced to mere units undergoing changes as purely physical as the setting stars of astronomy or the decomposing atoms of chemistry' (Hilts, 1970, 144). In the Christian tradition the recording angel is understood to record the names of the elect in the Book of Life.

This is not to be received as a figure of speech.

to have made a pursuing Fury of the Good Samaritan] In Greek mythology the Furies are the three avenging female deities who pursue criminals and those tortured with bad conscience. The story of the Good Samaritan is found in Luke 10.30–7. In *OT* the 'large brass buttons' of the beadle Mr Bumble are ornamented with ' "the porochial seal – the Good Samaritan healing the sick and bruised man" ' (4). In *HT* Mr Gradgrind would prove that 'the Good Samaritan was a Bad Economist' (2.12).

She caught up her basket as she spoke

the sign of the White Lion hanging across the road] The town is Hampton, where the sign of the Red Lion inn hung across the road; the parish church of St Mary was at the entrance to the village.

'I am the Deputy Lock, on job

this is the Lock-house.] The scene is probably Hurley Lock, three miles by river below Henley, where the paper-mill is. The river makes a bend between this lock and Henley so that the distance by road is about half that by water. Hence Betty, though very weak from starvation and exhaustion, might make her way to the vicinity of the paper-mill.

She was gone out of the Lock-house

the Samaritan had in the lonely night, 'passed by on the other side'] In the parable of the Good Samaritan, the priest and the Levite 'passed by on the other side' (Luke 10.31–2).

The time was come, now, when the wants

a table had been spread for her in the next field.] Psalms 23.5: 'Thou preparest a table before me in the presence of mine enemies.'

Sewn in the breast of her gown, the money

in the valley of the shadow of death]   Psalms 23.4: 'Yea, though I walk through the valley of the shadow of death, I will fear no evil: for thou art with me; thy rod and thy staff they comfort me.'

would appreciate our Poor Law more philosophically]   There is a suggestion of the 'philosophers', political economists and utilitarians, of *OT*.

By what visionary hands she was led

what infinite variety of forms of tower and roof and steeple the trees took] Enobarbus uses the phrase 'infinite variety' of Cleopatra: 'Age cannot wither her, nor custom stale/Her infinite variety' (*Antony and Cleopatra* 2.2.239–40). Two of Dickens's other characters see church-like forms in woods shortly before their deaths: Lord Verisopht in *NN* (50) and Montague Tigg in *MC* (47).

'Water-meadows, or such like

There now arose in the darkness, a great building, full of lighted windows.]   The paper-mill at which Lizzie works was the well-known Marsh Mill by Henley Lock, about half a mile up-river from Henley. The building does not survive, though a similar mill still stands at Hambledon Lock, between Henley and Hurley Lock. A *HW* article by Dickens and Mark Lemon described the operation of 'A Paper-Mill' (1.529–31) at Dartford in Kent. The paper was made from rags. The rags were first shredded, then boiled in cauldrons until they became 'a dense, tight mass'. This was taken to the cutting room where it was 'subjected to the action of large rollers filled with transverse knives' (530). It was then bleached, racked, and rolled into paper, and finally cut into various sizes. The article is an argument against excise duty on paper. It begins by remembering Wat Tyler, leader of the Peasants' Revolt of 1381, who was from Dartford: had he been able to wait for the benefits brought by printing and paper, there need have been no revolt. The relation of mental and industrial progress is suggested by the 'metempsychosis' of the narrator, who imagines himself becoming the rags and going through the process of manufacture. The mill is in 'beautiful order' and the women workers 'thriving' (531).

my journey's end!']   'Here is my journey's end, here is my butt,/And very sea-mark of my utmost sail' (*Othello* 5.2.270–1).

219

Book 3, Chapter 9

SOMEBODY BECOMES THE SUBJECT OF A PREDICTION.

' *"We give thee hearty thanks*

' "WE GIVE THEE HEARTY THANKS]   Milvey is reading from the Order for the Burial of the Dead in the Book of Common Prayer.

The words were read above the ashes

the diggers and hewers]   A variant of the biblical 'hewers of wood and drawers of water' (Deuteronomy 29.11; Joshua 9.21, 23).

in a registering age, if we ticketed their graves at the common charge]   The wordplay alludes to the Registrar-General and to the 'ticket' system of poor relief (chits for relief given in receipt of work performed). In *TTC* a petitioner asks for such consideration: ' "My petition is, that a morsel of stone or wood, with my husband's name, may be placed over him to show where he lies. Otherwise the place will be quickly forgotten" ' (2.8).

They left him undisturbed

The water-wheel of the paper-mill was audible there, and seemed to have a softening influence on the bright wintry scene.]   The pastoral scene is similarly undisturbed by industry in the *HW* article 'A Paper-Mill' (1.529–31).

'The gentleman certainly is a Jew

I think there cannot be kinder people in the world.']   Like that of the Jew money-lender, the stereotype of the Jewish capitalist who 'sweated' his workforce was well established by this time.

'Nor I neither, ' said Bella

Ma going on like the Tragic Muse with a face-ache in majestic corners]   Included in the decoration of the proscenium of many theatres were to be found the masks of two Greek Muses, Melpomene, the Muse of tragedy, on one side, and Thalia, the Muse of comedy, on the other (Hill). Dickens might also have been thinking of paintings in which the Tragic Muse appears: for instance, Reynolds's famous portrait of 'Mrs Siddons as the Tragic Muse' (1790) in the Dulwich Picture Gallery and his 'Garrick between Tragedy and Comedy' (1762).

'I should lose some of the best recollections

these hands . . . softened and made supple by this new work]   Women's work in paper-mills was hard and poorly paid. In the rag rooms, where the dust and foul atmosphere were especially annoying, and in the glazing and sorting departments, women earned from two to four shillings weekly for a twelve-hour working day (Neff, 1929, 100).

'You are cold; I felt you tremble.

this wrapper of mine]   The wrapper was a loose thigh-length coat, cut so as to wrap over in front, sometimes buttoning, but more usually held in place by hand. The collar was a deep 'shawl'; the sleeves were close-fitting.

The railway, at this point, knowingly

shutting a green eye and opening a red one]   Henley station was at the end of a branch line of the Great Western Railway, the London terminus of which was Paddington. The sequence of signals here has been much debated by Dickensians. It appears that the green light indicated that the train could proceed, the red light was to prevent another following too closely.

Book 3, Chapter 10

SCOUTS OUT.

'He's enough to break

He'd be sharper than a serpent's tooth]   Another aggrieved parent, King Lear, complains: 'How sharper than a serpent's tooth it is/To have a thankless child' (1.4.288–9).

'A muddling and a swipey old child

swipey]   'Swipes' is poor weak beer; hence small beer; hence beer in general. The *HW* article 'Slang' lists 'swipey' as one of 'the astonishing number of thirty-two' synonyms for 'drunk' (8.75).

'I'm going to the Italian Opera

the Italian Opera]   Covent Garden became the Royal Italian Opera House in 1847.

'Now you prodigal old son

prodigal old son]   The parable of the Prodigal Son in Luke 15.11–32. The Prodigal Son 'wasted his substance with riotous living'; having done so, 'he would fain have filled his belly with the husks that the swine did eat' (13, 16).

Eugene lounged slowly

Charing Cross]   For a long time one of the busiest intersections in London. Dr Johnson believed that 'the full tide of human existence is at Charing Cross'; in 1833 the poet Thomas Campbell called it 'a roaring vortex'.

'You have fallen into the hands

fallen into the hands of the Jews]   The biblical phrase is 'fallen into the hands of the Philistines'.

'I have had an interview to-day

in a shovel-hat]   Mortimer compares Riah's 'large-brimmed low-crowned hat' (2.1) to the stiff broad-brimmed hat, turned up at the side and projecting with a shovel-like curve at front and behind, worn by clergymen.

'By-the-by,' said Eugene

with an instinctive desire to receive him into the bosom of our Church – *I* gave him the name of Aaron!']   Aaron, the high priest and brother of Moses, is traditionally taken as the type of the Christian priest (but see also p. 189). Eugene alludes to missions to convert the Jews.

'Dear boy, I know it, but I can't give it.

"If Peter Piper picked]   The full tongue-twister is:

> Peter Piper picked a peck of pickled pepper;
> A peck of pickled pepper Peter Piper picked;
> If Peter Piper picked a peck of pickled pepper,
> Where's the peck of pickled pepper Peter Piper picked?

He took the shovel from the grate

a few pastiles]   Small lozenges of aromatic paste prepared to be burnt as a perfume, especially as a fumigator.

'We have changed the subject!'

Patience on a mantelpiece frowning at Dolls]   A variation of Viola's words in *Twelfth Night*: 'She sat like Patience on a monument,/Smiling at grief' (2.4.113–14).

being gone you are a man again.']   Macbeth's reaction to the ghost of Banquo:

> Hence, horrible shadow!
> Unreal mock'ry, hence!   (*Exit Ghost.*
> Why, so; being gone,
> I am a man again. Pray you, sit still. (3.4.105–7)

'*Observe the legal mind!' remarked Eugene*

'Observe the dyer's hand, assimilating itself to what it works in] Shakespeare, Sonnet 3: 'My nature is subdu'd/To what it works in, like the dyer's hand.'

The schoolmaster's abroad.']   In a speech made in 1825, Lord Brougham (1778–1868), the radical Whig politician and education reformer who in that year founded the Society for the Diffusion of Useful Knowledge, is supposed to have said: 'Look out, gentlemen, the schoolmaster is abroad!'

'*You charm me, Mortimer, with your reading*

that very word, Reading, in its critical use]   It would seem that Dickens was quick to notice a critical fashion, for the earliest example of this use of the word 'reading' in the *OED* is from 1882: 'His reading of Balzac's Mercadet . . . appeared somewhat airy and not tragic enough.'

'*Then soberly and plainly*

I study and get up]   'Get up' is both a lawyer's and a schoolboy's phrase.

With Venetian mystery I seek those No Thoroughfares at night, glide into them]   Dickens described arriving at Venice in a gondola at night in *PI*:

> Before I knew by what, or how, I found that we were gliding up a street – a phantom street; the houses rising up on both sides, from the water, and the black boat gliding on beneath their windows. Lights were shining from some of the casements, plumbing the depth of the black stream with their reflected rays, but all was profoundly silent. ('An Italian Dream')

hope springs eternal in the scholastic breast]   An adaptation of a well-known line from Pope's *An Essay on Man*: 'Hope springs eternal in the human breast:/Man never Is, but always To be blest' (1.95–6).

I know he watches at the Temple Gate]   The Temple was walled in on every side and protected with gates which were ordinarily shut at night and guarded by a watchman.

223

'Bravo! cried Eugene, rising too

Yoicks]   A call used in hunting to urge on the hounds.

Hey Ho Chivey]   The refrain of the hunting song 'Old Towler' by John O'Keefe, music by W. Shield. This is the third of three stanzas:

> Poor stag the dogs thy haunches gore,
>   The tears run down thy face;
> The Huntsman's pleasure is no more,
>   His joys were in the Chase.
> Alike the Sportsman of the Town
>   The Virgin game in view;
> Are full content to run them down,
>   Then they in turn pursue.
>   With their Hey ho Chivey
>   Hark forward hard forward tantivy.

'I am always serious

a southerly wind and a cloudy sky proclaim a hunting evening.]   A play on the opening words of another hunting song, 'The Fox Chase': 'A Southerly wind and a cloudy sky/Proclaim a Hunting Morning.'

As the two friends passed out

difficult country about Bethnal Green]   Bethnal Green is in the East End of London. It was at this time an area of 'numerous blind courts and alleys', inhabited by 'men and women sharpers, shoplifters and pickpockets' (Timbs 50).

Book 3, Chapter 11   Fourteenth monthly number

June 1865

IN THE DARK.

The state of the man was murderous

If great criminals told the truth – which, being great criminals, they do not]   In *MED* when Rosa cannot understand Jasper's character Dickens comments: 'what could she know of the criminal intellect, which its own professed students perpetually misread, because they persist in trying to reconcile it with the average intellect of average men, instead of identifying it as a horrible wonder apart' (20). Both generalizations recall his observations on the behaviour of the poisoner William Palmer at his trial in 1856 ('The Demeanour of Murderers', *MP*).

They buffet with opposing waves, to gain the bloody shore]　There is a recollection of Hamlet's words 'to take arms against a sea of troubles,/And by opposing end them' (3.1.59–60), and those of Macbeth: 'I am in blood/Stepp'd in so far that, should I wade no more,/Returning were as tedious as go o'er' (3.4.136–8).

The suspicion crossed him as he rested in a doorway

the many heads erst hoisted upon neighbouring Temple Bar]　Temple Bar was a gateway of stone separating the Strand from Fleet Street which marked the boundary between the City of London and Westminster. Above the centre of the pediment, upon iron spikes, were formerly placed the heads and limbs of persons executed for treason. The last heads were put up in 1746 and remained there until 1772.

'Yes, and I come to London

a Busted B'low-Bridge steamer]　Riderhood means 'below bridge'. Three lines of steamers sailed from above London Bridge, two from below, passengers having often to change at Old Swan Pier.

'But, T'otherest Governor,' urged Mr. Riderhood again

a mouthful of rum and milk]　A popular early-morning drink.

Yet more really bewitched

the miserable creatures of the much-lamented times]　The reference is to the persecution of supposed witches during the reign of James I (1603–25). In his story in *MHC* Mr Pickwick mentions the sad fate of those supposedly 'evil old women' who 'inflicted various dismal tortures upon Christian men; sticking pins and needles into them when they least expected it, and causing them to walk in the air with their feet upwards'.

ridden hard by Evil Spirits in the night]　The nightmare, sometimes called the 'night-hag', was supposed to be a monster that crouched on the oppressed sleeper's breast. It is the subject of Fuseli's famous painting *The Nightmare* (1782), of which there were many copies and parodies.

the most advanced of the scholars might have taken fright and run away from the master.]　This is the first of a number of parallels to Thomas Hood's poem about a schoolteacher murderer, *The Dream of Eugene Aram* (1829).

225

Work out Riah and Fledgeby?   ⎤ Yes
          and the power over the others? ⎦ ⎓⎓

Twemlow? Yes

And Mrs Lammle? Yes

And the chorus?   Next time

    Mr Venus and Mr Boffin. Yes

        Riderhood? Yes   With Bradley

              and Pleasant?   No

Chapter XI.

In the Dark | Bradley's state of mind |

Bradley Headstone and Riderhood

      Get them together

         Let him know where to find Riderhood

    Plashwater Weir Mill Lock

Chapter XII.

Meaning Mischief.

Mr and Mrs Lammle and their plot.   Lead on carefully, to Bella

                                      in N.º XV   Make all

                                        the ground

Fascination Fledgeby, and <his feet> his ingenuous use of a confidence.

      'Toddle, Judah!'

Chapter XIII.

Give a dog a bad name, and hang him

                                  Dolls' Dress Maker

  The Counting House in St. Mary Axe

        Twemlow in difficulties

           The Dog with the bad name | Work Fledgeby |

'You are not the Godmother – but the Wolf.'

Chapter XIV.

Mr Wegg prepares a grindstone for Mr Boffin's nose

Venus relents and honestly backs out of the Friendly Move

  Scene with him and Mr Boffin in the shop.

    Wegg overheard by Mr Boffin | Behind the Alligator |

Work round to Mrs Lammle, to close.

Aram was an usher who in 1745 killed a man named Clarke. For fourteen years the crime went undetected until the bones were accidentally dug up. In the poem he is troubled by the contrast between himself and his students:

> Anon I cleans'd my bloody hands,
>   And wash'd my forehead cool,
> And sat among the urchins young,
>   That evening in the school!
>
> O Heaven! to think of their white souls,
>   And mine so black and grim!
> I could not share in childish prayer,
>   Nor join in Evening Hymn;
> Like a Devil of the Pit I seem'd
>   'Mid holy Cherubim! (129–38)

Book 3, Chapter 12

MEANING MISCHIEF.

The chapter title is altered in the MS from 'In the Daylight'.

'The name of the Creditor is Riah,' said Mr. Fledgeby

a rather uncompromising accent on his noun-substantive.]   A 'noun-substantive' (here 'Creditor') is a noun which is not dependent on, subsidiary to, or referable to something else, but the supposed creditor Riah is in fact subsidiary and referable to Fledgeby.

In fact, Mr. Fledgeby sped on his errand

his feet might have been winged by all the good spirits that wait on Generosity.]   But Fledgeby's feet are winged like those of Mercury, the god of merchants.

'Yes you do,' said Fledgeby. 'Oh, you sinner!

that bill of sale at Lammle's]   A bill of sale gave the right to possess and sell the specified property. The Lammles have had an advance of money or postponed the demand for repayment of a debt by this means.

228

'You have been told that he might pull through it

go in to win]   A phrase from boxing: in *BR* Miggs's mother, 'in prize-fighting phraseology, always came up to time with a cheerful countenance, and went in to win' (22).

Book 3, Chapter 13

GIVE A DOG A BAD NAME,
AND HANG HIM.

'One of his dodges,' said Mr. Fledgeby

the dodgerest of all the dodgers.]   The superlative degree in Hebrew is represented in English by such phrases as 'holy of holies'. Carlyle used phrases like 'joy of joys', 'game of games', 'prodigy of prodigies'.

'As near as a toucher,' assented Fledgeby

'As near as a toucher]   A colloquial phrase from boxing meaning 'very nearly', 'all but'.

The chivalrous Twemlow,

Knight of the Simple Heart]   Cervantes's Don Quixote is 'the Knight of the Rueful Countenance'.

But, the confiding young man proceeded

to heap coals of fire on his sensitive head.]   Proverbs 25.21–2: 'If thine enemy be hungry, give him bread to eat; and if he be thirsty, give him water to drink; For thou shalt heap coals of fire upon his head.'

The confiding young man besought him

had 'given him his name']   Signed a bill which, in the event of the default of his friend, made him liable for the named sum. Meason described the case of a man whose friend fails to meet the date of payment. He is offered the choice of either taking out a loan at exorbitant rates of interest – the equivalent of 200 per cent per annum – or of accepting a 'bill of sale' on his furniture. Another man seeking 'accommodation' has to pay 'altogether one hundred and fifty pounds for the temporary advance of thirty-seven' (13.561).

to 'confess judgement'] A term used in actions to recover possession of property, and in county-court actions to recover debts; it shortened the legal proceedings.

his life was assured for somebody not wholly unconnected with the sherry trade ... he had a Stradiuarius violin ... and also a Madonna] The business of a wine merchant was the standard front for a money-lender. The use to which the wine and the fake antiques could be put is explained in the *AYR* article 'A Trial of Jewry':

> My first trial of Jewry was, if I mistake not, in connexion with a pressing call for money on my part, and the production of a stamped piece of paper on the part of Jewry. Ten pounds was the sum required; but ... Jewry ... proceeded to explain he had only a five-pound note in the house.
> Aghast at the information, I asked him what I was to do. He frankly confessed he did not know; at length, smitten with a sudden idea, he pointed to the oil-painting of a Spanish boy, which stood against the wall, and told me I might 'take the Murillo.' I represented to Jewry that my want was money, not Murillos; upon which he suggested the pledging of the Murillo for five pounds. 'Dicks'll do it for you in a minute,' Jewry said. 'Here, Dicks!' And Dicks presenting himself in the shape of a very evil-looking clerk, was told to take 'That round the corner,' and to bring five pounds back. Dicks returned in three minutes without the Murillo, and with three pounds, which was all, he said, he could get for it. (10.398–9)

Rawdon Crawley of *Vanity Fair* knows the system better than Twemlow. Arrested for debt he writes to Becky: ' "Drive to Nathan's – offer him seventy-five down, and ask *him to renew* – say I'll take wine – we may as well have some dinner sherry; but not *picturs*, they're too dear" ' (58). Stradivarius violins are those made by the famous violin-maker Antonio Stradivarius of Cremona (1644–1737). This one, of course, is a fake.

stalked the shadow of the awful Snigsworth, eyed afar off by money-lenders as Security in the Mist, and menacing Twemlow with his baronial truncheon.] The allusion is to Horatio's account of the appearance of the ghost in *Hamlet*:

> A figure likè your father . . .
> Goes slow and stately by them; thrice he walk'd
> By their oppress'd and fear-surprised eyes,
> Within his truncheon's length (1.2.199, 202–4)

The ghost had first appeared out of a mist, rather than walking across the front of the stage, in a production by Dickens's acquaintance, the dramatist Tom Taylor. Love-in-a-mist is a garden flower.

'To prison,' returned Fledgeby

'To prison] Imprisonment for debt was not finally abolished until 1869.

Book 3, Chapter 14

MR. WEGG PREPARES A GRINDSTONE FOR MR. BOFFIN'S NOSE.

The proverb is 'To keep one's nose to the grindstone' (to keep hard at work).

The Golden Dustman seemed

'Get behind the young alligator in the corner]   The alligator has not been mentioned before. Dickens may have recalled the alligator in the apothecary's shop in *Romeo and Juliet* (5.1.40–4). Garth's description of the shop of Horoscope the apothecary in *The Dispensary* (1699) gives the same detail:

> Here mummies lay most reverendly stale,
> And there the tortoise hung her coat of mail;
> Not far from some huge shark's devouring head
> The flying fish their finny pinions spread:
> Aloft, in rows, large poppy-heads were strung,
> And near a scaly aligator hung. (2.122–7)

Dickens would have known Hogarth's engraving 'Hudibras Beats Sidrophel and His Man Whacum', an illustration to Butler's satire, *Hudibras* (Part 2, 1664, 3; the shop interior is not described by Butler); and also Plate 3 of Hogarth's *Marriage à-la-Mode* (1745). The original of the latter scene was the 'museum' of Dr Misaubin, at 96 St Martin's Lane, Westminster. See Plate 6. Rackstraw's 'Museum of Anatomy and Curiosities' (see p. 68) contained two stuffed crocodiles (Altick, 1978, 55).

'If you please, partner,' said Wegg

"I wish to see it with your eyes]   Wegg adapts the first two lines of Ben Jonson's 'Song. To Celia': 'Drinke to me, onely, with thine eyes,/And I will pledge with mine.' The song was set to music many times in the nineteenth century.

'As you handsomely say again

like a thief in the dark]   1 Thessalonians 5.2–4: 'For yourselves know perfectly that the day of the Lord so cometh as a thief in the night ... But ye, brethren, are not in darkness, that the day should overtake you as a thief.'

'But,' said Wegg, possibly with some slight

Begone, dull Care!]   The title and opening words of a song by John Playford,

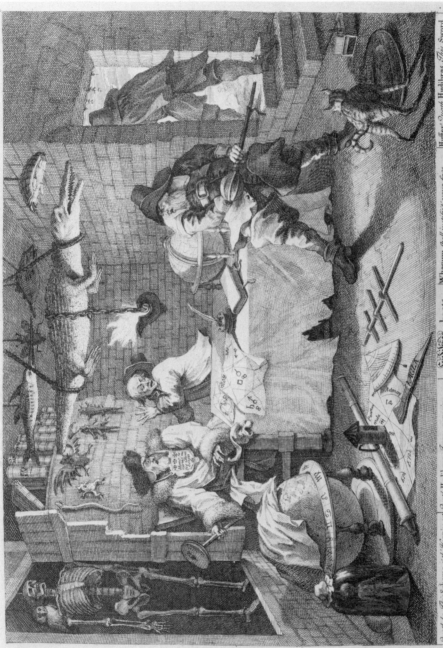

6 (a) William Hogarth's 'Hudibras Beats Sidrophel and His Man Whacum'

Marriage A-la-Mode, (Plate III)

6 (b) Plate 3 of William Hogarth's *Marriage-à-la-Mode*

published in *The Musical Companion* (1667): 'Begone, dull Care, I prithee begone from me,/Begone, dull Care, you and I shall never agree.'

"When the heart of a man is depressed with cares]   A song sung by Macheath in John Gay, *The Beggar's Opera* (1728):

> If the heart of a man is deprest with cares,
> The mist is dispell'd when a woman appears;
> Like the notes of a fiddle, she sweetly, sweetly
> Raises the spirits, and charms our ears.
>> Roses and lilies her cheeks disclose,
>> But her ripe lips are more sweet than those.
>>> Press her,
>>> Caress her,
>>> With blisses,
>>> Her kisses
> Dissolve us in pleasure, and soft repose.

'I am sure I don't know what to do

I was brought into the world to be dropped down upon]   1 Timothy 6.7: 'For we brought nothing into this world, and it is certain we can carry nothing out.'

Mr. Venus could only repeat

to betake himself to the paths of science, and to walk in the same all the days of his life]   An adaptation of the words of the Catechism: 'I should keep God's holy will and commandments, and walk in the same all the days of my life.'

'Not if I was to show you reason

good and sufficient reason?']   The phrase 'sufficient reason' is a philosophical term, from Leibnitz's *raison suffisante*.

Book 3, Chapter 15   Fifteenth monthly number
July 1865

THE GOLDEN DUSTMAN AT HIS WORST.

'Win her affections,' retorted Mr. Boffin

Mew says the cat]   Boffin adapts the nursery rhyme:

> Bow wow says the dog
> Mew mew says the cat
> Grunt grunt says the hog
> And squeak goes the rat

'I shall never more think well of you

Blackberry Jones]   The miser was known as Blewberry Jones (Blewberry is a place, not a fruit). Bella makes the same mistake in book 4, chapter 15.

'I would rather he thought well of me

he swept the street for bread . . . you splashed the mud upon him from the wheels of a chariot of pure gold.]   Crossing-sweepers, like Jo in *BH*, made their living by sweeping the mud from crossings for gratuities from pedestrians. Bella employs a version of a conventional contrast: for instance, Dickens's and G. A. Sala's *HW* article 'First Fruits' claims that we cannot forget our earliest experiences, 'for all that we may be riding in gold coaches, and denying that we ever trotted in the mud' (5.189).

She ran up-stairs, and sat down on the floor

selected only those she had brought with her]   In John Howard Payne's musical drama *Clari; or, The Maid of Milan*, which Dickens produced in amateur theatricals in 1833, Clari leaves the wealthy Duke's apartments to return to her poor father. She says:

> This to the Duke. (*bringing ornaments.*) And here are all his gifts – his diamonds – his detested wealth! (*puts the things on the toilet, and attaches the letter to a casket.*) Now, methinks, my heart feels lighter. (2.3)

Earlier in the piece she expressed the wish to exchange her rich attire for her old homely dress. When Edith Dombey and Lady Dedlock flee the homes of their respective husbands they also leave behind their fine dresses and jewels (*DS* 47, *BH* 55).

235

Work out the pious fraud concerted between Mrs
Boffin – Mr Boffin – and John Rokesmith

Make the most of Bella

Mr Twemlow? Yes
                And Mrs Lammle

Chapter XV.

The < triumph of the Monster > Golden Dustman at his worst

Mr Boffin, feigning indignation with the Secretary for what

Mrs Lammle has told him, affronts and discharges Secretary

Bring out Bella – 'I must go home. –

I can't stay here.

And goes away

No money – no Dresses – no anything.

Chapter XVI

The Feast of the Three Hobgoblins.

Bella goes to her father at Mincing Lane

John Rokesmith

The three pennyworths of milk and
the three cottage loaves

The return home.

Chapter XVII

A Social Chorus

The Veneerings and chorus generally

People going to smash, impossible to be accounted for

Mrs Lammle and Twemlow. Lead up to Fledgeby's corporal punishment

Lead up to Veneering's getting into Parliamentary scrape

Young Blight comes

And to Lizzie and Eugene. Close with that

The End of the Third Book

Book 3, Chapter 16

THE FEAST OF THE THREE HOBGOBLINS.

The old story of the Three Bears who came home to find that somebody had been eating their breakfast porridge was popularized by Robert Southey in *The Doctor* (1837). Dickens substituted hobgoblins for bears as he did in the allusion to the tale in *BH* (20).

The City looked unpromising enough

like the prostration of a spent giant]   In 'Jack and the Beanstalk' Jack steals various valuable articles away while the owner, the giant, is sleeping.

If Bella thought, as she glanced

the mighty Bank]   The Bank of England was then ' "the principal Bank of Deposit and Circulation, not in this country only, but in Europe" ' (Wheatley and Cunningham 1.95). The building, which was opened in 1734, covers an area of nearly four acres and has an imposing appearance. Dickens mentioned 'the bright copper shovels for shovelling gold' in *UT* (23).

The counting-house of Chicksey, Veneering

accounted for its humidity on natural principles . . . she had looked in . . . to see what o'clock it was.]   In 1797 clocks had been taxed beyond the reach of ordinary people, but public houses installed them for their customers: hence the euphemism.

'Now, does it really strike you

Rumty's Perch]   In *DS* the messenger in the Dombey counting-house is called Perch: his 'place was on a little bracket, like a timepiece' (13).

Bella playfully setting herself about the task

the once popular sign of the Saracen's Head, with a piece of Dutch clock-work]   The Saracen's Head inn sign first appeared in London in the fourteenth century, an inheritance from the Crusades. Dickens introduced the Saracen's Head inn at Snow Hill into *NN*. Dutch clocks, wooden clocks with brass workings made in Germany ('Deutsch'), were ornamented with Turks' or Saracens' heads:

'Miss Betsey, looking round the room . . . began on the other side, and carried her eyes on, like a Saracen's head in a Dutch Clock' (*DC* 1).

The cherub not presuming to address

A magnetic result of such glaring]   It was the belief of mesmerists that there was a 'human magnetism', which could be commanded and transmitted as a 'mesmeric force'. Mirrors were thought to focus and intensify this force. Dickens had a long-standing interest in mesmerism (Kaplan, 1975).

Then it's a pity she didn't know better

retiring into the ball of St. Paul's]   '*The Ball and Cross* stand on a cone between the cupola and dome . . . The ball is 6 feet 2 inches in diameter, and will contain eight persons, "without", it is said, "particular inconvenience." This, however, may well be doubted' (Wheatley and Cunningham 3.50).

Lavinia was about replying

washing her hands of the Boffins, went to bed after the manner of Lady Macbeth]   *Macbeth*, Act 4, scene 1, the famous sleepwalking scene:

> *Doctor.* What is it she does now? Look how she rubs her hands.
> *Gentlewoman.* It is an accustomed action with her, to seem thus washing her hands. (26–7)

As Lady Macbeth exits she says: 'To bed, to bed, to bed' (66).

'Listen, sir,' said Bella. 'Your lovely woman

she will marry on a hundred and fifty pounds a year.]   This was a typical lower-middle-class salary; it was also the income at which a man became a gentleman, though his wife did not become a lady until the income reached £250. It was not a large sum to marry on: in 1858, *The Times* conducted a debate on the question whether one could marry on less than £300 a year.

'Yes!' cried Bella, in high glee

the Knave of Wilfers]   In the nursery rhyme:

> The Queen of Hearts
> She made some tarts,
> All on a summer's day;
> The Knave of Hearts
> He stole the tarts,
> And took them clean away.

Book 3, Chapter 17

A SOCIAL CHORUS.

Amazement sits enthroned

Amazement sits enthroned]   *Hamlet* 3.4.112: 'But look, amazement on thy mother sits.'

For, it is by this time noticeable

to beat up people]   Officers and sergeants enlisting men were said to 'beat up (a town)' for recruits.

Perhaps, after all, – who knows?

Veneering may find this dining, though expensive, remunerative] Lavish dining created the impression of affluence. In the 1860s a conspicuous example of conspicuous consumption was D. Ward Chapman, the leading director of the doomed Overend, Gurney:

> 'Chapman lives in great style at Prince's Gate, Hyde Park, when he resides in London. He keeps ten horses. He has his house always full of visitors, and gives the most delicious dinners. He is the most splendid fellow I know. He lives at the rate of from £15,000 to £20,000 a year.'

'Twenty thousand pounds a year!' exclaimed I. (Xenos, 1869, 106)

Dickens's other fraudulent capitalists – Tigg Montague in *MC*, and Merdle in *LD* – both, in their different ways, entertain lavishly.

basked in the light of my countenance]   An echo of biblical phrases, such as Psalms, 4.6: 'Lord, lift thou up the light of thy countenance upon us.' In Moore's 'The Veiled Prophet of Khorassan' in *Lalla Rookh*, the prophet claims the 'gladden'd Earth shall, through her wide expanse,/Bask in the glories of this countenance' (1.181–2).

The camels are polishing up

having taken two advertised pills . . . on the faith of the printed representation . . . (price one and a penny halfpenny, government stamp included)]   Having got indigestion from eating adulterated food, Twemlow resorts to quack medicines. Then, as now, advertisers exaggerated: Beecham's Pills, for instance, were represented to be 'worth a Guinea a Box for nervous and Bilious Disorders . . . for a weak stomach, impaired digestion, and all disorders of the liver they act like "MAGIC"' (de Vries, 1968, 14). A *HW* article, 'The Methusaleh Pill', complained that the government duty conferred a spurious respectability on quack medicines (2.37–8). Carlyle, in *Past and Present* (1843), had used Morrison's famous and much-puffed Pill as an image of an imaginary quick cure for social evils.

Mr. Twemlow's little rooms

a full-length engraving of the sublime Snigsworth]　　The original would be hanging in the family gallery at Snigsworthy. Dickens burlesques the apparatus of the eighteenth-century and early nineteenth-century portrait: for instance, in Lawrence's well-known portrait of *HRH Prince Regent* (1818) the Prince Regent is depicted standing in front of curtains and a pillar with papers on a table at his hand.

'I don't know

we are bankrupt here, and must go abroad]　　The Lammles go to Boulogne, the Veneerings to Calais (4.'The Last'). Being near to England, and *en route* to Paris, Boulogne and Calais were the Continental towns most frequented by those who had left England to escape their creditors or scandal and to take advantage of the relatively low cost of living and the reputation for wealth of the 'English Milord': in *Vanity Fair* Thackeray ironically described Boulogne as 'that refuge of so much exiled English innocence'. He also described the 'second-rate dandies and *roués*, widow ladies who always have a law-suit' and sharpers who typically resided at the cheap Continental *tables d'hôte* (54). From 1853, Dickens frequently holidayed in Boulogne. Leaving there with a friend in 1863 he saw a famous exiled bankrupt, George Hudson, the former 'Railway King':

> Taking leave of Manby was a shabby man of whom I had some remembrance, but whom I could not get into his place in my mind. Noticing when we stood out of the harbour that he was on the brink of the pier, waving his hat in a desolate manner, I said to Manby, 'Surely I know that man.' – 'I should think you did,' said he; 'Hudson!' (Forster 3.244)

'Restraining influence, Mr. Twemlow?

till divorce do us part.']　　Mrs Lammle's words parody the marriage service: 'till death do us part'. Dickens and his wife Catherine lived apart after 1858. In 1854 he had used the character of Stephen Blackpool in *HT* to represent the suffering caused by the difficulty of obtaining divorces. There were *HW* articles, one with the title 'Marriage Gaolers' (13.583–5), on the same subject. Since then the Matrimonial Causes Act of 1857 had made divorce somewhat easier, though the grounds for divorce were few, and it remained very difficult for a wife to sue: for instance, what would now be regarded as gross brutality was not then sufficient grounds for a wife to divorce her husband. Mrs Lammle's predicament is intensified by the fact that she has no adequate means of supporting herself.

With those words, she walks out

slippery little horse-hair bolster]   The sofa and bolster of the period were stuffed with horsehair and covered with a shiny black fabric. The sofa on which Dickens died, preserved at his birthplace in Portsmouth, is of this kind (Hill).

Tippins the divine

to sup at last, and turn into bed]   The characteristic conclusion of entries in Samuel Pepys's diary, for instance, 4 March 1666: 'And so back home, and after supper, to bed.'

long overdue at the woolsack]   The woolsack is the official seat of the Lord Chancellor as speaker of the House of Lords. It is a large red square bag of wool, rather like an enlarged hassock; there were originally four, as symbols of England's staple trade. The term 'woolsack' is often applied to the office of the Lord Chancellor.

A new race of intimate friends

A new race of intimate friends has sprung up]   In Greek legend, the hero Cadmus sowed the ground with dragon's teeth, which sprang up as armed men who fought one another; the leading houses of Thebes claimed descent from the survivors.

a Contractor who (it has been calculated) gives employment, directly and indirectly, to five hundred thousand men.]   A railway contractor, like Hudson, the great Thomas Brassey (1805–70) or Sir Samuel Morton Peto (1809–89). In 1846, for instance, Peto employed nine thousand men on the Ely-to-Peterborough line; for the London-to-Birmingham railway he had fourteen thousand men on his payroll. Brassey's vast enterprises extended to four continents. Peto was ruined, and Brassey badly shaken, by the collapse of Overend, Gurney in 1866. Main contractors like Brassey or Peto subcontracted parts of a line. These subcontractors in turn appointed 'gangers', and the gangers took on the navvies.

a Chairman]   A chairman of boards of directors of companies, doubtless including railway companies.

hadn't a sixpence eighteen months ago]   ' "Capital!" ' exclaims a Greek to one of Meason's characters, 'that is what you Englishmen are always talking about, and the craving after it keeps you behind the rest of the world. Give me pen, ink, paper, and stamps, combined with commercial credit, *and I will never ask for capital*. Capital, my dear sir, *is merely nominal, and can be increased to any extent you like, in five minutes*' (*AYR* 14.87). Buffer's Genius has successfully 'bulled' the market, that is, speculated for a rise, a rise he has no doubt 'rigged'.

these Fathers of the Scrip-Church]   In his *Latter-Day Pamphlets*, Carlyle wrote of 'big Capitalists, Railway Directors, gigantic Hucksters, Kings of Scrip, *without* lordly quality, or other virtue except cash' ('The Present Time'). Hudson was the 'Ideal of the Scrip Ages' ('Hudson's Statue').

the word 'Committee' is occasionally heard] Veneering is bribed, probably with shares, to advance the interest of the railway company on a parliamentary committee. Railway lines could not be laid without an Act of Parliament. Such 'parliamentary expenses' could be considerable: a return of 1858 records that the Great Northern distributed some £1.4 million on that account, about 10 per cent of the company's authorized capital. In Dickens's view the railway system was 'so represented in Parliament by Directors, contractors, scrip jobbers, and so forth, that no minister dare touch it' (*Nonesuch* 3.430).

cut up the opposition, root and branch] Malachi 4.1: 'the day that cometh . . . shall leave them neither root nor branch' (here with a pun on 'branch').

Mr. and Mrs. Podsnap are of the company

those loves of Navvies] 'Navvies' (or 'navigators') was a term originally used for those labourers employed in the construction of canals, but which was then applied to those engaged in the heavy work of excavating, tunnelling, blasting and bridge-building on the railways and other public works. The men were renowned for their capacities for food and drink: they 'lived freely, and a myth grew up, that of the extraordinarily potent navvy man' (Coleman, 1965, 162).

BOOK THE FOURTH.
A TURNING.

The proverb is: 'It is a long lane that has no turning.' The title of book 3 is 'A Long Lane'.

Book 4, Chapter 1
Sixteenth monthly number
August 1865

SETTING TRAPS.

It was an amateur-sculler

a Wagerbut]   A wager-boat, a light racing sculling-boat used in contests between single scullers.

So imperturbable was the air

wooden objects by the weir . . . like huge teetotums]   The posts at which vessels moor whilst waiting for the lock to be opened. A 'teetotum' is a four-sided disc on a spindle, which is spun, like a top, as a toy.

'Ha ha! Don't be afeerd

where he lost the tide – say Richmond]   The tide ascends the Thames to Teddington ('Tide-end-town'), which is about fifteen miles above London Bridge and about two and three-quarter miles above Richmond.

Riderhood nodded, and the figure

the posts, bearing the dagger that slew Wat Tyler, in the City of London shield.]   The emblem is placed on the posts to show that the towing-path is the property of the City Corporation (Hill). The coat of arms of the City of London is a white shield bearing a red cross with a dagger, blade upright, in the upper left quarter. The dagger is popularly supposed to be that with which the one-time Mayor of London, William Walworth, slew Wat Tyler, one of the leaders of the Peasants' Revolt of 1381, a 'not very valiant deed' according to *CHE* (19).

The boat went on, under the arching trees

And then the red . . . mounting up to Heaven, as we say that blood, guiltily shed, does.] In *BH* Dickens commented that 'blood unlawfully shed, *will* cry aloud, and *will* be heard' (28). The idea derives from Genesis 4.10: 'the voice of thy brother's blood crieth unto me from the ground'.

'He has put up for the night

at an Angler's Inn] The Red Lion inn, situated north of Henley Bridge on the west bank of the river, 'a favourite resort for the disciples of Izaak Walton and boating men in general' (Allbut, 1899, 118). The lawn is a favourite standpoint for spectators at the Henley Royal Regatta.

'No!' said Riderhood, shaking his head

I've been brought out o' drowning] There are two superstitions: the first that someone who has nearly been drowned cannot be drowned; the second that someone who has nearly been drowned will in the end be drowned – that the water will have its own.

Riderhood, leaning back

water enough in all the Thames] *Macbeth* 2.2.60–3:

> Will all great Neptune's ocean wash this blood
> Clean from my hand? No; this my hand will rather
> The multitudinous seas incarnadine,
> Making the green one red.

'At his journey's end.

'At his journey's end.] *Othello* 5.2.270–1: 'Here is my journey's end, here is my butt,/And very sea-mark of my utmost sail.'

He dropped into a chair

a great spirt of blood burst from his nose.] Traditionally supposed to be a sign of misfortune:

> My nose bleeds.
> One that were superstitious, would count
> This ominous.
>
> (John Webster, *The Duchess of Malfi* 2.3.58–60)

245

The Runaway Match

    Wegg insults Mr Boffin: who seems to quail before him.

Eugene's pursuit

Mr Bradley Headstone	Yes
Riderhood?	
Charley Hexam?	No

Open at Plashwater Weir Mill Lock, and prepare for
the attack upon Eugene.

The Lammles fail with Mr Boffin?	Yes
Georgiana?	And end them.

Book the Fourth   A Turning

Chapter I

Setting <Two> Traps

Picture of Plashwater Weir Mill Lock
   Eugene coming up the river, after Lizzie
      Tracked by Bradley disguised
   'Why dressed like me?' thinks Riderhood. – Can't quite
make out.

          The Red Neck-kerchief

> 'The man as has been brought through drowning, can't be drowned.'

Chapter II

The Golden Dustman rises a little

Mr Boffin quietly disposes of the Lammles, nips their
designs in the bud –
      End of the Lammles
      –End of Georgiana.

Chapter III

The Golden Dustman sinks again

Mr Boffin seems to quail before the bullying Wegg
     Insolence of power on Wegg's part.
     Lead on to 'check-mate' chapter in N? XIX

Chapter IV

A Runaway Match

Bella runs away with her father – to marry John Rokesmith
   Greenwich
       And an old Pensioner.
Dinner at the hotel where the 'Innocent Elopement' came off.
     The ships 'sailing to us from the unknown seas.'

The thunder rolled

The thunder rolled]   Dickens underwrote the number by two and a half pages. Six passages, marked *A–F*, are added to the MS of the number. There are four short passages, the description of the storm beginning with these words and ending 'stealing a look at the man upon the bed' (passage *C*), and a long passage added to book 4, chapter 4 (see p. 252).

Book 4, Chapter 2

THE GOLDEN DUSTMAN RISES A LITTLE.

Mr. and Mrs. Lammle had come to breakfast

to breakfast]   Invitations to breakfast were quite fashionable; the usual hour was about nine.

'Sophronia, darling, Mr. and Mrs. Boffin

the old adage, that self-praise is no recommendation.']   A classic example, from which English proverbs derive, is Plutarch, 'Life of Cato': 'Self-praise and self-deprecation are alike absurd.'

'I haven't a minute

a dreadful old stony woman . . . in a turban]   The turban was worn as early as 1810; by 1830–40 it was twisted in a variety of shapes, often decorated with a plume; by 1840–50 it was small and had dangling ends falling to the shoulder on each side. In Thackeray's *Vanity Fair* the impressive Miss Pinkerton wears 'a large solemn turban' (1).

'Ma says chits and jewels

jewellers' cotton]   Cotton wool.

Book 4, Chapter 3

THE GOLDEN DUSTMAN SINKS AGAIN.

The evening of that day

a five-o'clock dinner]   Five o'clock was the fashionable dinner hour.

Mr. Boffin took his nose in his hand

a good man and true.]   'Are you good men and true?' Dogberry asks Verges and the members of the watch in *Much Ado about Nothing* (3.3.1).

'Oh no, Mr. Boffin,' was the ironical answer.

' **"If you'll come to the Bower I've shaded for you**]   Wegg adapts the first stanza of the song 'Will You Come to the Bow'r,' by J. Moore, music by J. E. Newell:

> Will you come to the Bow'r I have shaded for you,
> Our bed shall be roses all spangled with dew,
> Will you, will you, will you, will you, come to the Bow'r,
> Will you, will you, will you, will you, come to the Bow'r?

Mr. Boffin, entering the usual chamber

that man of might]   A phrase from the poem 'Tubal Cain' by Charles Mackay: 'Old Tubal Cain was a man of might/In the days when earth was young' (1-2).

'Any how, and every how

to the right-about.']   'Right about!' is a military command.

Mr. Boffin, as if he were about

to have his portrait painted, or to be electrified, or to be made a Freemason]   In each case the person was seated on a chair raised on a shallow dais: 'Kate Nickleby sat in a very faded chair raised upon a very dusty throne in Miss La Creevy's room, giving that lady a sitting for the portrait upon which she was engaged' (*NN* 10).

Mr. Venus, reminded of the duties

a Gum-Tickler]   An Americanism: the first drink, taken straight.

'Milk and water-erily you mean

"Along the line the signal ran]   From the refrain of 'The Death of Nelson' by
S. J. Arnold, music by J. Braham:

> 'Twas in Trafalgar's bay
> We saw the Frenchmen lay,
> Each heart was bounding then,
> We scorn'd the foreign yoke,
> For our Ships were British Oak,
> And hearts of oak our men!
>
> Our Nelson mark'd them on the wave,
> Three cheers our gallant Seamen gave,
> Nor thought of home or beauty,
> Along the line this signal ran,
> 'England expects that every man
> This day will do his duty!'

Book 4, Chapter 4

A RUNAWAY MATCH.

Were they expected at Greenwich?

the coaly (but to him gold-dusty) little steamboat]   'For the excursion to
Greenwich, there were sharp-nosed paddle steamers with tall black Puffing Billy
funnels' (Millicent Rose 188–9).

a gruff and glum old pensioner]   Greenwich Hospital, a magnificent
building by Wren and others, was opened as an asylum for disabled seamen in
1705. During the Napoleonic Wars there were as many as 2,700 pensioners. An
Act of 1865 offered the pensioners out-pensions, an option which the majority
preferred, and the buildings then became the Royal Naval College. The
pensioners were one of the sights of London: 'The happy, peaceful old men who
used to bask against the walls upon the stone benches . . . were pleasant fellows to
chat with. And they were picturesque withal; and gave a meaning to the galleries
under which they hobbled' (Doré and Jerrold, 1872, iv).

Say, cherubic parent

Say, cherubic parent] Mock-Miltonic.

for Greenwich church, to see his relations.] St Alphege's Church (1710), a fine work by Nicholas Hawksmoor. The stately and massive portico over the steps that lead to the main doors supports a magnificent pediment with a deep hollowed arch. The interior was destroyed by an incendiary bomb in the Second World War. There are large sculptured cherubs on Hawksmoor's huge stone urns in Church Street.

He was a slow sailor

in a car and griffins, like the spiteful Fairy at the christenings of the Princesses] A recollection of Perrault, 'Sleeping Beauty', though in that tale it is the good fairy, not the wicked fairy, who rides in 'a fiery chariot, drawn by dragons'.

a stealthy movement somewhere in the remote neighbourhood of the organ] There is a gallery at St Alphege's: the Boffins hide in the Royal Pew, which was immediately below the organ and, like the organ case, carved in the manner of Grinling Gibbons.

And now, the church-porch

a narcotic consciousness of having dreamed a dream.] Romeo says: 'I dreamt a dream to-night' (*Romeo and Juliet* 1.4.50).

Pa was, at first

a window of the Observatory . . . the Astronomer Royal] The observatory, a 'quaint old pile, with its familiar turrets and domes' (Thorne, 1876, 260), was built on the advice of Wren, and at the order of Charles II, in 1675. The Astronomer Royal in 1865 was Sir G. B. Airy.

cottage on Blackheath] Blackheath is in Kent, six miles from the centre of London, and south of Greenwich Park. By the 1860s the heath had been built up, too, and the town of Blackheath had churches, schools, assembly rooms, banks and several good shops (Thorne, 1876, 48–9).

A modest little cottage

a bunch of keys] The housekeeping keys: when Esther arrives at Bleak House the maid brings her 'a basket . . . with two bunches of keys in it, all labelled'; ' "The large bunch is the housekeeping, and the little bunch is the cellars" ' (6).

Then they, all three

a charming ride]   Thorne described the attractions of Greenwich Park:

> The park is only 190 acres in area, but it is greatly varied in surface, and hence its great charm. Everywhere the scenery is different, and everywhere beautiful; while from the high and broken ground by the Observatory and One Tree Hill the distant view of London and the Thames, with its shipping, are of matchless beauty and interest. (259)

It was a pleasant sight

the Infant Bands of Hope.]   By the 1850s the temperance movement had turned its attention to rearing children in sobriety. The first Band of Hope was founded in Leeds by Mrs Anne Carlile in 1847; by January 1860 there were 120 in London alone (Brian Harrison, 1971, 193–4). Dickens gave an ironic account of a Band of Hope meeting in *UT*, chapter 37, 'A Plea for Total Abstinence'.

The appearance of dinner

The appearance of dinner]   The passage from these words to 'I think it must be, Pa and John dear, because I look so happy' is passage *F* of the added material (see p. 248).

What a dinner!

What a dinner!]   Thackeray described the effect in 'Greenwich – Whitebait':

> At last we come to the bait – the twelve dishes of preparatory fish are removed, the India sauced salmon has been attacked ... the stewed eels have been mauled, and the flounder soup-tureen is empty. All those receptacles of pleasure are removed – eyes turned eagerly to the door, and enter
> Mr. Derbyshire (with a silver dish of whitebait).
> John (brown bread and butter).
> Samuel (lemons and cayenne).
> Frederick (a dish of whitebait).
> Gustavus (brown bread and butter).
> Adolphus (whitebait).
> A waiter with a napkin, which he flaps about the room in an easy *dégagé* manner.
> 'There's plenty more to follow, sir,' says Mr. D., whisking off the cover.

samples of the fishes of divers colours that made a speech in the Arabian Nights]   In 'The Fisherman and the Jinni' in the *Arabian Nights*, a fisherman catches fish of four colours: red, white, blue and yellow. The fish represent the Muslim, Persian, Christian and Jewish citizens of a city that has been placed under a spell. When the fish are cooked a young woman appears, calling on them to remember their covenant. The fish reply that they will.

So, she leaning on her husband's arm

And O what a bright old song it is]   Dickens concludes the chapter with the opening words of a song popular in his schooldays. The many versions were nearly all sung to the French air 'C'est l'amour' (Ley, 'Sentimental songs in Dickens' 316).

Book 4, Chapter 5   Seventeenth monthly number
September 1865

CONCERNING THE MENDICANT'S BRIDE.

'No. Your daughter Bella

bestowed herself upon a Mendicant.']   The term 'mendicant' was applied to vagabonds and other street people.

'The true point is

with some pew-opener or other]   Pew-openers were usually elderly women, like Mrs Miff in *DS*, 'a mighty dry old lady, sparely dressed, with not an inch of fulness anywhere about her' (31). At his wedding David Copperfield wonders 'why pew-openers must always be the most disagreeable females procurable' (43).

'As of course you would have done?

'Viper!']   The young of the viper are supposed to feed on the mother: hence they traditionally represent ingratitude.

'I shouldn't like it

the wishes in the Fairy story, that were all fulfilled as soon as spoken]   A feature of many fairy-stories.

Her married life glided

without pursuing the China house into minuter details]   Bella's idea of China is as vague as that of Flora Finching in *LD* (1.13). In the nineteenth century Britain traded with China in silk, porcelain, lacquer, carved wood, ivory and, above all, tea.

253

The Wilfers. – Miss Lavinia executes her first hysterics.

Bella at home   John Rokesmith's secret.   British Housewife

                The baby coming

The attack upon Eugene
    < Eugene app > Lizzie saves him
                  Back to the opening chapter of the story

Chapter V.

Concerning The Mendicant's Bride.

Mrs Wilfer is of the opinion that her child has united herself to 'a mendicant.'

Miss Lavvy's first hysterics

Then Bella's visit home.

Then her housekeeping and pleasant ways

Her husband harping on how she would like to be rich

And so to her being in the family-way.

Chapter VI.

A Cry for Help.

Open with the Paper Mill Village on a Saturday Night

And a wretched little Fair

Eugene alone, except for a Bargeman lying on his face. – And what's there in that?

Scene between Eugene and Lizzie

Attack on Eugene

Rescue by Lizzie

> Back to the opening chapter of the book. strongly.

Chapter VII

Better to be Abel than Cain.

Riderhood turns spie on Bradley.

Indication derived therefrom, how Bradley

did it. All his plot shewn.

Pursue Bradley, and unrepentant state of mind

Charley Hexam renounces him. The wretched creature afflicted by this selfishness.

Charley not wanted any more. Hints out his own future career.

tight-eyed people in more than double-soled shoes, with their pigtails pulling their heads of hair off, painted on transparent porcelain.] The vogue for chinoiserie, which began in the eighteenth century, inspired British pottery and porcelain manufacturers to produce breakfast, dinner and tea services decorated with imaginary Chinese scenes.

trim little wrappers] Outer garments used for housework, designed to envelop loosely the whole (or nearly the whole) figure.

putting back her hair with both hands, as if she were making the most business-like arrangements for going dramatically distracted] To represent their distraction, actresses conventionally let their hair down when they came to a mad-scene. In *NN*, for example, 'Miss Petowker of the Theatre Royal Drury Lane' is 'entreated to begin the Blood-Drinker's Burial, to which end, that young lady let down her back hair' (14).

The Complete British Family Housewife] There were numerous cookery books with titles like this for the guidance of ordinary women running modest homes. Mrs Beeton's immensely successful *Book of Household Management* (1861) was first published in sixpenny monthly parts in the 1850s. A selection of the more economical recipes was published as *The Englishwoman's Cookery Book* (1863 [1862]). Dickens encouraged his wife, Catherine, to publish a cookery book, *What Shall We have for Dinner? Satisfactorily Answered by Numerous Bills of Fare for from Two to Eighteen Persons. By Lady Maria Clutterbuck* (1851). This passage reflects his concern that women be educated in 'Common Things' – the basics of cookery, household management, accounts and needlework. See page 139.

Kamskatchan language] Kamchatka is a peninsula in north-east Siberia, with a population in 1870 of 5,846. The Kamchadale language has a very poor vocabulary and could not then be assigned to any known group. It had become something of a cliché to allude to Kamchatka. Prior to Eliza Acton's *Modern Cookery for Private Families* (1855) and Mrs Beeton's *Household Management*, most cookery writers gave only vague instructions, omitting accurate weights and measures, a complete list of ingredients, and precise directions for preparation.

There was likewise

salamander] A circular iron plate which is heated and put over a dish to brown it.

Another branch of study

the City Intelligence] The newspaper column.

how much gold had been taken to the Bank] Gold had been discovered in California in 1848 and in Australia in 1851, and the arrival in London of a bullion shipment was always news. The supply of gold underlay the economic prosperity of the era.

The cherub investing himself

Jack Horner]   A character in a nursery rhyme:

> Little Jack Horner
> Sat in the corner,
> Eating a Christmas pie;
> He put in his thumb,
> And pulled out a plum,
> And said, What a good boy am I!

Left to herself, she sat down

your first curtain lecture.]   A 'curtain lecture' is a reproof given by a wife to her husband (given in bed, thus bed-curtains).

the stool of repentance]   A common figurative expression: a stool was formerly placed in a conspicuous position in Scottish churches for the public repentance of offenders (especially against chastity).

'Pretty good!' said Bella

as you know your Catechism]   'What is your name?' and 'Who gave you this name?' are the first two questions in the Catechism in the Book of Common Prayer.

'It's not all, John dear

a dreadful Secondly, and a dreadful Thirdly to come – as I used to say to myself in sermon-time]   In *UT* Dickens described how as a child he was submitted to the sermons of 'Boanerges Boiler' and how at the end he was 'hauled out of the place of meeting . . . and catechized respecting Boanerges Boiler, his fifthly, his sixthly, and his seventhly, until I have regarded that reverend person in the light of a most dismal and oppressive Charade' (9).

Book 4, Chapter 6

A CRY FOR HELP.

It was a Saturday evening

Mrs. Hubbard's dog is said to have smoked]   In the comic nursery rhyme 'Mother Hubbard and Her Dog' by Sarah Catherine Martin, first published 1805:

> She took a clean dish
> To get him some tripe;
> But when she came back
> He was smoking a pipe.

Fearful to relate

even a sort of little Fair]   Dickens's defence of the amusements of the poor began with *Sunday under Three Heads* and continued through his writings, most notably in the *HW* articles 'The Amusements of the People' and in *HT*.

Some despairing gingerbread . . . had cast a quantity of dust upon its head in its mortification]   Icing sugar is commonly used by bakers to disguise stale goods. The Hebrews in the Bible placed dust or ashes on the head as a sign of mortification, a practice preserved in the Christian ceremony on Ash Wednesday.

a heap of nuts, long, long exiled from Barcelona . . . speaking English so indifferently as to call fourteen of themselves a pint.]   The nuts called 'Barcelonas', which were, in fact, from Tarragona, were kiln-dried and hence long-lasting. Political exiles from Spain had settled in numbers in north London after the destruction of the Spanish constitution by Ferdinand VII in 1823. This is a 'slang pint', a measure with a very thick, or false, bottom.

A Peep-show]   The Victorian showman 'Lord' George Sanger described the peep-show exhibited by his father:

> This was nothing more than a large box carried on the back, containing some moveable and very gaudy pictures, and having six peep-holes fitted with fairly strong lenses. When a pitch was made, the box was placed on a folding trestle and the public were invited to walk up and see the show . . . My father . . . could 'patter' in the most approved style, especially about the Battle of Trafalgar, scenes of which formed the staple feature of his little show. (Sanger, 19)

altering the Duke of Wellington's nose]   A prominent feature, of which cartoonists took full advantage; the Duke's popular nickname was 'Old Nosey'.

a Learned Pig]   Learned Pigs were among the most common of trained animals to appear at fairs and in taverns. A particularly famous one at the time of Dickens's childhood was the subject of an autobiography, *The Life and Adventures* *of Toby the Sapient Pig* (?1805). Among the dummy books at Gad's Hill was the 'Life and Letters of a Learned Pig' in six volumes.

hewers of wood and drawers of water]   The phrase derives from Joshua 9.21, 23, and Deuteronomy 29.11.

I will do anything within the limits

'See here! Napoleon Buonaparte at St. Helena.']   Napoleon was exiled to the island of St Helena after his defeat at Waterloo. His famous folded-arm stance was defined by the paintings of Benjamin Robert Haydon (1786–1846): 'I have painted nineteen Napoleons. Thirteen musings at St. Helena, and six other musings, and three Dukes and Copenhagens. By Heavens! how many more?' (diary, 5 March 1844).

Eugene Wrayburn went the opposite way

Eugene Wrayburn went the opposite way]   Eugene and Lizzie met on the towpath by the river about halfway between Henley and Marsh. Eugene begins by strolling along the west bank towards his inn at Henley but, instead, crosses the river at Henley Bridge, continuing his walk in the same direction along the other side of the river. It is here, opposite the town, that he is attacked by Bradley. Lizzie, meanwhile, has walked off towards Marsh, but crosses the river by the lock gates and walks along the east side of the river. She is, in fact, walking behind Eugene. When she hears the attack she rows downstream, past Henley (the 'hilly street' is New Street), finally bringing Eugene's body to the lawn of the Red Lion inn (Allbut, 1899, 123–4).

At length, she reached

broken splintered pieces of wood]   In *The Dream of Eugene Aram*, Aram attacks his victim with 'Two sudden blows with a ragged stick' (85). He then throws the body into a river.

Book 4, Chapter 7

BETTER TO BE ABEL THAN CAIN.

Cain complains: 'My punishment is greater than I can bear' (Genesis 4.13). In *The Dream of Eugene Aram* Aram comes upon one of his pupils reading ' "The Death of Abel" ' (48): he tells the pupil of 'how murderers walk the earth/Beneath the curse of Cain' (67–8) and of his own terrible dream: 'A dozen times I groan'd; the dead/Had never groan'd but twice!' (113–14).

Day was breaking

the cold eastern glare . . . the eye of the firmament quenched . . . the stare of the dead.]   There are echoes of Macbeth's description of the ghost of Banquo:

> Thy bones are marrowless, thy blood is cold;
> Thou has no speculation in those eyes
> Which thou dost glare with! (3.4.94–6)

Now, too, was he cursed

doing the evil deed again]   The paragraph recalls the words of Macbeth: 'If it were done when 'tis done, then 'twere well/It were done quickly' (1.7.1–2). In *MED* Jasper says: ' "I did it over and over again . . . it seemed not worth the doing, it was done so soon" ' (23).

The school reopened

all through the day.]   The MS continues:

He was neither sorry for having done it, nor pressingly afraid of being found out. His misery was, that he must think of it, must take himself to task for having done it ill, must incessantly reconstruct the scheme and redo the deed.

Again Mary Anne's telegraphic arm

telegraphic arm]   The pre-electric telegraph, invented by Chappe in France in 1792, consisted of upright posts with movable arms, the signals being made by positioning the arms according to a code.

'Where were you,' said the boy

Don't tell me.]   A MS passage is omitted:

> Don't tell me.'
>   Bradley Headstone for one brief moment threw up his arms and head as if he were about to shriek. The moment passing, he sat quite still.

Was it strange

unrelieved by a single tear.]   The MS continues:

> But he must be up and doing. He must be ever doing the deed again and again, better and better, with more and more of precaution, though never in a swifter way. His head had got to ache with the sound of the blows; in their monotonous repetition they had begun to go to a horrid tune; he could vary the preliminaries and the attendant circumstances in doing the act again, but the act, if his mind had ever been able to change the manner of it, would be changed no more. The same blows without diminution of number or force, the same effect from the blows, the same slipping of his foot upon the grass, the same strained face fallen back and turned up to the moon, the same face drifting down the stream.
>   The river ran in his thoughts distractedly. Whatever he planned in correction of the weak details of his scheme that could never be recalled, the river ran through all. On his way to do the murder the river was always meeting him as if to keep him back. On his way back from doing the murder, the river ran before him as if to tell the tale. Lock ho! Lock! But in recalling the cry (he in his fancy lying on the bed in the Lock-House) it was the river itself that seemed to call out to be let through to outstrip him.

Book 4, Chapter 8   Eighteenth monthly number
                                                                          October 1865

A FEW GRAINS OF PEPPER.

'Are you in the army?'

'Are you in the army?']   Though Fledgeby is a money-market man, he poses as a West End gentleman. One of Meason's figures attempts this effect:

> Mr. Hardy – for that was his name – had in appearance the combined characteristics of the guardsman and the stockbroker. His hat, shirt collar, scarf, pin, coat, trousers, boots, and umbrella, were undeniably and unmistakeably Westendish; his moustache, whiskers, and gloves would have

passed muster in the Household Brigade, or at Aldershot. Yet he had about him, habits and customs which savoured strongly of Capel-court. (*AYR* 11.13)

'Perhaps,' said Miss Jenny

which is Greek to me.]   The phrase was proverbial by the time Shakespeare used it in Casca's report of the speech of Cicero in *Julius Caesar* (1.2.283).

For the terrors undergone

a Gargantuan order]   In *La Vie très horrificque du Grand Gargantua* (1534) by Rabelais, the giant Gargantua eats and drinks in large quantities.

'Mr. Fledgeby in his shower-bath

his shower-bath]   The shower-bath was usually an ordinary lounge-bath or hip-bath with the addition of a small water-tank on legs. The shock from the cold water was intense.

'What do you think of vinegar

vinegar and brown paper]   A common treatment for bruises. In *NN* Squeers complains: ' "I was one blessed bruise, sir ... from *here* to *there*. Vinegar and brown paper, vinegar and brown paper, from morning to night ... you might have thought I was a large brown paper parcel" ' (34).

Miss Jenny got his Persian gown

extinguished his eyes crookedly with his Persian cap]   The cap is compared to the conical extinguishers used to extinguish candles and lamps.

The last thing Miss Jenny saw

took omnibus]   Horse-drawn omnibuses were instituted by a Mr Shillibeer in 1829. By this time there were about three thousand running on principal routes at about five-minute intervals. Fares were threepence or sixpence.

Book 4, Chapter 9

TWO PLACES VACATED.

'It looked so bad, Jenny

I was hateful in mine own eyes.]   Riah's words suggest a number of Old Testament phrases, particularly from Proverbs: for instance, 'The way of a fool is right in his own eyes' (12.15), and 'All the ways of men are clean in his own eyes' (16.2). Also Isaiah 5.21: 'Woe unto them that are wise in their own eyes.'

the unwilling necks of the whole Jewish people.]   The Jews are a number of times described as 'a stiffnecked people' in the Bible (for instance, Exodus 34.9).

I would that all our people remembered it! Though I have little right to say so, seeing that it came home so late to me.']   These sentences are not in the MS.

'On the contrary, godmother

what a pumpkin is]   In the story of Cinderella, the Fairy Godmother turns a pumpkin into a carriage.

'Godmother, godmother, godmother!'

the Good Samaritan]   Luke 10.30–7.

'Oh! Bother your people!'

it's a pity they ever got out of Egypt.]   Exodus 13–14.

The letter, which was scrawled

uphill and downhill and round crooked corners]   After the nursery rhyme 'Goosey, goosey gander':

> Goosey, goosey gander,
>   Whither shall I wander?
> Upstairs and downstairs
>   And in my lady's chamber.

This market of Covent Garden

Covent Garden . . . had the attraction for him which it has for . . . the drunken tribe.]   The opera house and other nightspots, as well as the market, provided as near as possible a 24-hour life:

Dolls' Dress Maker and her bad child
    The Jew
        Fledgeby? <u>Caned by Lammle.</u>

Eugene married to Lizzie, on his sick bed, by the Rev: Frank Milvey.
Eugene dying.

    Kill Mr Dolls?
        Funeral of Mr Dolls

        'I hope I should amend, if I recovered,' says Eugene, 'but
        I am afraid I shouldn't!'

Chapter VIII

A Few Grains of Pepper

Fascination Fledgeby soundly flogged by Lammle

Mrs Lammle keeping watch

Described through the Dolls' Dress Maker

who favours him with the title

of the chapter

Chapter IX

Two Places Vacated

Riah, the Jew

  Death of the bad child

    Dolls' Dress Maker fetched to Eugene

So: By Lightwood

  Get the Dolls' Dress Maker to nurse Eugene.

> Eugene, to clear her reputation, enjoins Mortimer never to punish Bradley.

Chapter X.

The Dolls' Dress Maker < finds > discovers a word

And the word is: 'wife'

    < The marriage chapter >

Chapter XI.

> The marriage chapter

Effect is given to the Dolls' Dress Maker's discovery

Open with Bella, and her husband's mystery.

Then, the Milvey's

Glimpse of Bradley in his misery. And

then the marriage: 'I think upon the whole I had better die, my dear.'

Early coffee-shops and taverns are gorged with customers, for the Covent Gardeners are essentially jolly gardeners, and besides, being stalwart men, are naturally hungry and athirst after their nights' labour ... among the hale, hearty, fresh-coloured market-people, you may see, here and there, some tardy lingerer at 'the halls of dazzling light,' who has just crawled away from the enchanted scene, and, cooling his fevered throat with soda-water, or whipping up his jaded nerves with brandy and milk, fancies, because he is abroad at six o'clock in the morning, that he is 'seeing life.' (Sala, 1859, 48)

There is a swarm of young savages

young savages always flitting about ... as the policeman hunts them] Dickens touched on this subject in *UT*:

Covent-garden Market, when it was market morning, was wonderful company ... But one of the worst night sights I know in London, is to be found in the children who prowl about this place; who sleep in the baskets, fight for the offal, dart at any object they think they can lay their thieving hands on, dive under the carts and barrows, dodge the constables, and are perpetually making a blunt pattering on the pavement of the Piazza with the rain of their naked feet. (13)

He returned to the subject in a later *UT* essay (21).

the Powers that be] Romans 13.1: 'the powers that be are ordained of God'.

in top-boots they would make a deafening clatter.] The high leather boots, formerly worn by farmers and country gentlemen. In a letter to W. F. de Cerjat, Dickens wrote: 'At this present moment I am on my little Kentish freehold (*not* in top-boots, and not particularly prejudiced that I know of)' (7 July 1858, *Nonesuch* 3.30).

As the load was put down

the nearest doctor's shop.'] An apothecary's shop, similar to a modern chemist's shop, though the apothecary himself would be the equivalent of today's general practitioner.

Thither he was brought

globular red bottles, green bottles, blue bottles] In Charles Lever's *A Day's Ride* (1863), an apothecary asks: 'What respect has the world any longer for the great phials of ruby, and emerald, and marine blue, which, at nightfall, were once the magical emblems of our mysteries, seen afar through the dim mists of louring atmospheres, or throwing their lurid glare upon passers-by?' (1).

as if Death had marked him: 'Mine.'] Perhaps an echo of a line from 'The Epitaph' in Gray's *Elegy Written in a Country Churchyard*: 'And Melancholy marked him for her own' (120).

Therefore, the police

the dolls with no speculation in their eyes ... Mr. Dolls with no speculation in his.] Macbeth's description of the ghost of Banquo:

> Thy bones are marrowless, thy blood is cold;
> Thou hast no speculation in those eyes,
> Which thou dost glare with! (3.4.94–6)

'I mean to go alone

the service in the Prayer-book says, that we brought nothing into this world] The Order for the Burial of the Dead reads:

'We brought nothing into this world, and it is certain we carry nothing out. The Lord gave, and the Lord hath taken away: blessed be the name of the Lord.'

a lot of stupid undertaker's things] Dickens detested the rituals of mourning. In his will he gave the instructions:

I emphatically direct that I be buried in an inexpensive, unostentatious, and strictly private manner ... that at the utmost not more than three plain mourning coaches be employed; and that those who attend my funeral wear no scarf, cloak, black bow, long hat-band, or other such revolting absurdity. (*Nonesuch* 3.799)

After that previous carrying

another blossom-faced man, affecting a stately stalk, as if he were a Policeman of the D(eath) Division] The characteristic manner of the policeman on his beat would seem to have developed early (see *BH* 11). The Metropolitan Police District was divided into seventeen police divisions, each designated by an appropriate local name and by a letter of the alphabet. D division was the Marylebone division.

At last the troublesome deceased

the stately stalker stalked] After the tongue-twister: 'Round the rugged rock the ragged rascal ran.'

Those Furies, the conventionalities] The Furies, normally represented as three black women with snaky hair, were the avenging spirits of Greek mythology.

'Not a funeral, never fear!'

Court mourning they are rather proud of.]　　Court mourning was worn by those with any connection with court. In Thackeray's *Vanity Fair*, Becky, in the days of her triumph, 'talked about great people as if she had the fee-simple of Mayfair; and when the court went into mourning, she always wore black' (52).

my name's Jack Robinson!']　　The saying 'before you could say Jack Robinson', meaning 'very quickly', seems to derive from a song called 'Jack Robinson', which told the story of a sailor jilted by his love, and which ended with the line 'And he was off before you could say Jack Robinson' (Ashton, 1888, 258).

In a few moments the black bonnet

in a chaise . . . posting out of town.]　　Mortimer has hired a post-chaise, a faster and more expensive vehicle than the ordinary chaise.

Book 4, Chapter 10

THE DOLLS' DRESSMAKER DISCOVERS A WORD.

'Don't tell me not to speak

those places -- where are those endless places]　　There may be a recollection of De Quincey's description of his visions of vast spaces whilst under the influence of opium: 'Buildings, landscapes, &c. were exhibited in proportions so vast as the bodily eye is not fitted to receive. Space swelled, and was amplified to an extent of unutterable infinity' ('The Pains of Opium', *Confessions of an English Opium Eater*, 1822).

Book 4, Chapter 11

EFFECT IS GIVEN TO THE DOLLS' DRESSMAKER'S DISCOVERY.

It was near John's time

a sort of dimpled little charming Dresden-china clock]　A mantel or bracket clock in the form of a Dresden china female figure in voluminous skirts, among the folds of which is the gilded clock. Mrs Rouncewell in *BH* and Mrs Crisparkle in *MED* are compared to them (Hill).

'In earnest, Blue Beard

Blue Beard of the secret chamber?']　'Blue Beard' is one of Perrault's tales. A man of great wealth disfigured by a blue beard marries Fatima. His reputation is suspect because his previous wives have disappeared. While he is away, his young wife finds the keys of his secret chamber and discovers the bodies of the previous wives. Bluebeard discovers she has disobeyed him but is prevented from killing her.

They started directly

they waited at a railway station]　The South Western line ran from Waterloo to Reading, passing through the built-up areas of Southwark and Battersea and then crossing the river between Richmond and Twickenham. A carriage takes the party from Reading to Henley; the road runs closest to the river at Shiplake and near Henley. Mortimer would take this route because it is easier and quicker to get from London Bridge (terminus of the Greenwich line) to Waterloo, and there take a train to Reading, than to cross the city to Paddington (terminus of the Great Western line) to take a direct train to Henley.

That worthy couple

the various lamentations of David]　Psalms, as appointed, are said in both morning and evening services. The images of 'pitfalls' and 'rods of iron' are found in them: for instance, 'Thou shalt bruise them with a rod of iron' (2.9) and 'they have digged a pit before me, and are fallen into the midst of it themselves' (57.7).

This very exacting member

a marplot]　In Mrs Centlivre's play *The Busybody* (1709) the well-meant officiousness of the character Marplot constantly endangers the love stratagems of the other characters.

269

(as Who begat Whom, or some information concerning the Amorites)]
'Who begat Whom' is an allusion to the genealogies in Genesis. The Amorites
were one of the tribes in the Bible.

myrrh and frankincense . . . locusts and wild honey.]   The Wise Men gave
the baby Jesus 'gold, and frankincense, and myrrh' (Matthew 2.11). When John
the Baptist preached in the wilderness 'his meat was locusts and wild honey'
(Matthew 3.4).

'Had no play

'Had no play in your last holiday time?']   In *The Dream of Eugene Aram*,
Hood ironically comments on Aram: 'Much study had made him very lean,/And
pale, and leaden-ey'd' (29–30).

Lightwood had by this time

the departure-bell]   Handbells were rung by station porters.

'I hope so, dearest Lizzie

There is a sharp misgiving . . . that I ought to die]   Dickens noted in his
Book of Memoranda:

> As to the question whether I, Eugene, lying ill and sick even unto death, may
> be consoled by the representation that, coming through this illness, I shall
> begin a new life, and have energy and purpose and all I have yet wanted: 'I *hope* I
> should, but I *know* I shouldn't. Let me die, my dear.' (24)

Book 4, Chapter 12   Final double number
                                                         November 1865

THE PASSING SHADOW.

The winds and tides rose

the earth moved round the sun a certain number of times]   Had the earth
travelled as far as Dickens says, this would have been an unusual baby. About
eighteen months have passed between the eighteenth and nineteenth numbers.

saving and excepting]   A legal phrase.

Mr. Inspector, in a dark-blue buttoned-up

a dark-blue buttoned-up frock coat and pantaloons, presented a service-able, half-pay, Royal Arms kind of appearance]　　Because of the traditional British dislike of military authority, the uniform chosen for the New Police in 1829 was a compromise: 'Uniform it was – military it was not . . . the blue coat, blue or white trousers according to season, and black tall hat were almost indistinguishable from those of the man-in-the-street of the day' (Cunnington and Lucas, 1968, 255–6). Half-pay was paid to military and naval officers not in actual service or after retirement.

Mr. Inspector declined eating

so gravelled]　　So confounded, puzzled.

The whitewashed room was pure

a kind of criminal Pickford's.]　　Thomas Pickford started the famous carrying service in the reign of Charles I. Its operations greatly expanded in the nineteenth century with the spread of canals and railways. The name was recognized as symbolic of efficient transport (Hill).

'And talk of Time slipping by you

as if it was an animal at rustic sports with his tail soaped]　　The greased or soaped piglet used at country sports. The idea is to make the game of catching it more fun.

The inexhaustible baby, hearing this

marble-hearted parent]　　'Ingratitude, thou marble-hearted fiend' (*King Lear* 1.4.259).

a pause. – opening   after Bella's child is born

<u>The Inexhaustible Baby</u>

Check-mate to the Friendly Move.
    Defeat and disgrace of Silas Wegg
John Rokesmith
        His supposed poverty
        He seems under suspicion of murder

<u>Bella always faithful</u>

<He Tells> how Mrs Boffin found him out:
    How she, and he, and Mrs Boffin plotted:
     –and why (To reclaim Bella).

<u>The Fellowship Porters</u>
<u>The Steward and the Fellow-
Passenger</u>

+over
Mr Boffin, and
his story, concerning
the Dutch bottle
and its contents

  –and how it proves Bella to be
    the best and dearest of girls
  –and how she is Mrs John Harmon, and
    comes into no end of money

Also how he feigned
and why, clearing him
and Mrs Boffin,
and shewing them to be
the best of honest creatures

++over++
Riderhood and Bradley at the Lock again. Riderhood turns on Bradley and shows him how he (Bradley)
plotted to throw the appearance of guilt on him (Riderhood). Swears
he'll know all about him, and will never leave him unless well
paid. Bradley seizes him on the brink of the Lock at last
'It's no use. I can't be drowned.' – 'We'll try!' Holds him
tight, falls in with him purposely. Still holds him tight. Both
drowned.
  <Silas Wegg> ∧Mr Venus∧ and Pleasant Riderhood become a couple
  Sloppy and Miss Wren   Ditto   in perspective
  Eugene and Lizzie Hexam. The dawn of their new life
  Total smash of the Veneerings. He retires to Boulogne, and says ∧thereafter∧
  of all the other Members of the House of Commons, that they were the
  six hundred and odd dearest friends he ever had in the world. –
  End of Social chorus generally.
  <u>Twemlow?</u>

  <u>Riah?</u>
  Mortimer Lightwood?

'And so,' says Mr Boffin radiantly, ∧quoting himself in his feigning:∧ 'Mew, quack quack, Bow wow!'

+
   In the Dutch Bottle was the latest will
of all (found by Mr Boffin), leaving him all the
Property, to the disinheriting and excluding of John
Harmon. 'No,' said Mr Boffin, on finding it, 'this
will shall never see the light. This slur shall never
be cast upon young John, through my instrumentality.'
But not knowing what to do with it, and fearful
that it might be a crime at law to destroy it,
buried it again for the time being. Finding certain
signs (through Sloppy) that Wegg was poking about
and delving into the Mounds, took it up again. So
the Friendly Move receives check-mate, and the
Move only shows Mr Boffin in a brighter light.

++
Mrs Boffin's uneasiness while their little plot with
John Harmon was working out, arose from her ∧wifely∧ affection
being perpetually at war against Mr Boffin's pretence
of being a Miser, and a man quite spoiled by
prosperity.

(The notes carry on to the reverse of the sheet)

Chapter XII.

The Passing < The > Shadow < of the Harmon Murder >

John Harmon under suspicion of his own murder

   Bella fully trusting

      Mr Inspector's eyes opened   Baby

Chapter XIII.

Showing how the Golden Dustman helped to scatter dust.

Unwind the Boffin mystery, chiefly through Mrs Boffin

      Baby

> with
> great care

Chapter XIV.

Check-Mate to the Friendly Move

Unwind Venus and Wegg.

     Sloppy

     Pitch Wegg into mud cart

> with
> great care

Chapter XV.

What was caught in the traps that were set

Bradley's state of mind. Riderhood in the school. And the black board

    The Lock House again   And the drowning of the two.

Chapter XVI.

Persons and Things in General

Pa and Ma and Lavvy and George

   Riah – Twemlow – Miss Wren and Sloppy   Work through to Eugene & wife

Chapter XVII The Last.

The < voice > voice of society

about Eugene's marriage   Is the voice Veneering's?   or Boots's?

Worked through Lightwood   Or Mrs Veneering's   / or Brewer's

                 or Lady Tippins's?   or the Directors'

                            or the Contractor's?

                            And is it worth much,

                            after all?

Book 4, Chapter 13

SHOWING HOW THE GOLDEN DUSTMAN HELPED TO SCATTER DUST.

At this, Mrs. Boffin fairly screamed

clapping her hands, and bobbing . . . like a demented member of some Mandarin's family.] Victorian ornaments included Chinese mandarin figures, made of glazed china richly coloured, often a foot or two high, with movable heads and hands. They were manufactured in Europe.

The house inspected

smiling Peace associated herself with that young olive branch.] Shakespeare used the phrase 'smiling peace' in *King John* (3.1.246). An olive branch was an ancient emblem of peace, but 'olive branch' was also a phrase for a child (Psalms 128.3: 'Thy wife shall be as a fruitful vine . . . thy children like olive plants'), usually used facetiously by this time: ' "the Kenwigses," were the wife and olive branches of one Mr Kenwigs' (*NN* 14).

Book 4, Chapter 14

CHECKMATE TO THE FRIENDLY MOVE.

Though disappointed

fantail hat] A fantail hat was a hat with a leather flap attached to the back which protected the shoulders of the wearer while carrying heavy burdens such as baskets of dust.

'No, Mr. Wegg,' said Venus. 'When I use it

cobblers' punch] 'Punch' as the name for a drink is from a Hindu word meaning 'five', as there should be five ingredients: wine, water, lemon, sugar and spice. In cobblers' punch, the principal ingredient is gin, so 'cobblers' punch' is a facetious name for sweetened gin and water with a slice of lemon (Hill).

'I don't want to guess

the diwision of labour]　　Wegg unwittingly refers to the principle which Adam Smith identified in *The Wealth of Nations* (1776) as fundamental to economic progress. The title of Smith's opening chapter is: 'Of the Division of Labour'.

'Mr. Wegg,' said Venus, 'in a case

There are strings that must not be played upon.]　　The observation is a favourite of Dickens's lower-middle-class lovers. In *BH* Guppy says: ' "Jobling, there *are* chords in the human mind" ' (20); and in *BR* Sim Tappertit proclaims: ' "There are strings . . . in the human heart that had better not be wibrated" ' (22).

'When is it to come off?' asked Silas.

to come off]　　The phrase was used of boxing matches, but some of Dickens's less romantic characters use it of weddings. In *PP* Jingle tells Rachael: ' "ceremony comes off to-morrow" ' (10).

'Bof-fin!' replied Wegg

so much smeary glass to see through]　　1 Corinthians 13.12: 'For now we see through a glass, darkly; but then face to face.'

'There was likewise,' resumed Wegg

a pair of trestles, for which alone a Irish person . . . offered five and six]　　Many poor Irish emigrated to England at the time of the famine (1845–52). Estimating the costermongers' capital, Mayhew valued 'stalls and standings' at an average of five shillings each (1.56).

The words were but out of his mouth

a scavenger's cart]　　Scavengers were responsible for cleaning the streets:

> By the ordinary method of scavenging, the dirt is still swept or scraped to one side of the public way, then shovelled into a cart and conveyed to the place of deposit. In wet weather the dirt swept or scraped to one side is so liquified that it is known as 'slop', and is 'lifted' into the cart in shovels hollowed like sugar spoons.

Like the dustmen, scavengers used 'a heavily-built high box cart . . . furnished with a short ladder' (Mayhew 2.201, 175). Dustmen often doubled as scavengers.

Book 4, Chapter 15

WHAT WAS CAUGHT IN THE TRAPS THAT WERE SET.

The title recalls Job 18.8–10: 'For he is cast into a net by his own feet, and he walketh upon a snare. The gin shall take him by the heel, and the robber shall prevail against him. The snare is laid for him in the ground, and a trap for him in the way.'

How Bradley Headstone

risen . . . out of the ashes of the Bargeman]   In legend, the mythical bird, the phoenix, every five hundred years burnt its body on a funeral pyre and was reborn out of the ashes.

First, he had to bear

the steady pressure of the infernal atmosphere]   The pressure of the earth's atmosphere is discussed in one of the *AYR* articles on the elements, 'Air': ' "As light as air" is a proverbial expression. Air, nevertheless, is heavier than is generally imagined. It presses on us with a load of fifteen pounds on every square inch of surface of our bodies, although we do not so much as suspect its weight' (12.399).

For, then he saw that

left him to crawl along his blasted course.]   An echo of Hamlet's words: 'What should such fellows as I do crawling between earth and heaven?' (3.1.128); perhaps also of the 'blasted heath' on which Macbeth meets the witches (1.3).

'Oh! It's in the way of school!'

'I'll pound it]   To be certain: ' "I'll pound it, that Barney's managing properly" ' (*OT* 26).

Wots the diwisions of water]   Riderhood parodies the classroom practice of question and answer. For example, the 'divisions' type of question was common in the question-and-answer books. Chambers, *Miscellaneous Questions*, has '*Into what is the land divided?* – Into continents and islands,' and '*Into what are the waters on the globe divided?* – Into oceans, seas, lakes, and rivers' (Shatto, 1974).

'That's a lie,' said Riderhood

a Savings-Bank book]   The Savings Bank systems were established in the early part of the nineteenth century, largely through the efforts of the politician George Rose (1744–1818). They were intended to encourage the poor to save; hence facilities were provided for small deposits.

Not until the late daylight

this decaying statue move.]   At the conclusion of Mozart's opera *Don Giovanni* the statue of the Commendatore takes Don Giovanni in its stony grasp and drags him down to hell. See page 36.

'I can be!' returned Bradley

I'll hold you living, and I'll hold you dead.]   In 'The Tale About the Queer Client' in *PP*, a delirious man imagines revenging himself on a cruel creditor by drowning him in this way (21). In *GE* Magwitch says of Compeyson: ' "If I had died at the bottom there;" and he made an emphatic swing at the ditch with his manacled hands; "I'd have held to him with that grip, that you should have been safe to find him in my hold" ' (5). Later, Magwitch pulls Compeyson into the river with him and Compeyson drowns (54). In *TTC* Miss Pross takes hold of the vengeful Madame Defarge 'and clung to her with more than the hold of a drowning woman'. She says: ' "I'll hold you till one or other of us faints or dies!" ' (3.14). This part of the story may owe something to Edgar Allan Poe's story 'William Wilson' (1839). Dickens and Poe exchanged letters at the time of Dickens's first visit to America. In this short story, Wilson is haunted by a physical double, who has the same name and was born on the same day. His double imitates his mannerisms and dress: 'In his rivalry he might have been supposed actuated solely by a whimsical desire to thwart, astonish, or mortify myself; although there were times when I could not help observing, with a feeling made up of wonder, abasement, and pique, that he mingled with his injuries, his insults, or his contradictions, a certain most inappropriate, and assuredly most unwelcome, *affectionateness* of manner.' The double has 'a weakness in his faucial or guttural organs, which precluded him from raising his voice at any time *above a very low whisper*'. Wilson finally kills his double, whose dramatic last words are: ' "*You have conquered and I yield. Yet henceforward art thou also dead – dead to the World, to Heaven and to Hope! In me didst thou exist – and, in my death, see by this image, which is thine own, how utterly thou hast murdered thyself.*" '

Book 4, Chapter 16

PERSONS AND THINGS IN GENERAL.

In all their arrangements

that transatlantic dram which is poetically named An Eye-Opener] 'America is fertile in mixtures: what do we not owe her? Sherry cobler, gin sling, cocktail, mint julep, brandy smash, sudden death, eye openers' (Charles Reade, *Hard Cash*, 1863, 7).

no longer ravening but mild] An echo of Juliet's words about Romeo after he has killed Tybalt: 'Dove-feather'd raven! Wolfish-ravening lamb!' (3.2.76).

'I am sure you look so

as if one's under-petticoat was a backboard] A backboard was a board strapped across the back to straighten the figure. In a speech in 1857, Dickens recalled the 'youthful enthraller' at dancing school whose 'arms, which should have encircled my jacket . . . those precious arms, I say, were pinioned behind her by an instrument of torture called a backboard' (*Speeches* 241).

'If you meant to say

never brought up a young gazelle] An allusion to famous and much-parodied lines from 'The Fire Worshippers' in Thomas Moore's *Lallah Rookh*:

> Oh! ever thus, from childhood's hour,
> I've seen my fondest hopes decay;
> I never loved a tree or flower,
> But 'twas the first to fade away.
> I never nursed a dear gazelle
> To glad me with its soft black eye,
> But when it came to know me well
> And love me, it was sure to die! (280–7)

It was the crowning addition

'Exotics, George] Plants of foreign origin grown indoors.

'Why, you're like the giant

the giant . . . when he came home in the land of Beanstalk, and wanted Jack for supper.'] In 'Jack and the Beanstalk', Jack climbs the beanstalk to the land of the giants in the clouds. Each day he hides in a giant's house and steals an object of great value. When the giant comes home it cries out in 'a voice of thunder': ' "Wife, I smell fresh meat." '

'Never was taught a stitch

'Just gobbled and gobbled]   A gobble stitch is one made too long through haste or carelessness: 'Miss M. the milliner – her fright was so strong –/Made a great gobble-stitch, six inches long' (Thomas Hood, 'A Blow Up', 57–8).

'And as concerning the nests

a comic song . . . with "Spoken" in it.]   Songs with interspersed passages of spoken 'patter'. In his *Book of Memoranda* Dickens recorded the idea of

> The two people in the Incurable Hospital. – The poor incurable girl lying on a water-bed, and the incurable man who has a strange flirtation with her – comes and make[s] confidences to her – snips and arranges her plants – and < repe > rehearses to her the Comic Songs (!) by writing which, he materially helps out his living. (16)

'I'll take more care of her

than if she was a gold image]   Nebuchadnezzar set up a 'golden image' in Daniel 3.

'Dear old fellow,' Eugene began

equivalent to a melodramatic blessing.']   As, for instance, the blessing bestowed by Rolamo on his daughter at the end of *Clari; or, The Maid of Milan* (1823):

> *Rolamo. (starting up wildly.)* . . . Let me see my child! – my lost child found! – my child that I can own! (*Clari is set before him; they spring into each other's arms. Rolamo takes her hand, and unites it to the Duke's – They both kneel. Rolamo extends his hands over them, his eyes turned upward, and streaming with tears, and with a choaked voice, exclaims –* Heaven bless ye! (3.3)

'There spake the voice of wisdom

We are shepherds both. In turning to at last, we turn to in earnest.]   'Shepherds' because inexperienced beginners: ' "Jupiter!" exclaimed Mr. Folair, "what an unsophisticated shepherd you are, Johnson!" ' (*NN* 29). There is perhaps an allusion to the concluding lines of 'Lycidas':

> At last he rose, and twitched his mantle blue:
> Tomorrow to fresh woods, and pastures new. (192–3)

'You think this thumped head

I can say to you of the healthful music of my pulse what Hamlet said of his.]   'My pulse as yours doth temperately keep time,/And makes as healthful music' (3.4.140–1).

Book 4, Chapter the Last

THE VOICE OF SOCIETY.

Behoves Mortimer Lightwood

it is written in the Books of the Insolvent Fates that Veneering shall make a resounding smash next week.]   Since 1825 there had been a financial crisis about every ten years, and Victorians had come to believe there was an inevitability in the pattern. By the mid-1860s there were many commentators who thought they saw 'the clouds gathering' (Evans, 1864, 169). There was, as Dickens remarked in a letter of 25 October 1864, 'apprehension of a commercial crisis' (*Nonesuch* 3.402). The fall of Overend, Gurney and the resultant crisis in 1866 bore out the predictions. Dickens may have known something about the desperate state of affairs of that great old house in which, interestingly, Gottheimer had become deeply involved. By the middle of 1865 there were many who did. In July, in a last effort to fend off disaster, Overend, Gurney became a limited company (when it 'sold itself to the unsuspecting public and charged £500,000 for the goodwill' it was already 'insolvent by at least four millions sterling': Shannon, 1930–3, 614). Though the public rushed for the shares, *The Economist* commented that at least now there would be some public account of how the house was run and how sound it was (1865, 845).

having over-jobbed his jobberies]   'Jobbery' is the corrupt use of public office. 'To offer any bribe of money to a member of the House though it be only a guinea fee to a lawyer and M.P. for drawing up a petition to the House, is breach of privilege. Members proved to have received money-bribes suffer expulsion' (*AYR* 1.151).

Veneering will accept the Chiltern Hundreds]   In accordance with the unwritten British constitution, a Member of Parliament cannot resign his seat unless disqualified or by accepting an office of honour and profit under the Crown. The stewardship of the Chiltern Hundreds is such an office and so, by a fiction, an MP who wishes to resign accepts this office and immediately resigns it.

the Veneerings will retire to Calais]   The Lammles went to Boulogne (3.17).

the six hundred and fifty-seven dearest and oldest friends]   After the Reform Act of 1832, there were 658 Members of Parliament, but the disfranchisement of Sudbury and St Albans reduced the number by four.

That fresh fairy

'We know what Russia means, sir . . . we know what France wants; we see what America is up to; but we know what England is.] In the *Times* summary for 1864, 'the prosperity and ambition of Russia' were seen to be 'visibly reviving' after the defeat in the Crimea (31 December, 6). By 1864, Napoleon III had successfully established Maximilian on the Mexican throne and had concluded a war against Austria over the question of Italian independence which had resulted in the French annexation of Nice and Savoy. America was embroiled in civil war, and there was tension between England and the North because of the disruption of supplies of Southern cotton to Lancashire. Dickens himself mistrusted America; he wrote in a letter to W. F. de Cerjat: 'If the Americans don't embroil us in a war before long, it will not be their fault' (13 November 1865, *Nonesuch* 3.445).

However, when dinner is served

'Long banished Robinson Crusoe] The hero of Defoe's *Robinson Crusoe* is not banished, but shipwrecked on the uninhabited island of Juan Fernandez. He rescues Friday, the man he makes his servant, from cannibals. In his *UT* essay 'Nurse's Stories', Dickens mentioned the vivid impression made on him when a child by 'the sandy beach . . . where the savages hauled up their canoes when they came ashore for those dreadful public dinners, which led to a dancing worse than speech-making'.

'How was the bride

In rowing costume?'] In the first half of the century, women were not a common sight on the river, at least as active rowers, though the wives and daughters of fishermen apparently engaged in races. Ladies who took to the river wore draped and kilted overskirts and skin-tight bodices, feathered and flowered hats, and woollen combinations.

'You shall not escape me

you morose backwoods-man] American fiction and the accounts of English travellers to America had made the backwoodsman a familiar object of reference for the English reader.

a Committee of the whole House] A parliamentary term for all of the Members sitting as a committee to consider the details of a measure.

'But, excuse me,' says Podsnap

ever a female waterman?'] Watermen were employed in the specific business of ferrying passengers. But Lizzie worked in a far less reputable business.

'And now, Mr. Lightwood

'a factory girl?']   Paper manufacture was not brought under government control until the Factory Acts Extension Act of 1867, so Lizzie was not technically a factory girl (David, 1982).

Lady Tippins next canvasses

These things are a question of beefsteaks and porter.]   The Contractor regards Lizzie as a female navvy.

The fair enslaver

the Wandering Chairman]   On the model of the Wandering Jew who, in legend, is condemned to wander the world until the Second Coming. He urged Christ to go faster on the road to Calvary.

in an Electric Telegraph Office, where young women answer very well.]   The electric telegraph, which had first been set in operation between Euston Square and Camden Town stations in 1837, had provided a new source of employment for women. By 1854 over 350,000 public messages were sent a year.

Buffer says he knows a man

a man who married a bathing-woman]   Bathing women, sometimes in partnership with their husbands, supervised the bathing machines used on beaches in Victorian times. They were usually 'middle-aged women, wearing dark voluminous dresses, slouch hats or bonnets and head scarves. Their function was to dip the timid ... and also to scare off inquisitive males' (Cunnington and Mansfield, 1969, 261–2).

'I say,' resumes Twemlow

I think he is the greater gentleman for the action and makes her the greater lady.]   It was the convention that a man could raise the woman he married to his own class, but that a woman was lowered if she married a man from a class beneath her.

POSTSCRIPT,
IN LIEU OF PREFACE.

When I devised this story

readers and commentators would suppose that I was at great pains to conceal exactly what I was at great pains to suggest]   It has been remarked (by Gill, 1971) that Dickens had before him Wilkie Collins's defence of such a method of plotting in the preface to the 1861 edition of *The Dead Secret*:

> I was blamed for allowing the 'Secret' to glimmer on the reader at an early period of the story, instead of keeping it in total darkness till the end. If this was a mistake (which I venture to doubt), I committed it with both eyes open. After careful consideration, and after trying the experiment both ways, I thought it most desirable to let the effect of the story depend on expectation rather than surprise; believing that the reader would be all the more interested in watching the progress of 'Rosamond' and her husband towards the discovery of the Secret, if he previously held some clue to the mystery in his own hand.

Collins made a similar defence in the preface to *No Name* (1862):

> it will be seen that the narrative related in these pages has been constructed on a plan, which differs from the plan followed in my last novel, and in some other of my works published at an earlier date. The only Secret contained in this book, is revealed midway in the first volume. From that point, all the main events of the story are purposely foreshadowed, before they take place – my present design being to rouse the reader's interest in following the train of circumstances by which these foreseen events are brought about.

To keep for a long time unsuspected

To keep for a long time unsuspected, yet always working itself out, another purpose originating in that leading incident]   Dickens's letters suggest that he was at pains to conceal that Boffin's good nature was unchanged. Early in 1865, he wrote to William Charles Kent:

> It amuses me to find that you don't see your way with a certain Mutual Friend of ours. I have a horrible suspicion that you may begin to be fearfully knowing about No. 12 or 13. But you shan't if I can help it. (17 January 1865, *Nonesuch* 3.412)

He was as confident of his effect in a letter to the Reverend William Harness written later in the year:

> I am, and have been, hard at work at your conversion – to the opinion that the story of Our Mutual Friend is very interesting and was from the first tending to a purpose which you couldn't foresee until I chose to take you into my confidence. Modest this – but true. (23 May 1865, *Nonesuch* 3.422)

Yet, that I hold the advantages of the mode of publication to outweigh its disadvantages, may be easily believed of one who revived it in the Pickwick Papers after long disuse]   In the 'Preface' to the 1847 edition of *PP* Dickens recalled that when approached about publishing in shilling numbers he had had 'a dim recollection of certain interminable novels in that form, which used, some five-and-twenty years ago, to be carried about the country by pedlars, and over some of which I remember to have shed innumerable tears, before I served my apprenticeship to Life'. When Dickens began to write, novels were usually published in three or four volumes, costing as much as half a guinea a volume, which made novel-reading very expensive to readers who did not belong to a circulation library (Butt and Tillotson, 1957, 13).

There is sometimes an odd disposition

the Prerogative Office]   Dickens described a visit to the Prerogative Office in 'Doctor's Commons' in *SB*.

In my social experiences

Circumlocution champions]   Like the officials of the Circumlocution Office in chapter 10 of *LD* whose idea of 'the whole Science of Government' is 'HOW NOT TO DO IT'.

My friend Mr. Bounderby ... turtle soup and venison out of gold spoons.]   See *HT*, book 1, chapter 11.

the late exposure of THE LANCET]   The *Lancet* announced a 'Commission to Inquire into the State of Workhouse Hospitals' on 15 April 1865 and reports were published each week throughout the remainder of that year. See page 217.

since the days of the STUARTS]   Dickens gave a critical account of the Stuarts in *CHE*: he referred to James I as 'his Sowship' and remarked of Charles I that, in his pursuit of the 'wrong idea' of the supremacy of the king, he 'never took a straight course, but always took a crooked one' (22–3).

On Friday the Ninth of June

Mr. and Mrs. Boffin (in their manuscript dress of receiving Mr. and Mrs. Lammle at breakfast) were on the South Eastern Railway with me, in a terribly destructive accident.]   On 9 June 1865, Dickens was travelling with Ellen Ternan, and perhaps her mother, on the boat train (or 'tidal train' as it was then called) from Folkestone to London. The engine leapt a 42-foot gap in the rails and ran to the farther end of a river-bed, dragging a number of carriages after it. Numbers of people were killed or injured. Dickens was later sent a 'Resolution of Thanks' by the directors of the railway company for his assistance to his fellow-passengers (Slater, 1983, 209; *Nonesuch* 3.429).

THE ILLUSTRATIONS TO
OUR MUTUAL FRIEND

The forty illustrations to *Our Mutual Friend* are by Marcus Stone. Marcus Stone was the son of Dickens's old friend Frank Stone. Frank Stone died in 1859, leaving Marcus dependent on his own efforts for support. Dickens immediately interested himself on behalf of Marcus: a letter to the publisher Thomas Longman recommends him as 'an admirable draughtsman' who wished 'to make an additional opening for himself in the illustration of books' (*Nonesuch* 3.138). Stone contributed illustrations to the *Cornhill Magazine, Good Words* and other periodicals. His major work as an illustrator, apart from that for Dickens, was on Trollope's *He Knew He Was Right*. For Dickens he illustrated the 1862 edition of *AN* and *PI* and the 1863 edition of *GE*. His work on *OMF* and a number of successes at the Academy made his name and he enjoyed a moderately successful career as a painter of gracefully sentimental genre pictures. Once his reputation was established, he abandoned book illustration: 'Mr. Stone had recognized, what few will dispute, that his "forte" did not lie in illustrating' (Robinson, 1869, 34).

Stone's illustrations are in the style that in the 1850s and 1860s was replacing the satiric tradition of Hogarth, Gilray and Cruikshank. They add little to the enjoyment and nothing to the understanding of the novel. Dickens gave Stone detailed instructions for the cover of the monthly parts (which is, significantly, in the earlier style of illustration) in which he made interesting comments on certain characters (see pp. 55, 138). His interest in Stone's contribution seems not to have been sustained, however: in 1912, Stone recalled in the *Dickensian* that he received proofs of *OMF* and selected his own subjects: 'I then sent them on for his approval, and I have no recollection that he ever rejected one' (7.217). On 13 September 1865, Dickens wrote to Stone from Paris:

> The sooner I can know about the subjects you take for illustrations the better, as I can then fill the list of illustrations to the second volume for the printer, and enable him to make up his last sheet. Necessarily that list is now left blank, as I cannot give him the titles of the subjects, not knowing them myself.

He added the suggestion that the frontispiece to Volume 2 be either 'Mr. Boffin digging up the Dutch bottle, and Venus restraining Wegg's ardour to get at him. Or Mr. Boffin might be coming down with the bottle, and Venus might be dragging Wegg out of the way as described' (*Nonesuch* 3.435–6).

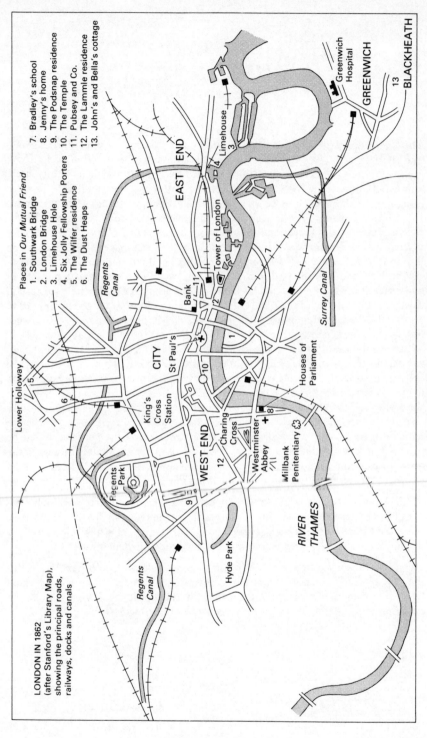

LONDON IN 1862
(after Stanford's Library Map),
showing the principal roads,
railways, docks and canals

Places in *Our Mutual Friend*

1. Southwark Bridge
2. London Bridge
3. Limehouse Hole
4. Six Jolly Fellowship Porters
5. The Wilfer residence
6. The Dust Heaps
7. Bradley's school
8. Jenny's home
9. The Podsnap residence
10. The Temple
11. Pubsey and Co.
12. The Lammle residence
13. John's and Bella's cottage

Lower Holloway

Regents Canal

Regents Park

Hyde Park

King's Cross Station

WEST END

Charing Cross

Westminster Abbey

Millbank Penitentiary

Houses of Parliament

St Paul's

CITY

Bank

Tower of London

EAST END

Limehouse

Regents Canal

Surrey Canal

RIVER THAMES

Greenwich Hospital

GREENWICH

BLACKHEATH

7 A map of the London of *Our Mutual Friend*

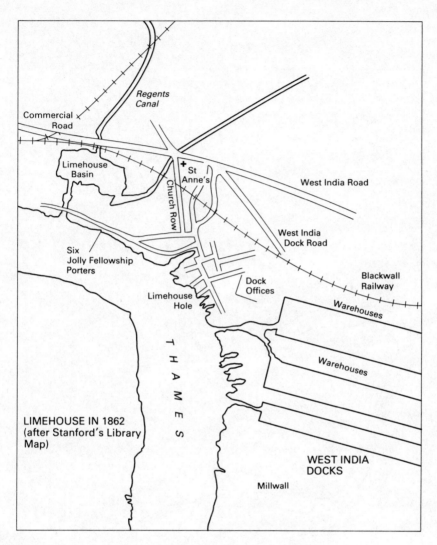

8   (*a*) Map of the East End of *Our Mutual Friend*

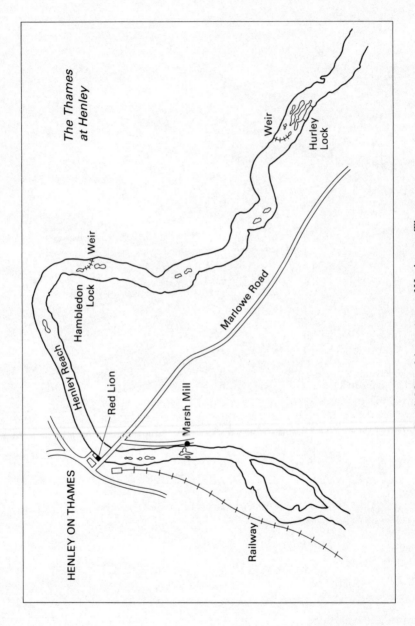

The Thames at Henley

HENLEY ON THAMES

Henley Reach

Red Lion

Hambledon Lock

Weir

Weir

Hurley Lock

Marsh Mill

Marlowe Road

Railway

8 (b) Map of the environs of Henley-on-Thames

SELECT BIBLIOGRAPHY

The manuscript and work plans of *Our Mutual Friend* are in the Pierpont Morgan Library, New York. A complete set of proofs is in the Berg Collection, New York Public Library.

(i) *Works by Dickens*

The Clarendon Dickens (Oxford: Clarendon Press, 1966–) is the edition cited in quotations from:
   David Copperfield, ed. Nina Burgis (1981)
   Dombey and Son, ed. Alan Horsman (1974)
   Little Dorrit, ed. Harvey Peter Sucksmith (1979)
   Martin Chuzzlewit, ed. Margaret Cardwell (1982)
   The Mystery of Edwin Drood, ed. Margaret Cardwell (1972)
   Oliver Twist, ed. Kathleen Tillotson (1966)
The Norton Critical Edition (New York/London: W. W. Norton) is cited in quotations from:
   Bleak House, ed. George Ford and Sylvère Monod (1977)
   Hard Times, ed. George Ford and Sylvère Monod (1966)
The Penguin English Library (Harmondsworth: Penguin Books) is the source of quotations for:
   Barnaby Rudge, ed. Gordon Spence (1973)
   The Christmas Books, ed. Michael Slater, 2 vols (1971)
   Great Expectations, ed. Angus Calder (1965)
   Nicholas Nickleby, ed. Michael Slater (1978)
   The Old Curiosity Shop, ed. Angus Easson (1972)
   The Pickwick Papers, ed. Robert L. Patten (1972)
   A Tale of Two Cities, ed. George Woodcock (1970)
The Oxford Illustrated Dickens, 21 vols (London: Oxford University Press, 1947–58) is the source of quotations for:
   American Notes and *Pictures from Italy*
   A Child's History of England (this volume includes *Master Humphrey's Clock*)
   The Christmas Stories (this volume includes *A Lazy Tour of Two Idle Apprentices*)
   Sketches by Boz (this volume includes *Sketches of Young Gentlemen* and *Sketches of Young Couples*)
   The Uncommercial Traveller and Reprinted Pieces (this volume includes *To Be Read at Dusk, Hunted Down, Holiday Romance* and *George Silverman's Explanation*)
Memoirs of Joseph Grimaldi, edited by Dickens, ed. Richard Findlater (London: MacGibbon & Kee, 1968).
Miscellaneous Papers, ed. B. W. Matz, 2 vols (Vols 35 and 36 in the Gadshill Edition) (London: Chapman & Hall, 1897–1908).
Collected Papers, Nonesuch Edition, 2 vols (London: Nonesuch Press, 1938).
The Letters of Charles Dickens, Pilgrim Edition, 5 vols to date (Oxford: Clarendon Press, 1965–). Vols 1 and 2, ed. Madeline House and Graham Storey; Vol. 3, ed. Madeline House, Graham Storey and Kathleen Tillotson; Vol. 4, ed. Kathleen Tillotson; Vol. 5, ed. Graham Storey and K. J. Fielding.

The Letters of Charles Dickens, ed. Walter Dexter, Nonesuch Edition, 3 vols (London: Nonesuch Press, 1938).

Letters from Charles Dickens to Angela Burdett-Coutts, 1841–1865, ed. Edgar Johnson (London: Jonathan Cape, 1953).

The Speeches of Charles Dickens, ed. K. J. Fielding (Oxford: Clarendon Press, 1960).

Charles Dickens' Book of Memoranda, ed. Fred Kaplan (New York: New York Public Library, 1981).

(ii)   *Articles in* Household Words

Capper, John, 'The Wonders of Mincing Lane', 5 (5 June 1852), 273–6.

Dickens, Charles, and Lemon, Mark, 'A Paper-Mill', 1 (31 August 1850), 529–31.

Dickens, Charles, and Morley, Henry, 'Boys to Mend', 5 (11 September 1852), 597–602.

Dickens, Charles, and Morley, Henry, 'Drooping Buds', 5 (3 April 1852), 45–8.

Hollingshead, John, 'New Puppets for Old Ones', 19 (29 January 1859), 210–12.

Horne, R. H., 'Dust; or Ugliness Redeemed', 1 (13 July 1850), 379–84.

Hunt, Frederick Knight, 'The Hunterian Museum', 2 (14 December 1850), 277–82.

Hunt, Frederick Knight, 'A Visit to the Registrar-General', 2 (30 November 1850), 235–40.

Morley, Henry, 'Parish Poor in London', 17 (5 June 1858), 577–8.

Morley, Henry, 'Something that Shakespeare Lost', 15 (17 January 1857), 49–52.

Morley, Henry, 'Use and Abuse of the Dead', 17 (3 April 1858), 361–5.

Morley, Henry, and Wills, W. H., 'Not Very Common Things', 14 (26 July 1856), 39–41.

(iii)   *Articles in* All the Year Round

'The Frozen-Out Poor Law', 4 (16 February 1861), 446–9.

Halliday, Andrew, 'Shakespeare-Mad', 11 (21 May 1864), 345–51.

Hollingshead, John, 'A New Chamber of Horrors', 4 (2 March 1861), 500–1.

'Jack's Castle Up the Lane', 3 (22 September 1860), 574–6.

Meason, Malcolm Ronald Laing, 'Accommodation', 13 (8 April 1865), 260–4.

Meason, Malcolm Ronald Laing, 'Amateur Finance', 14 (12 August 1865), 56–60; (19 August 1865), 87–91; (26 August 1865), 110–15.

Meason, Malcolm Ronald Laing, 'Bank of Patagonia', 13 (17 June 1865), 485–90.

Meason, Malcolm Ronald Laing, 'Going into Business', 13 (13 May 1865), 378–82; (20 May 1865), 404–8; (27 May 1865), 428–32.

Meason, Malcolm Ronald Laing, 'How I Discounted My Bill', 13 (8 July 1865), 557–61.

Meason, Malcolm Ronald Laing, 'How the Bank Came to Grief', 13 (25 February 1865), 102–6.

Meason, Malcolm Ronald Laing, 'How the Bank Was Wound Up', 13 (15 April 1865), 276–82.

Meason, Malcolm Ronald Laing, 'How We "Floated" the Bank', 12 (31 December 1864), 493–7.

Meason, Malcolm Ronald Laing, 'Insurance and Assurance', 13 (3 June 1865), 437–42.

Meason, Malcolm Ronald Laing, 'Promoters of Companies', 11 (12 March 1864), 110–15.

Meason, Malcolm Ronald Laing, 'Starting the Rio Grande Railway', 14 (11 November 1865), 368–72.

Meason, Malcolm Ronald Laing, 'Wanted to Borrow, One Hundred Pounds', 13 (11 March 1865), 164–8.

Meason, Malcolm Ronald Laing, 'Working the Rio Grande Railway', 14 (18 November 1865), 393–7.

'The Sensational Williams', 11 (13 February 1864), 14–17.
'Small-Beer Chronicles', 9 (23 May 1863), 309–12.
'A Sum in Fair Division', 1 (7 May 1859), 40–4.

(iv)   *Other Material*

Accum, Friederich, *A Treatise on Adulterations of Food and Culinary Poisons* (London: Longman, 1820).

Adams, William Bridges, *English Pleasure Carriages* (1837; reprinted Bath: Adams & Dart, 1971).

Allbut, Robert, *Rambles in Dickens' Land* (London: Freemantle, 1899).

Altick, Richard, *The English Common Reader: A Social History of the Mass Reading Public, 1800–1900* (Chicago: University of Chicago Press, 1957).

Altick, Richard, 'Education, print and paper in *Our Mutual Friend*', in Clyde de L. Ryals (ed.), *Nineteenth-Century Literary Perspectives: Essays in Honor of Lionel Stevenson* (Durham, NC: Duke University Press, 1974).

Altick, Richard, *The Shows of London* (Cambridge, Mass./London: Harvard University Press, 1978).

Arnold, Matthew, *Reports on Elementary Schools, 1852–82* (London: Macmillan, 1889).

Ashton, John, *Modern Street Ballads* (London: Chatto & Windus, 1888).

Beames, Thomas, *The Rookeries of London* (London: Thomas Bosworth, 1850).

Beeton, Isabella, *The Book of Household Management* (London: S. O. Beeton, 1861).

Berridge, Virginia, and Edwards, Griffith, *Opium and the People* (London: Allen Lane, 1981).

Best, Geoffrey, *Mid-Victorian Britain, 1851–75* (1971; revised edn St Albans: Panther, 1973).

Birch, John Godfrey, *Limehouse through Five Centuries* (London: Sheldon Press, 1930).

Boll, Ernest, 'The plotting of *Our Mutual Friend*', *Modern Philology*, (November 1944), 96–122.

Booth, Charles, *Life and Labour of the People in London*, 17 vols (1902–4; reprinted New York: AMS Press, 1970).

Brettell, Thomas, *A Topographical and Historical Guide to the Isle of Wight* (London: Leigh & Co.; Ollivier, 1840).

Brown, Captain Thomas, *The Taxidermist's Manual* (Glasgow: Archibald Fullarton, 1836).

Browne, Alexander Montagu, *Practical Taxidermy: A Manual of Instruction to the Amateur* (London: 'The Bazaar Office', 1878).

Butt, John, and Tillotson, Kathleen, *Dickens at Work* (London: Methuen, 1957).

Clapham, Sir John, *An Economic History of Modern Britain: Free Trade and Steel, 1850–86* (Cambridge: Cambridge University Press, 1967).

Coleman, Terry, *The Railway Navvies* (London: Hutchinson, 1965).

Collins, Philip, *Dickens and Crime* (London: Macmillan, 1962).

Collins, Philip, *Dickens and Education* (revised edn London: Macmillan, 1964).

Collins, Philip, 'Dickens and the ragged schools', *Dickensian*, 55 (1959), 94–109.

Collins, Philip (ed.), *Dickens: The Critical Heritage* (London: Routledge & Kegan Paul, 1971).

Copley, Esther, *Cottage Comforts, with Hints for Promoting Them* (London: Simpkin & Marshall, 1825).

Cotsell, Michael, 'The book of insolvent fates: financial speculation in *Our Mutual Friend*', *Dickens Studies Annual*, 13 (1985), 100–14.

Cotsell, Michael, ' "Do I never read in the newspapers": Dickens's last attack on the Poor Law', *Dickens Studies Newsletter*, 14 (September 1983), 81–90.

Cotsell, Michael, 'Mr Venus rises from the counter: Dickens's taxidermist and his contribution to *Our Mutual Friend*', *Dickensian*, 80 (Summer 1984), 105–13.

Cowper, B. H., *A Descriptive Historical and Statistical Account of Millwall* (London: Robert Gladding, 1853).

Coxhead, A. C., *Thomas Stothard, RA: An Illustrated Monograph* (London: A. H. Bullen, 1906).

Cunnington, Phillis, and Lucas, Catherine, *Costumes for Births, Marriages and Deaths* (London: A. & C. Black, 1972).

Cunnington, Phillis, and Lucas, Catherine, *Occupational Costume in England from the Eleventh Century to 1914*, revised edn (London: A. & C. Black, 1968).

Cunnington, Phillis, and Mansfield, Alan, *English Costume for Sports and Outdoor Recreations* (London: A. & C. Black, 1969).

David, Deirdre, *Fictions of Resolution in Three Victorian Novels* (New York: Columbia University Press, 1981).

Davies, James A., 'Forster and Dickens: the making of Podsnap', *Dickensian*, 70 (September 1974), 145–58.

Davis, Earle, *The Flint and the Flame: The Artistry of Charles Dickens* (London: Victor Gollancz, 1964).

Doré, Gustave, and Jerrold, Blanchard, *London: A Pilgrimage* (London, 1872).

Evans, David Morier, *Speculative Notes and Notes on Speculation* (London, 1864).

Feltes, N. N., 'Community and the limits of liability in two mid-Victorian novels', *Victorian Studies*, 17 (June 1974), 355–69.

Fielding, K. J., 'Dickens's work with Miss Coutts: I. "Nova Scotia Gardens and What Grew There"', *Dickensian*, 61 (1965), 112–19.

Fitzgerald, Percy, *Bozland* (London: Downey, 1895).

Forster, John, *The Life of Charles Dickens*, 3 vols (London: Chapman & Hall, 1872–4).

Gill, Stephen (ed.), *Our Mutual Friend* by Charles Dickens (Harmondsworth: Penguin, 1971).

Harrison, Brian, *Drink and the Victorians: The Temperance Question in England, 1815–72* (London: Faber, 1971).

Harrison, J. F. C., *The Early Victorians, 1832–51* (London: Weidenfeld & Nicolson, 1971; reprinted as *Early Victorian Britain,* London: Fontana, 1979).

Heads of the People; or, Portraits of the English, drawn by Kenny Meadows (London: Willoughby, 1841).

Hill, T. W., 'Notes to *Our Mutual Friend*', *Dickensian*, 43 (1947), 85–90, 142–9, 206–12.

Hilts, Victoria L., 'William Farr (1807–1883) and the "human unit"', *Victorian Studies*, 14 (1970), 143–50.

Himmlefarb, Gertrude, 'Mayhew's poor: a problem of identity', *Victorian Studies*, 14 (1970–1), 307–20.

House, Humphry, *The Dickens World* (London: Oxford University Press, 1941).

Hutter, Albert D. (1983), 'Dismemberment and articulation in *Our Mutual Friend*', *Dickens Studies Annual*, 11 (1983), 135–76.

Johnson, Edgar, *Charles Dickens: His Tragedy and Triumph*, 2 vols (London: Hamish Hamilton; Boston, Mass./Toronto: Little, Brown, 1952).

Kaplan, Fred, *Dickens and Mesmerism: The Hidden Springs of Fiction* (Princeton, NJ: Princeton University Press, 1975).

Kay-Shuttleworth, Sir James, *Letter to Earl Granville on the Revised Code* (London/ Manchester, 1861).

Keith, Norman M., 'The Anatomy Acts of 1831 and 1832', *AMA Archives of Internal Medicine*, 99 (May 1957), 678–94.

King, W. T. C., *History of the London Discount Market* (London: Wilfred King, 1936).

Kitton, Frederick G., *The Novels of Charles Dickens* (London: Elliott Stock, 1897).

Knowles, Owen, 'Veneering and the age of Veneer: a Source and Background for *Our Mutual Friend*', *Dickensian* 81 (1985), 88–96.

Lanham, Richard A., '*Our Mutual Friend*: the bird of prey', *Victorian Newsletter*, 24 (Autumn 1963), 6–12.

Lawson, John, and Silver, Harold, *A Social History of Education in England* (London: Methuen, 1973).

Ley, J. W. T., 'More songs of Dickens's day', *Dickensian*, 28 (1932), 15–26, 97–104.

Ley, J. W. T., 'Sentimental songs in Dickens', *Dickensian*, 28 (1932), 313–21.

Ley, J. W. T., 'The songs of Silas Wegg', *Dickensian*, 26 (1930), 111–17.

Ley, J. W. T., 'The sporting songs of Dickens', *Dickensian*, 28 (1932), 187–9.

Lohrli, Anne (ed.), *Household Words: A Weekly Journal, 1850–1859, Conducted by Charles Dickens. A Table of Contents, List of Contributors and Their Contributions Based on the 'Household Words' Office Book* . . . (Toronto: University of Toronto Press, 1973).

McMaster, R. D., 'Birds of prey: a study of *Our Mutual Friend*', *Dalhousie Review*, 40 (1960), 372–81.

Matz, B. W., *Dickensian Inns and Taverns* (London: Cecil Palmer, 1922).

Mayhew, Henry, *London Labour and the London Poor*, 4 vols (1861–2; reprinted London: Frank Cass, 1967).

Meason, Malcolm Ronald Laing, *The Bubbles of Finance: Joint-Stock Companies, Promoting Companies, Modern Commerce, Money Lending, and Life Assurance* (London: Sampson Low, 1865).

Meason, Malcolm Ronald Laing, *The Profits of Panics* (London: Sampson Low, 1866).

Metz, Nancy Aycock, 'The artistic reclamation of waste in *Our Mutual Friend*', *Nineteenth-Century Fiction*, 34 (1979–80), 59–72.

Montague, C. J., *Sixty Years in Waifdom; or, The Ragged School Movement in History* (London: Chas. Murray, 1904).

Morley, John, *The Struggle for National Education* (London: Chapman & Hall, 1873).

Neff, Wanda, *Victorian Working Women* (London: Allen & Unwin, 1929).

Nelson, Harland S., 'Dickens's *Our Mutual Friend* and Henry Mayhew's *London Labour and the London Poor*', *Nineteenth-Century Fiction*, 20 (1965), 207–22.

Opie, Iona and Peter, *The Oxford Dictionary of Nursery Rhymes*, revised edn (Oxford: Clarendon Press, 1973).

Patterson, Annabel M., 'Dickens as the Compleat Angler', *Dickens Studies Annual*, 1 (1980), 252–64.

Pope, Norris, *Dickens and Charity* (London: Macmillan, 1978).

Purton, Valerie, 'Dickens and Bulwer Lytton: the dandy reclaimed?', *Dickensian*, 74 (1978), 25–9.

Qualls, Barry V., 'Savages in a "bran-new" world: Carlyle and *Our Mutual Friend*', *Studies in the Novel*, 10 (1978), 199–215.

Rich, R. W., *The Training of Teachers in England and Wales during the Nineteenth Century* (Cambridge: Cambridge University Press, 1933).

Robinson, Lionel G., 'Marcus Stone', *Art Journal*, NS, 8 (1869), 33–5.

Robson, Edward Robert, *School Architecture* (1874; reprinted Leicester: Leicester University Press, 1972).

Rose, Michael E., *The English Poor Law, 1780–1930* (Newton Abbot: David & Charles, 1971).

Rose, Michael E., *The Relief of Poverty, 1834–1914* (London: Macmillan, 1972).

Rose, Millicent, *The East End of London* (1951; reprinted Bath: Cedric Chivers, 1973).

Russell, Norman, 'The literary response to capitalism in England, 1840–80', 2 vols, University of London dissertation, 1979.

293

Sala, G. A., *Twice round the Clock* (London, 1859).

Sala, G. A., *Gaslight and Daylight* (London, 1859).

Sanger, 'Lord' George, *Seventy Years a Showman* (1910), with an introduction by Colin MacInnes (London: MacGibbon & Kee).

Shannon, H. A., 'The first five thousand limited companies and their duration', *Economic History*, 2 (1930–3), 396–424.

Shatto, Susan, ' "A complete course, according to question and answer" ', *Dickensian*, 70 (1974), 113–20.

Shea, F. X., 'Mr Venus observed: the plot change in *Our Mutual Friend*', *Papers in Language and Literature*, 4 (1968), 170–81.

Shea, F. X., 'The text of *Our Mutual Friend*: a study of the variations between copy text and the first printed edition', University of Minnesota dissertation, 1961.

Sinclair, Robert, *East London* (London: Robert Hale, 1950).

Slater, Michael, *Dickens and Women* (London/Melbourne/Toronto: Dent, 1983).

Smith, Frank, *The Life and Work of Sir James Kay-Shuttleworth* (London: John Murray, 1923).

Stang, Richard, *The Theory of the Novel in England, 1850–70* (London: Routledge & Kegan Paul, 1959).

Stephen, Sir James Fitzjames, 'The relation of novels to life', in *Cambridge Essays* (London: J. W. Parker, 1855).

Stephen, Sir Leslie, *The Life of Sir James Fitzjames Stephen* (London: Smith, Elder, 1895).

Stern, Walter M., *The Porters of London* (London: Longmans, 1960).

Stone, Harry, 'Dickens and the Jews', *Victorian Studies*, 2 (1958–9). 223–53.

Stonehouse, J. M., *Catalogue of the Library of Charles Dickens from Gadshill* . . . (London: Piccadilly Fountain Press, 1935).

Sucksmith, Harvey Peter, 'The dust-heaps in *Our Mutual Friend*', *Essays in Criticism*, 23 (1973), 206–12.

Thornbury, Walter, and Walford, Edward, *Old and New London*, 6 vols (London: Cassell, 1873–8).

Thorne, James, *Handbook to the Environs of London* (1876; reprinted Chichester: Godfrey Cave, 1970).

Tillotson, Kathleen, *Novels of the Eighteen-Forties* (Oxford: Clarendon Press, 1954).

Timbs, John, *Curiosities of London* (London: J. S. Virtue, 1885).

Tropp, Asher, *The School Teachers* (London: Heinemann, 1957).

Vries, Leonard de, *Victorian Advertisements* (London: John Murray, 1968).

Wheatley, Henry, *London Past and Present, Based upon The Handbook of London by Peter Cunningham*, 3 vols (London: John Murray, 1891).

Wilson, David Alec, *Carlyle to Threescore and Ten (1853–1865)* (London: Kegan Paul, 1929).

Young, George F., 'Noddy Boffin's misers', *Dickensian*, 43 (1947), 14–17.

Young, George F., 'The Six Jolly Fellowship-Porters: a new view', *Dickensian*, 21 (1935), 119–24.

Xenos, Stefanos, *Depredations; or Overend, Gurney, & Co., and the Greek & Oriental Steam Navigation Company* (London, 1869).

INDEX

A NOTE ON THE INDEX

This is an index to *The Companion to 'Our Mutual Friend'*; it is not an index to Dickens's novel. Variant readings in the manuscript and proofs are not indexed, nor are the work plans.

Literary allusions and references are indexed only when a note gives a probable allusion by Dickens: references which are merely illustrative, or which are examples of typical phrases, are not indexed. Allusions and references are given title entries in the following cases only: (i) anonymous works other than books of the Bible, nursery rhymes, nursery tales, and songs; (ii) works by Dickens.

Because of the density of information contained in the text, it has not been possible to index all *mentions* of names, places and so on. Acts of Parliament are not indexed; see under the subject, for example: 'companies: limited liability'.

Notes on the names of characters are entered under the character's surname.

Filing order is word by word rather than letter by letter: thus 'lime works' precedes 'Limehouse'.

Sub-headings are arranged alphabetically, with the following exceptions: (i) entries for the Bible (arranged in canonical order); (ii) entries for costume and appearance, London, public houses, and songs (each of these headings has a distinct and self-explanatory sub-class or sub-classes).

The abbreviation *OMF* is used for *Our Mutual Friend*.

INDEX

315